35.00

C000279449

Governments, Managers and Industrial Relations

Warwick Studies in Industrial Relations
General Editors: G. S. Bain, R. Hyman and K. Sisson

Also available in this series

Governments, Managers and Industrial Relations

Public Enterprises and their Political Environment

Anthony Ferner

Basil Blackwell

Copyright © Anthony Ferner 1988

First published 1988

Basil Blackwell Ltd
108 Cowley Road, Oxford, OX4 1JF, UK

Basil Blackwell Inc.
432 Park Avenue South, Suite 1503
New York, NY 10016, USA

All rights reserved. Except for the quotation of short passages for the purposes of criticism and review, no part of this publication may be reproduced, stored in a retrieval system, or transmitted, in any form or by any means, electronic, mechanical, photocopying, recording or otherwise, without the prior permission of the publisher.

Except in the United States of America, this book is sold subject to the condition that it shall not, by way of trade or otherwise, be lent, re-sold, hired out, or otherwise circulated without the publisher's prior consent in any form of binding or cover other than that in which it is published and without a similar condition including this condition being imposed on the subsequent purchaser.

British Library Cataloguing in Publication Data
Ferner, Anthony
    Governments, managers and industrial relations : public
    enterprises and their political environment — Warwick
    studies in industrial relations
    1. Great Britain. Public sector. Industrial relations. Political
    aspects
    I. Title   II. Series
    331'.041'35441

    ISBN 0-631-15978-9

Library of Congress Cataloging in Publication Data
Ferner, Anthony.
    Governments, managers, and industrial relations : public
    enterprises and their political environment / Anthony Ferner.
        p.   cm -- (Warwick studies in industrial relations)
    Bibliography: p. Includes index.
    ISBN 0-631-15978-9
    1. Government business enterprises. 2. Industrial relations.
    3. British Railways. 4. Red Nacional de los Ferrocarriles
    Españoles.   I. Title.   II. Series.
    HD3845.6.F47 1988
    331'.04135--dc19

Typeset in 10 on 11½ pt Times
by MHL Typesetting Ltd, Coventry
Printed in Great Britain by Bookcraft Ltd, Bath, Avon

In memory of my father, Robert Ferner

Contents

Contents

Editors' Foreword

The University of Warwick is the major centre in the United Kingdom for the study of industrial relations, its first undergraduates being admitted in 1965. The teaching of industrial relations began a year later in the School of Industrial and Business Studies, and it now has one of the country's largest graduate programmes in the subject. Warwick became a national centre for research into industrial relations when the Social Science Research Council (now the Economic and Social Research Council) located its Industrial Relations Research Unit at the University. Subsequently, in 1984, the Unit was reconstituted as a Designated Research Centre attached to the School of Industrial and Business Studies. It continues to be known as the Industrial Relations Research Unit, however, and now embraces the research activities of all members of the School's industrial relations community.

The series of Warwick Studies in Industrial Relations was launched in 1972 by Hugh Clegg and George Bain as the main vehicle for the publication of the results of the Unit's projects, as well as the research carried out by staff teaching industrial relations in the University and the work of graduate students. The first six titles of the series were published by Heinemann Educational Books of London, and subsequent titles have been published by Basil Blackwell of Oxford.

In recent years, the efforts of governments in many advanced industrial countries to control public expenditure have led to an emphasis on greater 'commercialism' in public enterprises. This could be expected to have profound consequences for industrial relations as managements try to cut costs, raise productivity and become more 'market-oriented'. Yet public enterprises are as much political as economic entities; they operate within a formal framework of political control, and also have to take account of a broader political environment that emits diffuse, complex and often conflicting signals. This means that the enterprises' response to new demands on them is not straightforward and mechanical. Likewise, the response of industrial relations to the challenges of commercialism is far from automatic. It depends on the way broad economic pressures are translated into political programmes and how these are in turn 'transmitted' to the enterprise.

The aim of the present book is to use a comparative case study of the railways in Britain and Spain to unravel some of the threads that link change in the external environment to changing patterns of industrial relations within the enterprise. It shows how the particular response of industrial relations to commercialism in different countries is fashioned by variations in political institutions and ideologies, as well as by existing industrial relations structures and patterns of trade union organization. But, in addition, it tries to generalize beyond the industry and the country to explore the common underlying logic of public enterprise industrial relations — a logic deriving from the nature of public enterprises themselves and their position within the state. The book will therefore be of value to students of comparative politics and of the role of the state, as well as to specialists in industrial relations.

George Bain
Richard Hyman
Keith Sisson

Preface

This book grew out of an earlier study by Eric Batstone, Mike Terry and myself of industrial relations in the British postal and telecommunications services. Our research examined the influence of the political environment on management's industrial relations strategies. Exploring a relatively uncharted area, we raised possibly more questions than we answered. For example, to what extent were our findings typical of other public enterprises, such as those dependent on government subsidy? What were the longer-term implications of the Conservative government's radical policies for encouraging 'commercialism' in the public sector? What are the precise mechanisms by which political pressures are 'transmitted' to the enterprise and become integrated into managerial policies? How typical was the British case, when compared with developments in other countries with different political traditions? The present study is an attempt to get to grips with some of these questions.

A project like this incurs considerable intellectual debts. Sadly, the first debt I must record is to Eric Batstone who died in 1987. His warm personality, intellectual vigour, imagination and consummate fieldwork skills provided constant stimulation to his co-workers. Many of the concerns, as well as the research methods, of the present book owe much to my period working with Eric.

The second debt is to the unparalleled research environment provided by the Industrial Relations Research Unit. I would like to thank my colleagues in the Unit for their support, advice and helpful criticism. I would particularly like to acknowledge those who have read and commented on the book in manuscript: Pete Armstrong, George Bain, Paul Edwards, Richard Hyman, Ewart Keep, Keith Sisson and Mike Terry. Their advice has been perceptive, constructive and often invaluable. Outside the Unit I also received extremely useful comments from Philip Bagwell, Eduardo Encinas, Gerry Orbell, John Holroyd of British Rail, and from the National Union of Railwaymen. I am grateful to Willy Brown, then director of the Unit, for his help in the early stages of the project, and to Norma Griffiths, Conny Bussman and Jasbir Bains for typing up large quantities of fieldnotes.

Many people helped with the practical problems of making the right contacts and gaining access to railway management and unions. Among them, I would especially like to thank Bill McCarthy in Britain, and Alvaro Espina and Julio Revenga in Spain. A special role was played by the director and staff of the railway-funded Fundación de los Ferrocarriles Españoles. They not only helped greatly in making contacts but also gave me access to the invaluable archival material in the Foundation's documentation centre.

I am also most grateful to the many other people who eased the problems of living and researching in a foreign country. I would like to thank Lluis Fina for his friendship, support and intellectual collaboration, and for the frequent hospitality that he and his wife Elena Blanchar offered me. Felipe Sáez gave me the use of an office at the Instituto del Empleo y de la Seguridad Social during my stay in Madrid in the spring of 1984. It is perhaps unfair to pick out individual names among the many other people who helped me, but I would like to mention Pepe Aznar, Cecilia Castaño, Eduardo Encinas, María Eugenia Martín, Fausto Miguélez, Miguel Rodríguez Piñero, and Víctor Pérez Díaz.

My final debt, and certainly not the least important, is to all those managers, trade unionists, and others who participated in the research, giving up their time to answer my intrusive questions. In both Britain and Spain there were some who went far beyond the call of duty, spending many hours with me explaining the intricacies of the organization, helping with data collection, offering advice and arranging contacts. Although the conventions of anonymity prevent me from naming them, I am most grateful for their courtesy, helpfulness and patience.

Anthony Ferner

List of Abbreviations

ACAS	Advisory, Conciliation and Arbitration Service
ADG	Assistant Director General
ASLEF	Association of Locomotive Engineers and Firemen
BR	British Rail
BRB	British Railways Board
BREL	British Rail Engineering Limited
BTC	British Transport Commission
BTOG	British Transport Officers Guild
CCOO	Comisiones Obreras (Workers' Commissions)
CEFE	Comisión para el Estudio de los Ferrocarriles Españoles
CGI	Comité General Intercentros
DB	Deutsche Bundesbahn
DOO	Driver Only Operation
EFL	External Financing Limits
FEVE	Ferrocarriles de Vía Estrecha
GDFCF	Gross Domestic Fixed Capital Formation
GDP	Gross Domestic Product
INI	Instituto Nacional de Industrias
LDC	Local Departmental Committee
MMC	Monopolies and Mergers Commission
NUR	National Union of Railwaymen
PSO	Public Service Obligation
PSOE	Partido Socialista Obrero Español
PT&R	Promotion, Transfer and Redundancy
PTF	Plan de Transporte Ferroviario
RENFE	Red Nacional de Ferrocarriles Españoles
RSJC	Railway Staff Joint Council
RSNC	Railway Staff National Council
RSNT	Railway Staff National Tribunal
SLF	Sindicato Libre Ferroviario
TSSA	Transport Salaried Staffs' Association
TUC	Trades Union Congress
UCD	Unión Centro Democrático
UGT	Unión General de Trabajadores
USO	Unión Sindical Obrera

1

Introduction: Changing Industrial Relations in the Public Enterprise

Politics, Public Enterprises and Industrial Relations

This book is a study of how change comes about in the industrial relations of public enterprises. In recent years, the outbreak of major industrial relations conflicts in public enterprises has attracted attention not only in Britain but in France, Spain and elsewhere. During the 1980s, there have been serious confrontations in the British railways and steel and an epic struggle in the coal industry. The winter of 1986–7 witnessed an intensity of public sector conflict in France not seen since 1968, while a massive, prolonged wave of strikes and demonstrations affected Spanish railways and other public industries in the spring of 1987. These conflicts have, of course, had diverse and individual causes, but common to them has been a change in the political environment in which public enterprises operate.

Public policy in a number of countries has been increasingly exercised since the mid-1970s by the problems of controlling state expenditure and increasing the efficiency of the state's activities. The background to these concerns has been a deepening crisis in the capitalist economic system — to which some argue the growth and behaviour of the state sector has itself contributed. The crisis has brought, to varying degrees, recession, mass unemployment, high rates of inflation, and widespread industrial restructuring (see, e.g., Armstrong *et al.* 1984: part III).[1]

There has also been a political debate over whether the state should play a role in production or whether its presence should be reduced in order to clear the way for greater private initiative. Governments have tried to introduce the disciplines of the market into the management of public enterprises, and in many cases, have returned companies to the private sector. One of the main arguments used by politicians in the debate has been that the typical industrial relations practices of public enterprises have impeded efficiency. In Britain, for example, John

Moore, Financial Secretary to the Treasury (and later Secretary of State for Transport) in the 1983 Conservative government, argued that

> The [nationalized] industries' performance on both productivity and man-power costs has also been disappointing. Public sector trade unions have been extraordinarily successful in gaining advantages for themselves in the pay hierarchy by exploiting their monopoly collective bargaining position. ... We have consciously tried to place responsibility on the management of nationalized industries and to make it clear that pay negotiations are matters for them and their employees. But public sector trade union experience of previous administrations has given their leaders a taste of political power without responsibility (1986: 82, 89).

Government's belief that 'the character of management−union relationships have provided a substantial blockage to the adoption of entrepreneurial behaviour by [nationalized] industry managers' (Pendleton 1987a: 2) has focused political interest directly on the industrial relations of public enterprises. But the political pressure for greater efficiency and 'commercialism' has also had more indirect but far-reaching consequences for industrial relations through its impact on management strategy.

The book explores these consequences by asking how industrial relations in state enterprises respond to economic crisis and to attempts of governments to formulate political programmes to combat that crisis. The heart of the study is an examination of state railways in two countries, Britain and Spain, but it is not intended to be a book primarily 'about railways'. It aims to use detailed empirical observations both to draw out general trends and processes that occur in state enterprise industrial relations, and to illuminate the factors that create different responses in similar industries. It will, I hope, show that political processes and structures are important variables mediating between underlying economic trends and pressures, and industrial relations outcomes within the state enterprise. In doing so, it should contribute to the debate about the nature of the capitalist state and its degree of 'relative autonomy' from the processes of capitalist accumulation. Too often that debate has been conducted in a vacuum, uninformed by detailed empirical information on how states and their component parts actually operate.

But the principal aim of the study is to help develop at least a framework of analysis, in a seriously neglected area of research: the nature and logic of industrial relations in state enterprises. In particular, the study concentrates on the strategies of the chief industrial relations actors − managers, politicians and unions − and the way they respond to changing political pressures on them. It is frequently assumed that large corporations act in roughly the same manner, whether they are part of the public or the private sector, and that their industrial relations follow the same pattern, too. A notorious illustration of this assumption was the failure of the influential Donovan Report on trade unions and employers' associations to address public sector industrial relations at all (Donovan 1968). But, in the words of Grant (1987: 56−7), 'the distinctive relationship that the nationalised industries have with government, and the politically charged environment in which they operate, means that they cannot simply be treated as

a special case of the close relationship that many large privately owned enterprises have with government.' The comment was made in the British context,
but as will be seen in later chapters, it is of general applicability.

Students of the British public sector have attempted to set down the 'typical'
features of industrial relations in nationalized industries. For example, Thomson
and Beaumont argue that the 'public market sector' is characterized by high
unionization for both manual and white-collar staff, with relatively clear union
jurisdictions. Bargaining is centralized, highly formalized, and wide-ranging
with highly codified agreements, and there is extensive joint consultation. Job
security is relatively high and attention is paid to relocation and the easing of
redundancy when job loss occurs. Finally, conflict resolution procedures are
formal and centralized, there is frequent resort to third party intervention, and
the pattern of conflict is one of occasional large strikes having a very high impact
on the 'public at large and related production' (1978: 14−15).

Other writers (e.g. Bell 1975; Beaumont and Leopold 1982; Clegg 1979:
passim; Winchester 1983) have also attempted to identify 'key features' of nationalized industries, although few (with the exception of Bell) have dealt with
the state enterprise sector specifically rather than the public sector as a whole.
Leaving aside the question of whether these descriptions may be generalized
beyond the British context, a problem with the approach is that writers have
tended to concentrate on the 'outward and visible signs', the more manifest differences in collective bargaining structure, unionization, pay determination,
conflict and so on, without providing a more general framework within which
these phenomena may be seen. The picture drawn is a static one, and it has been
unable to provide a convincing account of how and why changes have occurred
in the pattern of industrial relations. As a result, writers have often resorted to
ad hoc explanations of changes in the typical characteristics, or confined their
explanations to changes in institutional industrial relations variables, as, for example, in accounting for the outbreak of conflict in hitherto peaceful industries.

This study will take a different approach to identifying the peculiarities of
public enterprise industrial relations. It will be more concerned with how industrial relations practices are related to the distinctive logic of operation of
public enterprises, and how they have changed as the enterprises themselves
have come under the political pressures referred to above. It will be argued that
the enterprises' distinctiveness is to be found in their relationship to the state.
They are under some degree of political control but they also need to have
enough autonomy to carry out complex productive activity in an efficient way.
The continuing conflict between control and autonomy has profound consequences for industrial relations and it will therefore be examined in detail in
subsequent chapters.

The Aims of Comparative Research

Writers have frequently attributed to cross-national research the important advantage of throwing light on one's own country and helping one to understand
it better, undermining the 'in-bred prejudices or preconceived ideas' that attend

a parochial approach (e.g. Schregle 1981: 28). It has also been suggested that the comparative approach may help to develop explanatory theory of greater power and generality (e.g. Bean 1985: 7; Shalev 1980). These arguments apply with particular force to the study of state enterprises. For, to anticipate the argument of later chapters, the nature of the political process and the relationship between state enterprises and other state agencies are crucial for an understanding of the evolution of industrial relations. It will also be argued that the history of the labour movement, its degree of internal coherence, and its relationship with the state and political parties are significant explanatory factors. It is therefore important to have a sufficient range of variation in these 'independent variables', and this can only be achieved by means of cross-national study.

The value of the approach is illustrated by Weaver's illuminating study (1985) of public enterprise in the United States and Canada; coincidentally it is also about railways. Weaver convincingly explains differences in the use of nationalization as a 'policy instrument', and in the subsequent pattern of industrial restructuring, by reference to differences in the political system. The checks and balances of the US system lead to a fragmentation of power both within the executive and between it and the legislative branch, while executive dominance within the Canadian parliamentary system assures a more unitary approach. By contrast, the Canadian polity is riven by conflict between federal and regional interests, a conflict more muted in the US case. These distinctions have major consequences for the way in which public railway enterprises are controlled, and the way in which their objectives are negotiated. For example, the existence of 'multiple veto points' in the American system leads to pressure to distribute widely the benefits of a proposed enterprise strategy, in order to build a winning coalition from potential allies in Congress, the labour unions, rail users' organizations and so on. This has sometimes led to rail company policies of resisting cutbacks, restoring services (e.g. in the home states of influential congressmen) and avoiding staff reductions.

The comparative approach allows two major tasks to be carried out. First, the factors that explain differences in the response of enterprises to similar environmental pressures (in Weaver's study, the crisis of private railways in North America) can be identified. Second, it also enables general features of public enterprise behaviour to be explored. Weaver shows, for example, that a certain peculiar kind of process is occurring when public enterprise objectives are being determined. In his analysis, this relates to patterns of negotiation and conflict adjudication within political systems. Thus a cross-national study can tell us something at a more general level about how public enterprises 'work'.

The logic of cross-national comparative study suggests the value of carrying out research within a single industry, a strategy long recognized by students of industrial relations. By holding technological and market factors more or less constant, comparison allows one to 'highlight the relative influence of the national power contexts' (Dunlop 1958: 129); or as Bean puts it, 'to test for any separate impact of environmental forces appertaining to the national level, in terms of broader social and political influences' (1985: 14).

Holding the industry constant in this way is of course only possible in broad terms. The organization and development of an industry from country to country may vary significantly enough for factors such as firm size, management strategy, introduction of new technology and market structure to be important variables explaining differences in the nature of industrial relations in a single industry. For example, Elbaum and Wilkinson (1979) explain differences in industrial relations in the United States and British steel industries from the late nineteenth century in terms of the increasing differences in the size of the market, the rate of technological innovation and the degree of industrial concentration in the two countries. Thus a comparative analysis must be sensitive to an 'industry effect' even within what is broadly the same industry. This is made easier by confining the study to a small range of detailed case studies.

The case study approach also mitigates the classic problem of cross-national comparisons, of comparing like with like (see, e.g., Schregle 1981: 18−19), which is acute in the case of public enterprises. As an OECD study notes, 'the borderline between public and private enterprises is difficult to draw ... some enterprises are more public than others, some are only nominally public and have all the essential characteristics of private organizations' (1985: 75). National practices in the definition and classification of enterprises vary widely (Pathirane and Blades 1982: 284−91) and rarely are the criteria made fully explicit in national accounts (263). For example,

> Some countries − Spain, Portugal and Austria for example − appear to classify enterprises as public if they are owned 50 per cent or more by government. Other countries − France, Italy and the United Kingdom for example − appear to use a stricter definition based on ownership *plus* some other criteria, such as the degree of control exercised by government, the enterprise's monopolistic position, or the way in which the enterprise came under public ownership (OECD 1985: 76).

A detailed case study approach is also called for by the nature of the explanatory variables that will be proposed. Since these have to do with complex processes of political control and relationships between industrial relations actors and the state, an adequate understanding of them and their historical context requires more than a superficial acquaintance with the countries concerned. As Kassalow argues, 'without a fair understanding of the social, economic and political setting of the industrial relations system in a given country one can make errors of analysis or judgment, or, even more likely, learn only half truths about the significance of particular industrial relations policies or practices in a foreign country' (1968: 99; cf. Shalev 1980: 40).

A detailed comparison should make it possible to filter out the effects of 'intervening variables' from more 'fundamental' determinants of variations in the 'dependent variables'. This relates to a more basic question concerning the sorts of explanations that are to be given of the cross-national variations that are discovered. One tradition in industrial relations research concentrates on differences in the character of industrial relations institutions in different countries. Clegg's attempt (1976) to relate variations in trade union behaviour to the nature of collective bargaining is perhaps the best-known example of the general approach. Among single industry analyses, Derber's study (1976) of five metalworking industries concentrates on the differences in union organization, collective bargaining structures and industrial relations 'rule-making' processes. Such studies generally refer to wider determinants or concomitants of the national industrial relations variables with which they explain their findings. Clegg refers (1976: ch. 8) to the role of the state and the strategy of employers; Derber to such all-embracing national characteristics as size, GNP, politics, economic history and cultural values. But on the whole these broader factors do not form an integral part of the explanation of observed differences.

The strategy of explaining certain industrial relations phenomena in terms of other features of an industrial relations 'system' may be both legitimate and appropriate; it is partly a question of where one chooses to stop the analysis. But equally, in explaining observed differences in features of industrial relations, it may be more productive or apposite to go beyond industrial relations variables to consider explanatory 'factors in the social, political and economic environment' (Shalev 1980: 29). This is the strategy pursued in a second tradition in cross-national industrial relations research. A notable example is found in the attempt (e.g. Korpi and Shalev 1979) to explain the incidence of industrial conflict by reference to the political action of the working class and its representatives[2] rather than to institutional industrial relations features as in Clegg and others; while Dore's (1973) study of Japanese and British factories suggests that variations in the way that capitalist societies order the 'world of work' are a function of the nature, pace and timescale of industrialization — differences in industrial relations reflect aspects of early or late development.

However, the present study also sees industrial relations variables as having a certain 'functional autonomy' (Shalev 1980: 29). The institutions and processes of industrial relations are, to use Wright's distinction, 'mediating' rather than merely 'intervening' variables. An intervening variable is 'simply a variable which is causally situated between two other variables. X causes Y which in turn causes Z'; while a mediating variable 'is one which shapes the very relationship between the two other variables: Y causes the way in which X affects Z' (1979: 23). Thus the industrial relations outcomes of external pressures on state enterprises will be filtered through existing industrial relations structures (which may themselves have been partly determined by the same external pressures).

A common theme emerging from much of the second tradition of cross-national research is that it becomes possible to examine the complex ways in which national industrial relations variations are bound up with wider processes of political and economic development, particularly the phasing of industrial development (as in Dore's work), the nature of the state and underlying class relations. For example, the way in which the labour movement relates to political parties and the state has been seen as a function of when industrialization occurs (e.g. Maier 1984: 55; Badie and Birnbaum 1983: 77–8).

A related advantage of the case study method is that it more readily allows the exploration of *interaction* between variables. In other words it enables one to modify the artificially simplistic notion of clear-cut dependent and independent variables having one-way causal links. It will be argued in later chapters, for example, that processes within state enterprises act back upon the wider political context and modify its impact.

The idea of looking at variations in political response to a common economic crisis has provided the starting point for recent comparative studies, examining, for example, differences in the political strategies of the labour movement, its relation to the state and to other social classes (notably Goldthorpe 1984a). One of the major themes of the present study is that variations in the political response to economic crisis profoundly affect readjustments in the public enterprise sector. Political responses are dependent on the nature of the state, the political process and class relations. The theme goes to the heart of recent debate about the capitalist state and its degree of 'relative autonomy' from the interests of any one class in society.

This concern influences the choice of comparator. Within the overall group of advanced industrialized, capitalist market economies, it is necessary to choose a pair of countries that gives sufficient interesting variation in the 'independent variable'; that is, in the nature of the political system (including the place of state enterprise within it), and in the relationship between social classes and the state. Of major industrial countries, certainly within Europe, Britain and Spain provide perhaps the widest variation on these factors. The comparison does not set up the neat, formal differences such as those exploited by Weaver (1985) between the executive dominance of the Canadian parliamentary system and the checks and balances of the United States constitution. But it does allow the exploration of the effect of political factors at several different levels of analysis.

First, there are differences in the historical nature and development of the British and Spanish states. Spain is, together with Portugal, marked out from other European countries by its ambiguous historical engagement with the New World and with Africa (for example, the Moorish conquest in the eighth century led to a domination that lasted for up to eight centuries in some regions). Broad historical developments leave a distinctive legacy of political assumptions and behaviour.

Second, there is the very different trajectory of recent political history in the two countries. In Britain, most of the post-war period was marked by 'Butskellite' consensus within the continuity of a long-established parliamentary tradition. Spain by contrast has had a 40-year dictatorship which unlike those of Japan, Germany or Italy, is part of very recent history. The period of authoritarian rule has given way during the last decade or so to a democratic system that is still consolidating itself. Spain has the added advantage as a comparator, therefore, that it contains its own recent 'internal comparison' between markedly different political systems. Moreover, the 'transition to democracy' has occurred at exactly the time when the international economic crisis was making its presence felt with greatest intensity. It thus provides an unusually good opportunity to try to disentangle the general cross-national effects of the crisis from the influence of national political factors.

Third, the choice of Spain provides an important short-term political variable. The major political responses to the economic crisis have taken place under governments of a very different stripe in the two countries: the 'Thatcherite' Conservatives in Britain, and the Socialists of the PSOE (Partido Socialista Obrero Español) under Felipe González in Spain. This allows exploration of the impact of differing political ideologies and political alliances on the readjustments taking place in the state enterprise sector.

There are also more pragmatic reasons behind the choice of Spain. The vast majority of cross-national case studies confine themselves to a narrow range of countries: United States, Japan, Scandinavia, France, West Germany, Italy and the United Kingdom; and to a lesser extent, Canada and the smaller northern and central European countries (notably Holland and Austria). Comparative industrial relations studies which involve Spain are virtually non-existent, the only exception springing to mind being Dunlop's analysis in the 1950s (when Spain could hardly be considered an 'advanced' capitalist country) of the 'web of rules' in the construction industry (1958: ch. 6).[3] Yet Spain, with a population approaching 40 million, is now one of the major industrialized nations, eighth in the OECD group of countries in terms of GDP and fifth within Europe. Increasingly it is turning away from its relative isolation and facing towards the rest of Europe, a move symbolized by its accession to the European Economic Community on 1 January 1986 (and in quite another sense by its debates concerning its membership of the NATO alliance). If this by itself were not sufficient grounds for paying Spain more attention than it has hitherto received, the development of the country's industrial relations over the last decade provides ample material for fertile investigation. In particular, the transition to democracy has seen a condensed and accelerated process of institutionalization of industrial relations, and of accompanying political exchange between the labour movement, employers and the state that would normally only be observable over a far longer period. These processes have a relevance to academic and practical debates that go far beyond the confines of the Spanish case.

Plan of the Book

Public enterprises are part of the state, and its typical forms of organization and behaviour will be mirrored in them. Chapter 2 therefore explores the nature of the capitalist state, examining its 'relative autonomy' from the so-called needs of the economic system, and its complex internal organization. It is argued that political programmes have to be worked out by actors within the state, rather than emerging automatically from the 'needs' of the economic system. The nature of the state affects the way enterprises are controlled and their objectives are set. As well as examining the general pattern, the sources of variability within the state are analysed, and pertinent differences in the nature of the Spanish and British states are briefly described.

Chapter 3 examines in detail the characteristic logic of state enterprises and argues that the relationship of these enterprises to the state is marked by conflicting and changeable political objectives and an oscillation between pressures for political control and enterprise autonomy. The chapter focuses on the effect on this pattern of recent efforts to make the enterprises more 'commercially oriented'. A central theme is that the 'transmission' of state objectives to the enterprises is problematic, and that this gives rise to typical patterns of negotiation over changes in business strategy and in industrial relations. The form of these transmission processes is affected by variables such as the effectiveness of political control structures, as well as by differences in the organization of management and unions within the corporations. Again, broad differences between the British and Spanish public enterprise sectors, and in the respective government policies towards them, are outlined.

The first part of the book therefore establishes a framework of analysis for the detailed case studies of British and Spanish railways in chapters 4–9. Chapter 4 examines the changing political pressures on the railways, stressing the differences in the political process in Britain and Spain. It explores how the rise of public sector 'commercialism' has encouraged new management strategies in both countries. The consequences of these developments for industrial relations are the subject of the following chapters. Chapter 5 describes the similarities and differences in the 'institutional' background of industrial relations in British Rail (BR) and the Red Nacional de Ferrocarriles Españoles (Spanish Railways Network – RENFE), relating these to broader political and social developments. It emphasizes the direct and indirect effects of political control and intervention on the pattern of industrial relations. But it also suggests that industrial relations have a relative autonomy of their own, and hence are an independent influence on the railways' response to the pressures of commercialism. Management's efforts to devise new industrial relations strategies and styles appropriate for the changing circumstances are the subject of chapter 6. It is suggested that the timing and the content of new strategies differed markedly between BR and RENFE.

The underlying reasons for these differences are explored in depth in chapters 7 and 8. Chapter 7 shows how the nature of management strategy has been influenced by the success of the government in changing the 'rules of the game' – the set of political signals that forms the environment for managerial decision-making and determines the broad costs and benefits of different courses of action. It is argued that differences in the political agendas and ideologies of the British and Spanish governments lie behind the variable pressures – and opportunities – for industrial relations change experienced by railway management. Chapter 8 takes up another theme from chapter 6: why managerial strategies concentrate on particular issues rather than others. It argues that this reflects the inherent character of the relationship between the public enterprise and the political controllers. In order to retain political support, management has to address the preoccupations and objectives of the government as well as pursuing an internal managerial rationale. This leads to a concentration on politically symbolic items. Differences in the content of industrial relations strategies between BR and RENFE is thus again related to the different agendas of the British and Spanish governments.

The analysis stresses that managerial strategy in public enterprises develops by a process of negotiation between the enterprises and the state. Chapter 9 explores this theme by looking at the role of the trade unions in political bargaining over new industrial relations strategies. The limits and possibilities of such bargaining are shown to depend on complex interactions between the actors' strategies. The differences between the Spanish and British cases are used to highlight these processes.

The final chapter summarizes the themes of the book and attempts to synthesize the arguments about the nature of state enterprise industrial relations at a time of change. It assesses both the general processes affecting the public

enterprise sector, and the variations between countries resulting from differences in the political environment and in institutional industrial relations
factors.

A Note on Data Sources

The book is based on research that was carried out in British Rail and RENFE
between 1983 and 1986. The period of intensive fieldwork lasted from the summer of 1983 to the summer of 1984, but there was continuing contact with both
companies over the following two years. The detailed cases described in
chapters 7—9 concentrate heavily on the events that took place during that
period.

Since the aim of the research was to illuminate the industrial relations of state
enterprises by examining two corporations in considerable detail, there was a
need to collect material rich enough to illustrate the nature of the processes at
work. This dictated the extensive use of in-depth interviews. Over 100 interviews were carried out, lasting some 170 hours in all, as well as several shorter,
informal conversations. The great majority of them were with the management
and unions of the railways, the remainder with politicians, civil servants and
others closely involved with the railways and their industrial relations. Management interviews were conducted primarily with senior personnel and industrial
relations managers, though individuals involved in finance, planning and operations were also interviewed, as were managers at regional and local area level.
The purpose of the interviewing programme was to collect background information on the nature of the railways and their industrial relations, and to examine
a number of key issues and events with the actors who had participated in them.
Where possible, information on an issue was collected from several different
respondents to minimize the risk of bias.[4]

The interviews were supplemented by as much documentary information as
could be collected. This consisted of management data on pay, productivity,
hours, .staff numbers and so on, minutes of negotiating and consultative
meetings, and internal plans and reports. Annual reports and accounts were a
fruitful source of information.[5] The unions also provided copious material.
Finally, extensive use was made of published sources which for BR in particular
are quite voluminous. As well as a wide range of books on all aspects of the
railway question there are numerous official sources, from special commissions
of inquiry, to House of Commons select committee reports and minutes of
evidence, and debates in parliament. The relative lack of equivalent material on
RENFE (reflecting, among other things, the newness of the tradition of
democratic scrutiny in Spain) was partly compensated for by carrying out additional interviews.

Notes

1   For example, for the seven major capitalist nations (Canada, France, West Germany,
    Italy, Japan, United Kingdom and United States), the unemployment rate more than
    doubled, from 3.4 per cent to 8.4 per cent between 1973 and 1983 (Armstrong *et al.*

1984: 324), and the rate in the EEC more than trebled from 3.0 per cent to 10.1 per cent over the same period. GDP in the seven major countries rose by an average of only 1.9 per cent per annum during the period 1973−82, compared with a figure of 5.5 per cent for the period 1960−73 (ibid.: 336). The *origins* of the crisis are of course the subject of much debate, the evaluation of which is beyond the scope of the present study. The assumption implicit in the arguments that will be presented below is that the crisis was the outcome of forces inherent in the capitalist system (see, e.g., Mandel 1978, Armstrong *et al*. 1984: ch. 11), rather than of exogenous 'shocks' such as the Vietnam war or the 1970s oil price rises (see Goldthorpe 1984b: 2).

2 For a summary of explanations in these terms, see Bean 1985: 136−56.

3 Anecdotal, but striking, evidence for the almost total neglect of Spanish industrial relations is the absence of a single article on the subject in the main British academic industrial relations journal, the *BJIR*, from the time of its foundation in 1963 to the end of 1986 (with the solitary exception of a piece on the Mondragon workers' co-operative).

4 Extracts from interview notes are referred to in the text as 'fieldnotes'. The notes, although not strictly verbatim, are detailed and close approximations of the words used by the respondents.

5 For the sake of brevity in referencing, annual reports are referred to in the text by the year to which they refer, followed by the suffix 'r' in the case of British Railways Board's *Annual Report and Accounts*, and 'm' for RENFE's *Memoria* (e.g. BRB 1979r; RENFE 1980m).

2

The State and Relative Autonomy

Introduction

The task of the next two chapters is to provide a framework and some analytical tools for exploring public enterprise industrial relations. Public enterprise is part of the state; its logic of action, and hence the functioning of its industrial relations, must be understood in terms of the place that it occupies within the state. Yet most accounts of public sector industrial relations ignore the nature of the state. It is treated, if at all, only in the most descriptive terms. This chapter considers, therefore, the nature of the state, its internal composition, and its relationship to the groups, classes and interests of 'civil society'. Chapter 3 examines the place of public enterprises within the state, the nature of their objectives, the logic of their functioning, including their patterns of industrial relations, and the dynamic of their development over time. Within this broad picture, the factors that lead to different patterns in different states are considered, and some broad comparisons are made between the state and public enterprise in Britain and in Spain.

Relative Autonomy of the State

The nature of the capitalist state has been the subject of exhaustive argument in recent years, particularly among Marxist scholars (see, e.g., Jessop 1982). A central question in the debate concerns the relationship between the nature of the state and the development of the capitalist economic system as a whole. Early approaches which saw the state as the 'instrument' or tool of the dominant class, faithfully tending to its needs, were soon seen to be inadequate. Another approach, exemplified by the work of a number of German theorists (see Holloway and Picciotto 1978), derived the functions of the capitalist state from the 'needs' of capitalist accumulation. Thus the role of the state was to provide the economic, legal and administrative infrastructure; ensure adequate supplies of labour resources through education, health and welfare; and maintain the working of the market system. In short, it was to supply the framework for economic activity, especially in areas where private capital, operating according to the logic of profitability, would be unable to provide it. Other writers were quick to point out the inherent functionalism of this approach. There were no grounds for assuming that the capitalist state would work in such a way as to meet the needs of the system. First, these needs were themselves ambiguous and often contradictory. They had to be 'processed' or interpreted in the political sphere through the cut and thrust of political debate and conflict. Moreover, writers such as Poulantzas (e.g. 1978) pointed out that the state was not just called upon to meet the needs of capitalist accumulation; in a class-divided society the long-term stability of the system depended on the state's being able to act as a force of cohesion and stand as a 'symbol of legitimacy' for all sections of society. It was the argument of writers such as Offe (e.g. 1975b) that such demands on the state could lead to state policies that conflicted with the other needs of capitalist development.

Second, the contradictions inherent in the demands made on the state were likely to intensify as capitalist development proceeded. The growth of industrial concentration and the size of firms, the acceleration of technological innovation, and the increased costs of restructuring sectors of private capital (that is concentrating resources in more efficient units and transferring resources from declining to more profitable sectors of production) all tended to undermine the effectiveness of the market as an 'automatic' regulator of the processes of capitalist accumulation. As a result, the state was increasingly expected to intervene in order to provide the basic requirements of the system and to 'socialize' the costs of economic development. In the words of Mandel (1978: 484), 'there is thus an inherent trend under late capitalism for the state to incorporate an ever greater number of productive and reproductive sectors into the "general conditions of production" which it finances'. Increasingly, the state was financing the research and development costs of private industry, and subsidizing the activities of the private sector through grants, tax regimes, the provision of cheap inputs and so on (552−5).

At the same time, the development of the division of labour, the growth of the labour movement, the increased education of the working class, and so on, were leading classes and social interests other than those of capital to make more insistent demands on the state (e.g. Lehner and Widmaier 1981; Gough 1979). The ability of pressure groups and class interests to make use of the parliamentary political system has been interpreted by conservative critics of the expansion of the state's role as giving rise to an 'overload' of demands on the state (e.g. Brittan 1976). In other words, the demands on the state in its capacity as the focus of the system's legitimacy were increasing over time.

The two sets of pressures on the state − to meet demands for social welfare and other expenditure tied up with the legitimacy of the political system, and to provide the conditions for capitalist accumulation − were seen as leading to a growing 'fiscal crisis of the state' (O'Connor 1973). The quantitative growth of advanced capitalist states in recent years may be illustrated by the proportion of GDP represented by general government expenditure in OECD countries, shown in table 2.1.

The state's expanding role threatened capitalist development by drawing funds from the sector of production for profit into the state sector. Non-Marxist critics of the growing state intervention described this phenomenon as one of 'crowding out', whereby the state's activity starved the private sector of financial, physical and labour resources (e.g. Bacon and Eltis 1976). Even where the state's activities were productive, in the sense of producing a surplus, the capitalist logic of accumulation was undermined by the fact that the production of that surplus did not respond to the signals of profitability characterizing private capitalist activity (Frankel 1979; Offe 1975a).

The Sources of Relative Autonomy
The critique of functionalism led writers to stress the 'relative autonomy' of the capitalist state, manifested in its existence as a set of institutions separate from the classes of civil society. Originally, in the hands of Poulantzas (e.g. 1969; 1978) and others, the concept had a distinctly functionalist tinge. It was seen to derive directly from the dual functions of the state, the securing of accumulation and legitimation. The latter was only possible if the state was seen to be separate from direct control by capital. But the concept need not be functionalist, as writers such as Jessop and Offe have indicated. First, the fact that the 'needs' of accumulation and those of legitimation may be contradictory or confused, both internally and with respect to each other, gives an independent role to the political sphere in the formation of policy. Second, the form of the state allows the interests of groups and classes other than the dominant class to find expression within it. This is especially the case with the liberal democratic form of the state whose claim to legitimacy rests on the access to the political system which it grants to non-dominant interests. As a result, the interests of the subordinate social groups may at times prevail over those of capital; at the very least, such interests affect the form and outputs of the policy process. Thus, the very nature

TABLE 2.1
Public Expenditure/GDP Ratio for Selected OECD Countries

	1960	1965	1970	1975	1980	% Increase 1960–1980
France	34.6	38.4	38.9	43.5	46.2	33.5
Italy	30.1	34.3	34.2	43.2	45.6	51.2
Japan	20.7	22.7	19.3	27.3	32.7	58.0
Spain	13.7	19.6	22.2	24.7	32.4	136.5
UK	32.6	36.4	39.3	46.9	44.6	36.8
W. Germany	32.0	36.3	37.6	47.1	46.9	46.6
All OECD	28.5	30.1	32.6	38.2	39.4	38.3

Source: Heald 1983, pp. 30–31.

of the demands made upon the state by the capitalist system leads to a form of the state that cannot necessarily ensure that capitalist interests are furthered.

The notion of relative autonomy raises the question of the limits within which the state's autonomy may vary. Writers such as Zeitlin (1985: 22−5) argue that, if the autonomy is real, there is nothing to stop the state from *not* pursuing capitalist interests. However, several writers have postulated plausible mechanisms limiting the degree of autonomy of the state. Block (1980) and Offe (e.g. 1974), for example, have argued that there are structural 'selection mechanisms', notably the dependence of the state's activity on resources generated by the private sector, and the nature of capitalism as an international competitive system, that prevent the state from mounting a threat to the continuation of the capitalist mode of production (cf. also Poulantzas 1978: 190−3). It is appropriate therefore to see the state and its actors as facing strategic choices within constraints.

Nonetheless, the limits of the state's autonomy would seem to be very wide, and Block goes so far as to postulate a 'tipping mechanism' which could allow the state to take a social formation away from the capitalist mode of production. Taking their lead from Marx's classic account (1926) of the regime of Louis Bonaparte, writers (e.g. Miliband 1984; Ferner 1983) have argued that stalemate between classes or fractions of classes gives the state abnormal freedom of action, loosening the impact of the usual structural constraints and enabling it to prevent the interests of civil society from being expressed. The dominant class's grip on the formation of state policy may be weakened, for example in times of economic recession, giving the state heightened autonomy, as in the experience of the New Deal in the United States (Edwards 1986: ch. 4).

If the state is autonomous, within wide and variable limits, what determines how the state actually behaves, in other words the logic of state action? For many if not most writers in the Marxist or neo-Marxist tradition, the state is an 'arena of class struggle'. Class interests are represented within and through the state, and from their clash emerge state policies (e.g. Edwards 1986: ch. 4); the state represents the 'crystallization' of a relationship of class forces (Therborn 1978; Poulantzas 1978: part II), although it is not reducible to class relations. Thus state policies and actions reflect the balance of class forces and the way that balance is represented within the state. This implies that when the balance is temporarily favourable to the working class, the demands that it espouses, whether or not they are in the interests of the dominant class, may be translated into state policy − for example, on social welfare (see Gough 1979; Esping-Andersen and Korpi 1984), workers' rights and so on.

However, the nature of the state's action cannot be understood solely by reference to what happens outside the state. The notion of relative autonomy and the idea that the state faces choices suggests two further lines of inquiry, both of which have been relatively neglected in the mainstream of Marxist debates on the state, although they have been explored in the traditions of political science and public administration.

First, the state has its own institutional interests distinct from those of the classes and groups of civil society (Skocpol 1979; Zeitlin 1985: 16−26; Miliband 1983: 62−4). Skocpol (1979: 24−32) has strongly criticized the idea of the state as 'nothing but an arena in which conflicts over basic social and economic interests are fought out' (25). Against the arguments of writers such as Poulantzas, that the state is not an intrinsic entity, a subject capable of exercising power in its own right (e.g. 1978: 128), she maintains that it is 'an organization-for-itself' (Skocpol 1979: 27), which extracts resources from society and uses them to support coercive and administrative organizations. The state has two specific tasks: to maintain social order and to compete with other states. Its interest in maintaining 'sheer physical order and political peace' (30) may lead it to act against existing economic interests and class structure; moreover, its involvement with other states is a basis for potential autonomy of action over and against groups and economic arrangements within its jurisdiction. Thus Skocpol sees the state's autonomy as deriving from the specific political functions that it performs. Although it might be objected that Skocpol's analysis courts the danger of falling into another version of functionalism, since it postulates some inherent functions of the state, it has the benefit of drawing attention to processes within the state and the specific logic which guides them.

Second, the state is composed of separate agencies concerned with the formulation and implementation of policy, that is, it has an *internal structure* (Therborn 1978). In liberal democracies, there is, to varying degrees, a functional differentiation between legislative and executive tasks, although this has been seen as increasingly eroded by the growth of executive policy-making powers, whether *de facto* or statutory, and the emergence of policy-making 'communities' within the state administration. The main formal channel of representation of interests is through the elective process and the organization of political parties around programmes and ideologies.

The state administration is itself highly differentiated into agencies responsible for different aspects of policy. For example, policy is divided into different issue areas such as state finance, production and distribution (industry and trade), social welfare, foreign relations, labour management and so on. These policy areas are located in different parts of the state, each with its own 'institutional relative autonomy' (Palmer 1985: 528) and distinct organizational interests and policy agendas.

In more purely administrative and policy terms, the interests of different state agencies may be in conflict with each other, for example the interest of the treasury (finance ministry) and central bank in controlling government expenditure may, and frequently in real states does, conflict with the interests of production ministries such as industry and energy in promoting the development of their sector. This functional differentiation of the state apparatus leads potentially to the fragmentation of political authority, because of the problems of coordination and direction by the central executive authority, the government.

Fragmentation depends on factors such as the nature of political representation. States such as Italy with a preponderance of coalition government or with marked factional organization within political parties have seen the phenomenon of the parcelling up of different parts of the state administration among different parties or factions (e.g. Donolo 1980). In such cases, the functional differentiation between parties and the permanent state administration becomes blurred; a dominant political party may 'occupy' the state, but at the same time, becomes itself 'institutionalised' (167—8). This interpenetration of party and state machinery further complicates internal state relations, and also the relations between the political party and the interests of civil society that it represents.

Further, fragmentation is encouraged in many states by the relative transience of the political authority compared with the permanent state administration. Thus government ministers and other political appointments within the bureaucracy are frequently replaced, and governments themselves have a relatively short lifespan compared with the timescale for the generation and implementation of policy.

Fragmentation also results from the need for different 'regions' of the state to act according to different logics. As Offe (1975a: 136—40) argues, the classic Weberian model of bureaucratic rationality is suitable for applying predetermined rules in a universal, undifferentiated manner through a hierarchical structure composed of 'neutral' officials. This rationality is well described by a former head of the British civil service, Sir Douglas Allen: 'The desire for uniformity of treatment, coupled with accountability for decisions, require elaborate codes and rules so that a multiplicity of decision-makers can produce acceptably similar results in similar cases' (cited in Thomson 1983: 141). But it is not adequate for many of the tasks of the modern capitalist state which has to intervene increasingly according to a 'substantive' rather than 'formal' rationality (Therborn 1978: 54, 89) based on highly specialized forms of expertise (e.g. Dunleavy 1982: 196—205) — for example, in production itself. As a result the hierarchical structure of the state has been increasingly broken up by horizontal structures of working parties, *ad hoc* reviews, and above all, semi-autonomous government agencies (see, e.g. Barker 1982). Palmer (1985: 527) has argued that these 'quasi-government organisations', 'being relatively independent of normal public service rules, ... have a greater flexibility in operations and decision-making'. They increasingly operate in 'complex and dense networks of cross-cutting territorial, functional, and hierarchical organisational relationships' (Hood 1982: 66). The outcome of these developments is, therefore, a 'highly differentiated and fragmented form of government' (Dunleavy 1982: 185), in which co-ordination is achieved as much by negotiation and bargaining between agencies as by imperative, bureaucratic control mechanisms.

The fragmentation of the state, and the relative autonomy of its constituent agencies, also depends on the degree of permeability of the state to the interests of civil society. In the model of liberal democracy, interests are aggregated through political parties and expressed within the parliamentary system. But there are also forms of direct access of interests to the state, notably through relationships with individual state agencies. In some parts of the state, notably the quasi-autonomous organizations, the distinction between public and private is blurred (e.g. Dunleavy 1982: esp. 188—92). State agencies may enter into alliances and negotiate with private interest groups, and such alliances may provide the agencies with the leverage to resist, or act independently of, centrally co-ordinated state policy. However, the permeability of state agencies to external influence may lead them to serve the interests of private groups, and in extreme cases to become 'colonised' by them. Thus increased autonomy *within* the state may imply reduced freedom of manoeuvre with respect to outside interests;

though conversely, private interest organizations may become 'semi-private extensions of government' (Dunleavy 1982: 189). But the point is that the degree of autonomy is not static, determined *a priori*, but rather is negotiated within and outside the state. As with the state as a whole, the permeability of state agencies to civil society depends upon the balance of power between classes and interest groups, a point that will be returned to in the following chapter in connection with state enterprises.

The Variability of the Capitalist State

The discussion of relative autonomy suggests that to say that a state is capitalist is to make a statement at a very high level of abstraction. The constraints of the capitalist mode of production still permit a great degree of variability in actual historical states. The variability, which reflects both the relationship of the state to civil society and the internal organization of the state, operates at distinct, although interacting, levels of analysis. First, writers such as Badie and Birnbaum (1983) or Moore (1967) operating from a broad historical perspective suggest that states have a distinct character resulting from long-term processes of political development. In particular, the nature of class relationships and the degree of political centralization under feudalism affect the subsequent character of the state under capitalism, particularly forms of representation and the balance of power between state and civil society. Strong interventionist states with powerful centralized bureaucracies and institutions of state coercion, for example, may be contrasted with those of countries where the interests of civil society are stronger and state institutions are moulded to its purpose. Below, the main points of contrast between the British and Spanish states are briefly sketched.

Variations in the 'Historical Character' and Development of the State in Britain and Spain

The British state, compared, for example, with the powerful French state, developed in line with the interests of the dominant groups of civil society. Political centralization under the Tudor monarchs enabled the early creation of a unified national state. The tendency to royal absolutism was halted by the English revolution of the seventeenth century which reflected the dynamism of civil society and firmly established its pre-eminence. The centralized bureaucratic apparatus of the state became subordinated to the interests of the dominant economic groups that were already creating a commercial agriculture and would subsequently promote industrial development: 'for the first time a state had been created whose policies and activities were shaped in response to the needs and movement of civil society' (Gamble 1981: 67).

Subsequently the British state evolved with a remarkable degree of stability and continuity when compared with the state in Spain. Emerging groups, including the subordinate classes, were more or less successfully incorporated into political life, first by successive extensions of the suffrage and political 'citizenship', later by the evolution of well-organized institutions of interest mediation.

During the present century these have gained broad access to the policy process within the state.

Badie and Birnbaum (1983: 77–8) have argued that in countries where the working class has to organize in the context of a strong state, the labour movement has often been preoccupied with state power, giving rise to a powerful strand of revolutionary syndicalism as in France or Spain. By contrast, the British labour movement was more interested in shopfloor and trade union organizational issues than with politics or revolution: the ' "trade union model" is seen to be a perfectly logical development in a civil society with considerable capacities for self-organisation'. Another consequence is seen to be the lower degree of legal regulation of industrial relations in Britain compared with countries where the labour movement developed in the context of a strong state (see Bean 1985: ch. 5 for a summary of the literature).

The general subordination of the British state to the interests of civil society has limited the relative autonomy of state groups, although they have had a certain freedom to 'navigate' between the competing demands of different groups and classes, for example in the realm of industrial relations (Edwards 1986: 168–72). The internal organization of state policy-making has tended to reflect the lines of cleavage within dominant economic groups of civil society. For example, the dominant role of the Treasury and the Bank of England in economic policy-making and the absence of administrative counterweights in the ministries concerned with industrial policy is often said to reflect the dominance of British financial capital (e.g. Longstreth 1979).

The British pattern of development has limited the extent of corporate interests within the state, certainly when compared with Spain (see below). Notably, the Northcote–Trevelyan reforms helped to root out political patronage and corruption in the state bureaucracy in the second half of the nineteenth century, and to establish a public administration that operated according to principles of professionalism and the ethos of 'public service'.

While, as suggested earlier, the different time horizons of elected politicians and civil servants allow scope for the fragmentation of policy-making and group interests, limits are placed on this by the openness of the British state to organized interests. This gives rise to the typical 'policy style' of consultation and negotiation between different state agencies; each is at the centre of a 'policy community' composed of government officials, professional advisors and representatives of outside pressure groups (Jordan and Richardson 1981; 1987).

The historical character of the Spanish state, by comparison, falls into the pattern, exemplified by France, of a centralized, interventionist institution that developed before strong independent economic forces in civil society had time to emerge.[1] The feudal institutions of the *ancien régime* began to be dismantled under the bureaucratic reforms of the eighteenth century Carlist monarchy, and the process was hastened by the Napoleonic invasion, rather than by the pressure of new economic interests and the emergence of commercial agriculture. A polity grew up in the nineteenth century that, through changes of regime, was characterized by its narrow social base and the 'exclusion of subordinate classes from any form of participation in the political sphere' (Giner 1985: 311). The military played an important role as arbiter of conflicts between the restricted political groups, leading to the era of 'pronunciamientos' in mid-century. The army was, of course, to play a recurring part in Spanish political life in the twentieth century with the Nationalist insurrection against the second republic, and before that, the dictatorship of General Primo de Rivera from 1923 until 1931.

Spanish industrialization was relatively weak, late, and often under foreign control, and indeed the country remained a largely agrarian and underdeveloped society during the nineteenth century and well into the twentieth. In 1930, 50 per cent of the population still depended on agriculture, compared with 10 per cent in Britain. This development path led to a pattern of state interests markedly different from that in Britain:

> The political class controlling the state under the different regimes . . . was relatively independent of civil society. The control of the state apparatus, the manipulation of elections, the granting of privileges, and the control of violence often rendered the political class relatively autonomous and independent of interests or at least able to discriminate among them (Linz 1981: 368).

The unusual degree of relative autonomy of the Spanish state has continued into recent times. The Franco regime was able to control interest groups by means of the hierarchically ordered syndicate system which organized the different branches of the economy under the direction of the state. Autonomous interest representation, even of dominant economic groups, was successfully prevented. Instead, the state was organised by the political 'families' that provided the base of support for Francoism: the Falangists, the military, the monarchists, and later the lay Catholic 'Opus Dei' technocrats (Carr and Fusi 1981: ch. 2). These groups tended to divide up the different parts of the state machinery, with the Falangists, for example, controlling the ministry of labour, while the technocrats were in charge of economic policy from the 1960s. The relationship between state groups and civil society was thus fundamentally different from that in Britain, a point brought into focus by Linz's comment that the 'access of the political elites, the military, bureaucrats, Catholics and Opus Dei to positions of economic power in the public sector, and increasingly in the private sector, poses the interesting and difficult question of the extent to which political power can be transformed into economic power rather than the reverse' (1981: 392–30). This is of relevance to the distinctive origin and role of the public enterprise sector in Spain, a question that is considered in chapter 3.

Nonetheless, rapid economic development, which led to real income per head tripling during the 1960s and quintupling again during the 1970s, strengthened private economic interests.[2] Although these groups were often closely associated with the Francoist regime, their interests could not be expressed through the limited channels of the Francoist state. Economic development was also creating massive changes in the subordinate classes. The proportion of the population living and employed in rural areas declined sharply. Industrialization inevitably led to the expansion of the urban working class. These forces introduced unresolvable contradictions into the political model of hierarchical, authoritarian control of civil society. In the words of Giner (1985: 338), Spain, like the other authoritarian regimes of southern Europe, 'sheltered a "liberal" economy within an illiberal polity'. Well before the death of Franco, the model was breaking down. For example, autonomous grass roots organization at the workplace was officially tolerated at certain times, despite continuing repression, and the introduction of collective bargaining from the 1960s, particularly in the modern, foreign-controlled sectors of manufacturing, loosened the state's tight control over the regulation of labour.

The contradictions of the model help explain why the transition from Francoism to democracy did not take place by a process of radical 'rupture', but through a more consensual evolution in which elements of the regime's own institutions and key political figures played a central role.[3]

The historical growth of the state in Spain in combination with the weakness of economic development gave rise to a middle class connected with state employment and 'overloading of the public administration by parasitical personnel' (Giner 1985: 318). Giner adds that this phenomenon, common to the Southern European states, continues to be felt to the present day. 'Empleomanía' or the 'rage for office' as Dyson translates it (1980: 61), together with clientelistic politics based on 'enchufe' or personal contacts, came to characterize the public administration. Successive reforms failed to end patronage and to establish the sort of professional, rationally organized state bureaucracy loyal to the notion of public service that the Northcote–Trevelyan reforms made possible in Britain. The weakness of countervailing forces enabled state employees to pursue their corporate interests through the hundreds of specialist 'cuerpos'. These corps arose from the middle of the nineteenth century in response to the chronic insecurity caused by a Spanish version of the 'spoils system': each change of government would lead to the replacement of all those appointed under the previous government by individuals loyal to the new party in power.[4]

The corps have become, according to Medhurst (1973: 113), 'a means of transforming administrative structures to serve private ends'. They established considerable control over recruitment and promotion, and even collected special levies to supplement their basic pay. While the bureaucracy was highly centralized, with control being exerted from Madrid (at least until the devolution of functions to the new autonomous regions in recent years), fragmentation and lack of co-ordination resulted from the fiercely protected interests of the corps and their hermetic structure which allowed virtually no mobility between them.

To this day, the Spanish civil service is more politicized than its British counterpart. A modified version of the spoils system continues, since the senior civil service posts of under-secretary, director general and deputy director general within ministries remain political appointments. Under Franco, they used to be distributed among representatives of the different political groups that made up the regime's base of support; under democracy, incumbents in such posts have tended to be replaced with each change of government. There is also a much closer interconnection than in Britain between political elites and administrative elites within the state. The political class under Franco – ministers, political appointees in the civil service and members of the Cortes (Spanish Parliament) – was drawn to a marked extent from the ranks of civil servants (Beltrán 1977: ch. 2). During the early years of the transition back to democracy, politicians of the governing party moved repeatedly between ministerial posts, civil service appointments and management positions in public enterprises.

Variability of Political Responses to Economic Crisis in Britain and Spain

A second level of analysis of state variability is the response to much more short-term balances of political forces and economic conjunctures. As was suggested in chapter 1, a major theme of the present study is to examine differential reactions within two different states to a common economic crisis. Goldthorpe and others (Goldthorpe 1984a) have argued that these reactions express forms of political accommodations and alliances between social classes, allowing states to construct widely differing political strategies for confronting the crisis. Cameron (1984) argues, for example, that in countries where the labour movement is capable of reaching a political accommodation based on collective restraint in its economic demands, the rate of inflation is lower and employment higher than in countries where the working class is more militant. In turn, the ability of the working class to pursue a strategy of class co-operation depends upon its internal organization, strength and unity (Cameron 1984: 163–70; Regini 1984). State conjunctural policies respond, similarly, to variations in the strategies and internal organization of the dominant class. Thus Esping-Andersen and Korpi (1984) argue that cross-national variations in social welfare policy reflect factors such as the strength and homogeneity of the bourgeoisie and its political representatives.

The effects of the general economic crisis were being acutely felt in Britain and Spain by the mid-1970s or earlier. In both countries the crisis superimposed itself on more chronic economic problems. The decline of British manufacturing and the problems of relatively low growth, productivity and competitiveness had concerned policy makers for decades, while the Spanish 'economic miracle' of rapid growth during the 1960s concealed major structural weaknesses of the economy.

The world recession and the oil shocks of the 1970s exposed these weaknesses and precipitated effects that were often considerably worse than those in other advanced capitalist countries. The growth of GNP stagnated. During the second half of the 1960s, GNP had been rising at about 3 per cent a year in Britain. Between 1971 and 1976, the annual growth rate fell to 1.8 per cent and in the following five-year period it was only 0.5 per cent. From 1961 to 1973, Spain's growth had been 7 per cent a year, faster than in any capitalist economy except Japan; by 1976–81, growth was down to 1.4 per cent a year. Following the first oil shock, inflation rose from a figure of about 5 per cent in both countries in the early 1970s to an annual average of 16 per cent in Britain and 19 per cent in Spain in the period 1973–8. Spain was especially affected by its dependence on imported oil. Unemployment rose sharply. The number out of work in Britain which had stood at little more than half a million in 1969, had more than doubled by the end of the 1970s (then almost doubled again in the following two years). In Spain, unemployment rose from 2.1 per cent in 1972 to over 17 per cent in 1982.[5]

As has been suggested in this chapter, the relative autonomy of the state from the mode of production means that the jump from tendencies in the economy to a political response to those tendencies is problematic. The timing and content of political strategies for confronting the economic crisis within individual countries will depend on the kinds of interrelated factors that have been examined: the balance of social forces, class strategies and alliances and their expression within the state through the medium of political parties and their ideologies. Thus a political response does not arise automatically and fully formed out of the needs generated by crisis.

Thus it was that Britain and Spain produced two distinct political responses to the crisis. The Conservative government of 1979 represented a break with the post-war Keynesian consensus in economic management. Although the move away from Keynesianism had begun during the mid-1970s under a Labour government, the Thatcherite programme explicitly rejected the previous consensus and embraced a liberal political economy based on the restoration of market forces and market values.

Much of Conservative policy was therefore devoted to getting rid of 'imperfections' in the market. This lay behind the government's attacks on the power of trade unions. The union movement's informal channels of political influence became blocked, and the role of 'tripartism' in economic policy-making was diminished. The Conservatives' legislation to impose legal constraints on picketing, industrial action, the closed shop, the use of political funds, and so on, was justified as a means of removing impediments, both to the flexible operation of the labour market, and to the 'rights' and liberties of individual workers.

The freeing of markets also meant 'getting the state off people's backs'.[6] State expenditure supposedly 'crowded out' private enterprise by making use of scarce physical and financial resources, and by sapping the spirit of enterprise; while the rise of the 'public sector borrowing requirement' (PSBR) − the gap between government revenue and expenditure − was considered to be a major factor in inflation. The government's strategy led to policies to control public expenditure and to reduce the provision of goods and services by the state. This was to have major consequences for public enterprise.

Spain's response to economic crisis was dominated by the transition from an authoritarian regime to a liberal parliamentary democracy. After Franco's death at the end of 1975, the overwhelming political preoccupation was the creation of new democratic institutions. This process was initiated just as the economic crisis began to make itself felt in Spain. But economic problems were put into abeyance; in the words of Carr and Fusi (1981: 219), 'politics had an almost obsessional priority'. Attempts by Franco's supporters to limit change had to be defeated, and a coalition of democratic forces had to be assembled. The political agenda was dominated by issues of basic liberties, the legalization of parties, the introduction of democratic elections and a new constitution, and a decentralization of power to the regions. At the same time, serious threats to the stability of the infant democracy also had to be confronted. Campaigns of terrorist violence from the anti-democratic right and from Basque separatists had a destabilizing effect, while elements in the military remained strongly attached to Franco's authoritarian vision. The vulnerability of democracy was sharply illustrated by the failed coup d'état of February 1981, in which detachments of the civil guard, acting as the stalking horse for plotters in the armed forces, took control of Congress and held members of parliament hostage.

Within the political mainstream, the spirit of these times was consensual. The need to establish the legitimacy of the political system after the years of repression and apathy meant that previously excluded groups such as the organized working class had to be brought into the political process. Trade union liberties were re-established. Strikes were made legal, and a new framework of industrial relations was established. The individual and collective rights of the labour force were codified in the 1980 Workers' Statute.[7]

The consensual politics of the transition was manifested in a number of national compacts involving at different times government, opposition parties (including the Spanish communist party), national unions and employers. The first of these were the Moncloa Pacts of 1977. These agreements aimed to secure widespread support for pay moderation and other austerity measures, but real wages nevertheless increased significantly faster in Spain than in EEC countries (Fina and Hawkesworth 1984). The national agreements also granted important concessions to the labour movement. For example, annual working hours were successively reduced from the equivalent of a 48-hour week to a 40-hour week by 1984. Such compromises and concessions, necessary for maintaining consensual politics, exacerbated the economic pressures; for example, the growth of social provision and the socialization of the losses of large sectors of private capital through nationalization (see chapter 3) was reflected in a rapid rise in public expenditure from 25.0 per cent of GDP in 1975 to 35.4 per cent in 1982 (Donges 1984: 111); the public sector deficit rose from zero to 5.9 per cent of GDP over the same period.

There was, therefore, a significant lag before the newly emerging political system in Spain could turn its attention to the questions raised by the economic crisis. It was only once the basic political problems of the transition had been resolved that a coherent strategy could emerge for confronting the immediate economic crisis, and for dealing with serious underlying questions such as the restructuring of basic sectors of industry and the modernization of state finances and administration. Such a political strategy was crystallized in the programme of the Spanish Socialist party (PSOE) which came to power in 1982. Progress, change and modernization were the key ideas of its programme (PSOE 1982; Maravall 1984: 235−6).

In practice, the economic policies of the Spanish socialists had much in common with those of the Conservatives in Britain. The emphasis was on reducing inflation, increasing the competitiveness of the private sector, controlling the public deficit, and increasing the efficiency of the state sector. Monetarist ideas had considerable influence among economics ministers. A harsh restructuring of basic industries, particularly steel and shipbuilding, took place under the Socialists' rule, although it relied less than in Britain on the power of the 'market' and more on the intervention of the state.

Despite this, there were significant differences, reflecting the PSOE's social base of support as a party of the left, and the particular dynamic of the transition to democracy. Where Thatcherism sought to limit the power of organized labour, the PSOE was closely allied to the socialist segment of the union move-ment and promised to extend the rights of unions and workers. It committed itself to reduce inequality and increase social provision. The party's most impor-tant electoral commitment was the creation of 800,000 jobs over four years, and although it was to fall lamentably short of the aim, the reduction of unemploy-ment remained an important point of reference for the party in power and for its political allies (see, e.g., PSOE 1983: 43–4).

Thus the economic crisis evoked political responses in Britain and Spain that, despite their similarities, differed both in their timing and in their substance. They emerged from different ideological traditions, and had different social bases of support. Above all, one was premised on the rejection of a consensual pattern of post-war politics and of the role of organized labour in policy-making, while the other grew out of consensual politics in a vulnerable phase of political development.

Conclusions

This chapter has identified some features of the advanced capitalist state that are relevant for an understanding of the logic of state enterprises. The state is called on to perform a number of functions necessary for the smooth development of the capitalist system. But far from being logically and mechanically derived from the 'needs' of capitalist accumulation, state policies are the outcome of very complex and contradictory processes. First, even the theoretical basic re-quirements of the system, for policies to further accumulation and to guarantee political legitimacy, are mutually and internally contradictory. Second, the form of the political system means that non-dominant classes have access to the state and hence may influence state policy in directions antipathetic to the interests of capital. Third, the state has its own historically developed 'interests' which it can express to a greater or lesser degree depending on the balance of external class forces and their forms of representation within the state. Finally, the state is fragmented, both in terms of political authority and the organizational form and logic of its component parts.

Two important implications follow from the analysis. In the first place, the internal structure of the state leads to processes of bargaining within the state and between its agencies and interests of civil society, and this in turn raises fur-ther questions on the nature and coherence of state policy. In particular, when the nature of the tasks that state agencies are intended to perform leads them to act with relative autonomy within the state, how is political control to be main-tained without undermining the agencies' freedom of action? This is, of course, a problem of central importance to the case of state enterprises, and forms a major thread of the following chapter.

In the second place, the relative autonomy of the state from the mode of pro-duction means that the jump from tendencies in the economy to a political response to those tendencies is problematic. The formation of a strategy for con-fronting the current crisis of accumulation in the world capitalist system will de-pend on the factors that have been examined in this chapter: the balance of social forces, class strategies and forms of political representation; the broad historical character of the state; and its internal composition, organizational interests, and dynamic. As a result, a political response to economic crisis does not arise automatically, but may only emerge with a considerable lag, and its content will be highly variable from polity to polity.

Notes

1   For accounts of Spanish political development see especially Carr 1982. See also, Linz 1981; Giner 1985; Vilar 1983; Carr and Fusi 1981.
2   On Spain's recent economic development, see, e.g., Lieberman 1982: ch. 4; Harrison 1978: ch. 8; Wright 1977.
3   On the transition to democracy, see, e.g., Carr and Fusi 1981: chs. 9—11; Preston 1986: chs. 3—4; Share 1987.
4   On the role and organization of the 'cuerpos', see especially Beltrán 1977; Medhurst 1973; IBRD 1963: 74—9.
5   On the end of the Spanish 'economic miracle' see Lieberman 1982: ch. 5; Harrison 1982. On the economic crisis in Britain, see, e.g., Gamble 1981; Smith 1986; Williams *et al.* 1983.
6   On the Conservative government's policies and their philosophical underpinnings, see, e.g., Heald 1983: ch. 3; Smith 1986; Keegan 1984.
7   On the development of trade unions and of new industrial relations institutions under democracy, see Fina and Hawkesworth 1984; Fishman 1982; García de Blas 1985; Lawlor and Rigby 1986; Rijnen 1985; Sagardoy and León 1982; Zufiaur 1985. See also *European Industrial Relations Review* (EIRR), especially nos. 53, 74—7, 91.

3

'Commercialism' and the Logic of State Enterprise

Introduction: the Rise of Commercialism in the State Enterprise in Britain and Spain

This chapter first describes how the British and Spanish political strategies discussed in the previous chapter have created pressures for change in the public enterprises, pressures encapsulated in the idea of 'commercialism'. It then explores at a more fundamental level the relationship between public enterprise and the state, in an attempt to understand the ambivalence, tensions and even contradictions that are embodied in the pursuit of commercialism. It also examines some of the general implications for industrial relations that flow from the characteristic 'logic' of the state enterprise.

The new political programmes of the Conservative government in Britain and the PSOE government in Spain have had major consequences for public enterprises. The state productive sector is at the centre of a web of current policy concerns, for a mixture of economic and political or ideological reasons. The state enterprises in both countries have had a considerable economic weight in terms of contribution to GNP, employment and investment. Their activities have made major calls on state expenditure, both because they are operating in politically desirable but unprofitable areas, but also because of their presence in economic sectors like coal and steel that are undergoing a process of profound restructuring. The enterprises have also come to play a symbolic role in broader governmental strategies, epitomizing, for example, certain styles of managerial behaviour and of labour relations which both the Conservative and the PSOE have aimed to reform.

As a result of these concerns, there has been a major drive in both countries to reduce the burden placed on state finances by public enterprises. This has taken the form of the encouragement of 'commercialism', that is a rationality akin to that of the private corporation. In practice it has involved efforts to cut the size of the public enterprise sector and to make the remainder more efficient and more attentive to financial rather than public service criteria of viability.

The development of the public enterprise sector has been a major cause of the crisis of state expenditure in Spain. In the period 1972−83, government transfers to companies (of which state enterprises absorbed about three-quarters) rose from 8.8 per cent to 12.5 per cent of government expenditure. For most of this period, transfers to the state enterprises amounted to more than the total public deficit (Gimeno 1984: 88−92). The losses of the state sector had grown as a result of the explosion of labour costs with the return to democracy, and because the state holding company INI (Instituto Nacional de Industrias) became a 'hospital' for near-bankrupt private companies; these accounted for more than 40 per cent of its losses in 1983.[1] This reflected the pressures of the transition. Politicians were not prepared to risk the fragile social consensus by allowing troubled firms to go to the wall.

Thus the rationalization of the state enterprise sector became a major priority of the post-1982 PSOE government. According to a study by the finance ministry, the government's aim was to 'liberate the considerable financial resources which [these enterprises] absorb and employ them in financing activities and companies with a future and capable of generating stable employment' (cited in El País, 6 July 1983). The PSOE's restructuring programme in the steel, shipbuilding, mining, vehicles and capital goods industries led to a reduction in public enterprise employment and the sale of a number of major companies (notably the INI-owned car firm SEAT) to the private sector. The government also tried to reduce the deficits and increase the efficiency of other public enterprises, including the railways, by tightening mechanisms of control and introducing French-style 'programme contracts' between government and enterprise (see below).

The victory of the Conservatives in the British general elections of 1979 led to a radical questioning of the role of the public enterprise sector. As suggested in chapter 2, one of the main aims of the Conservative government's political programme was to reduce the weight of the state in economic activity, because of its belief in the superiority of market mechanisms. It was also concerned with the effect of nationalized industry deficits on public borrowing and hence on inflation and interest rates. By 1987, the government had 'privatized' half a dozen major public corporations including the telecommunications and gas utilities and the state airlines, and many smaller enterprises (including the hotel and shipping interests of the British Railways Board). The privatized companies had together employed well over half a million people when the Conservatives came to power. The government's programme for its third term of office contained provisions for further major privatizations, notably of the water and sewerage authorities and the electricity industry.

As a result of the government's programme, the weight of the public enterprise sector was significantly curtailed. In 1978, the 'public corporations' accounted for 20 per cent of GDP, employed 2.1 million people, or 8 per cent of the total working population, and were responsible for 16 per cent of gross domestic fixed capital formation (GDFCF) (Central Statistical Office 1987). By 1986, the proportion of GDP had fallen to under 15 per cent, employment to 1.2 million (less than 5 per cent of the total), and GDFCF to 9 per cent.[2]

The government also pursued policies designed to encourage a commercial ethos in the remaining public enterprises. It brought in new financial controls to limit spending and borrowing, and introduced competition by weakening the statutory monopolies of some of the major public services. To a greater extent than its predecessors, it attempted to intervene directly to undermine what it saw as union resistance to greater efficiency. This led to serious confrontations in steel, coal and the railways, on which the government had a major influence. The nationalized industries became a battleground in the government's fight to promote a change in the balance of power between management and workforce in British industry as a whole.

There was, then, a clear political strategy in both countries for dealing with the public enterprises.The pursuit of the new 'commercialism' was the response, albeit 'lagged and variable', to the forces engendered by the general economic crisis and its attendant crisis of state expenditure. Commercialism clearly created major tensions in industrial relations in the public enterprises, since it involved cost cutting, the search for greater efficiency and productivity and in some instances an attack on the very idea of public enterprise. One of the main questions that the following chapters try to address is how these pressures fed through into changes in industrial relations strategies and practices in the enterprises.The rest of this chapter lays the groundwork for this examination by considering how the general relationship between public enterprise and the state has evolved under the pressures of 'commercialism'. It will be argued that despite the obvious impact of government policy, the way in which policies are converted into practice within the enterprise and the precise form they take are problematic. Government intention does not transform itself into public enterprise action in a mechanical and straightforward way.

The Logic of State Enterprise: the Problems of Political Control

State enterprises are hybrid organizations, as their name implies, being in some ways akin to private enterprises while still being part of the state. Like private enterprises, they are concerned with the production of goods and services to be traded on the market. This distinguishes them from the state agencies that provide health, education or other services on the basis of bureaucratic criteria such as need and entitlement, rather than as commodities to be bought and sold in the market. But they differ from private enterprise in that their defining characteristic, indeed the rationale for their existence, is that they are subject to some form of political control. Their areas of activity are defined by politicians, they are given objectives, constraints are imposed on them, their performance is monitored. In this way, they are led to pursue goals that would not be achieved by leaving the activity to the private enterprise sector.

In the private sector, the imperative need to be profitable acts as an external discipline on the activities of enterprises. The operation of the market may be modified, of course, by government intervention, but in general the 'market' functions as a sort of semi-automatic, impersonal control device. Public enterprises, because they are subject to political control, are at most only partially affected by the discipline of the market; as manifested, for example, in the often quoted platitude that public enterprises do not go bankrupt (e.g. NEDO 1976: 42). The way in which their objectives are defined through the political process and then 'transmitted' into the enterprise raises fundamental problems. First, the political demands on public enterprises lead to objectives that are confusing, changeable and often mutually at odds. Second, partly for this reason, but for others as well, the relationship between the state and public enterprises is dogged by difficult questions of enforcement: how can the political authorities ensure that the objectives set for state enterprises are effectively pursued? These issues are discussed in the following paragraphs.

The Political Definition of Public Enterprise Objectives

The objectives of public enterprises mirror the complexity of the role of the state as a whole. As the discussion of the previous chapter would suggest, their objectives do not arise ready made in response to some supposed 'needs' of the accumulation process; they emerge out of the complex interplay within the state of organized political interests. Although the public enterprises have a primary economic task, such as the provision of railways, energy, postal services and so on, they also lend themselves to a wide range of other economic goals, precisely because they are under political control. First, their 'basic' economic function is supplemented by a major role in economic restructuring. They are themselves prominent actors in the rationalization of a number of industries in crisis, notably steel and shipbuilding. Second, they support private industry not only through the provision of often subsidized inputs but also by providing guaranteed markets and assisting export endeavours. Third, state enterprises provide governments with an important tool for implementing macroeconomic policies, for reducing inflation through price and wage controls and for controlling public expenditure by tariff policy and financial restraints.

Thus, while the principal economic function of state enterprises is usually quite well-defined and stable over time, they also perform many other economic functions which may place complex and often contradictory demands on them. For example, supporting a sector of national industry may increase the costs of the goods or services provided to industry as a whole; or the use of state enterprises to control inflation may increase the state's fiscal problems because of the need for higher subsidies. Most fundamentally, there is a constant tension between the need to provide the basic economic conditions under which capitalist accumulation can proceed, and the danger of upsetting the accumulation process through an increasing transfer of resources from the private to the state enterprise sector, thus undermining the logic of profitability that powers the accumulation process.

In addition, public enterprises also lend themselves to tasks that have more to do with political legitimation than with the needs of the economic system, and which increase the contradictory pressures on them. For example, they may frequently be given a role in maintaining employment and thus helping to preserve the political accommodations between classes upon which a successful response to the crisis depends; this may conflict with their central role in the restructuring of industries in crisis. In Spain, for example, the political and economic pressures of the transition to democracy saw the workforce employed in the companies controlled by INI rise from 219,000 to 244,000 between 1975 and

1980, at a time when the real value of sales was falling sharply (Crossier 1985: 24—6). Similar conflicts arise in the case of regional development policy, which again is important in countries such as Italy, Spain, France and Britain for maintaining bases of political support and consensus.[3] Another example is the conflict engendered by providing universal 'non-discriminatory' services in transport, communications or energy supply which may increase the cost of essential inputs to the capitalist sector (since costly services such as rural train lines will be subsidized by profitable services or by direct state subsidy).

This multiplicity of objectives, and the way in which they are defined through the political process and change in response to changing political priorities, distinguishes state enterprises from private firms. The position is neatly summarized by a former chairman of the British Railways Board, Lord Beeching:

> In the case of private industry there is a single, clear and unchanging primary objective, and management is free to optimise its behaviour in pursuit of that objective within a general framework of conditions imposed by law, practice, and opinion, which it hopes and expects will also be reasonably stable. Therefore, its actions can and should be compatible and coherent.
>
> In the case of a nationalized industry, on the other hand, objectives are more numerous, more ambiguous and less distinguishable from qualifying conditions. Moreover, they fluctuate in their supposed order of priority, not merely from Government to Government, nor even from year to year, but almost from day to day at the whim of public and parliamentary opinion. Imposed policy decisions which are bound to increase losses or limit capacity may be followed within days by a howl of anguish about the financial state of the organization, or about shortage of supply. Management does not have the freedom to optimise its own performance in pursuit of a single objective, or even in pursuit of a number of stable and compatible ones ... (cited in Edwards 1967: 10).

As this passage suggests, the contradictory pressures on the state enterprise are increased by the way objectives are defined through the political process. Multiple, changing objectives arise out of the very logic and internal organizational structure of the state. The functional division of policy-making responsibilities among different central government departments and agencies means that public enterprises may experience political pressures from several distinct authority sources within the state. For example, an enterprise may be subject to some form of political control from ministries or agencies responsible for finance, employment, defence and regional policy in addition to its principal 'sponsor' or 'tutelary' ministry (see, e.g., Feigenbaum 1985: 87—92). As Vernon (1984: 8) writes of the French case, 'in actual practice, managers have found themselves dealing with half-a-dozen ministers or more, each with some capacity to reward or punish'. In Spain in the 1960s, INI found itself with representatives of the ministries of finance, commerce, industry, public works, agriculture, as well as the ministries of the army, navy and airforce, on its board of directors (Fernández 1970: 951—2).

Thus state enterprises are faced, in Aharoni's phrase (1981a: 1342), with 'multiple principals'. This fragmentation of the state, with the 'coexistence of a great number of autonomous centres of power, all weakly linked to each other' (Burgi 1985: 137) makes more difficult the definition and co-ordination of public enterprise objectives. Conflicts among these state power centres are common, leading to confusion of objectives, or even mutually conflicting political messages for state enterprises. For example, ministries responsible for control of government expenditure may oppose the sponsor ministry's sectoral strategy on the grounds of cost. A notable example, provided by Eisenhammer (1985: 48—51), is of the refusal of the Italian finance minister to authorize release of the massive funds approved by the industry ministry for the restructuring of the steel firm Finsider.

The effects of functional differentiation of policy-making are exacerbated by the relationship between the government and the permanent machinery of the state. Co-ordination of enterprise objectives is impeded by the time cycle of political authority. In other words, governments, which formally at least set the political agenda, have relatively limited lifespans. The turnover of individual government ministers responsible for setting objectives of state enterprises in their domain is even more rapid (e.g. Grassini 1981: 75). Furthermore, the nature of political authority in representative democracies means that governments are bound by doctrines of accountability.[4] As a result, ministers are subject to a range of *ad hoc* and constantly changing pressures from parliamentary representatives and interest groups that create a substratum of secondary political considerations to be taken into account.

The Dilemma of Control and Autonomy

The nature of public enterprise objectives makes it difficult for political authorities to evaluate and control the activities of the enterprises. When there are few clear, constant priorities, it is difficult to hold management to account for its actions. For example, as will be argued in more detail below, performance targets, such as rates of return on capital, are undermined as a means of control when other politically imposed demands, such as the requirement to keep prices down, provide management with a plausible alibi for failing to meet them. Even where targets are met, it may be for the 'wrong' reasons; for example, where an enterprise has considerable monopoly power, it can achieve its targets by manipulation of prices or a reduction in the quality of service.

But even if political authorities were clear about what they expected from public enterprises, political control would remain problematic. One reason for this is that the enterprises must have a 'relative autonomy' within the state if they are to operate efficiently. Their functions — the production of goods and services — require, in Therborn's terms, substantive rather than formal rationality, that is rationality based on managerial technical skill rather than bureaucratic competence and predetermined general rules. Thus the model of bureaucratic central state organizations such as ministries is unsuitable. Public enterprises are usually separate from the central administrative bodies and have a legal identity and accounts independent of the central government department to which they are formally accountable (see, e.g., Shirley 1983: 2). Some public trading activities, notably posts and telecommunications, have operated as parts of central government departments. But this is more a reflection of historical functions and

origins, as with the role of postal services as a source of revenue for the state
and as an instrument of state security. With the growing pressures to develop
more efficient, flexible and 'commercial' state organizations, the tendency has
been to transfer trading activities from departments of state to public corporations, as with the British Post Office at the end of the 1960s and the Italian
railways in the mid-1980s.

This need for 'distance' from political control has given rise to the doctrine
of the 'arm's-length' relationship in countries such as Britain where the classic
form of the state enterprise has been the 'public corporation' under the control
of a 'sponsor' department. The original conception of the public corporation was
that it had only to be given its 'marching orders' by the political authority and
could then be left to pursue the 'national interest' as management saw fit (SCNI
1968: 34). In countries where state-owned enterprises have typically been scattered among different economic sectors alongside private capital, the conventional form of public enterprise directly responsible to a ministry has been supplemented by the state holding company; for example, IRI in Italy, and INI and
INH (the oil and gas sector holding company) in Spain. The holding company
form has been used to provide a buffer between the state enterprises themselves
and political direction by the state.

Management autonomy has led to serious problems of control. Merely giving
management its 'marching orders' proved insufficient to ensure that the principal economic function of producing goods and services was carried out efficiently and without becoming an additional strain on state finances. Indeed, a
major concern of many state enterprises in early post-war Europe was the physical reconstitution of the depleted or war-damaged infrastructure of railways,
power stations and so on. Financial constraints on investment were relatively
unimportant and only developed subsequently as political concern with state
enterprise deficits prompted efforts for greater commercialism.

The greater is managerial freedom on questions of pricing, internal organization and investment, the more likely are public enterprises to act in ways in-
imical to the political objectives of government, or as Feigenbaum (1982: 109)
puts it, 'to pursue strategies dysfunctional to the public weal'. Feigenbaum cites
examples of the role of French oil enterprises and banks speculating against the
national currency, refusing to divert deliveries from foreign customers during
the 1973−4 oil embargo, and making excess profits at the expense of the con-
sumer (1982; 1985). In Spain, the policies of the enterprises controlled by the
holding company INI have been said to follow those of their private sector
counterparts, to the detriment of the national interest in areas such as pricing
policy and import controls (e.g. Tamames 1986: 177−80). Feigenbaum, in
common with many others, also notes the problems when public enterprises are
given unbridled autonomy to 'ride the waves of the market' in conditions of
market imperfection and monopoly power.

The response of governments to such problems has been to redefine the relationship between control and autonomy by providing a more formal framework
for enterprises to operate in. One major thrust of such efforts has been to introduce proxies for market signals, in the form of financial targets and constraints. Enterprises have been required to achieve financial targets concerning
rates of return on capital or revenue, and to attain minimum rates of return on

investment programmes. Other market proxies have laid down rules for pricing according to marginal cost. More recently, governments have imposed financial constraints limiting the call of state enterprises on public funds. These targets have been the subject of successive initiatives in Britain, for example, since the 1960s.[5] Attempts have also been made to clarify political control by means of 'contractual' arrangements between government and state enterprise. These date back to the recommendations of the 1967 Nora Report in France. The essence of a 'contrat de programme' or 'contrat d'entreprise' is that a state enterprise agrees to achieve targets for economic performance, physical output, productivity, quality of service, and so on in return for a commitment from the government to provide necessary finance, and to provide compensation for obliging the enterprise to undertake non-commercial activities in the public interest (Durupty 1986b: 357–96).

Such moves, however, have tended to restate rather than resolve the tension between control and autonomy. One problem is that the pressures for commercialism have brought about two divergent policy responses from governments. On the one hand, there has been a redefinition and tightening of formal controls, but on the other, there has been a simultaneous and sometimes incompatible thrust towards more management autonomy. Public enterprises have been forced into a greater orientation to the market by increasing exposure to competition and a relaxation of their statutory monopolies: a strategy used most notably by the post-1979 Conservative government in Britain. But the more genuine the competition, the more ineffective do government-imposed controls become as a way of affecting enterprise behaviour, since it must increasingly be governed by the 'logic' of the market rather than of political control.

Problems of Enforcing Political Control

The increasing use of market proxies and targets of various kinds to control the activities of public enterprises brings problems of its own. The central issue is how to turn political objectives into actual behaviour by enterprises. In other words, how is political control to be made effective?

A major problem has been the complexity and variability of political objectives discussed earlier. First, as long as other politically defined goals may override them, the power of market proxies to control management behaviour is limited. For example, attempts to introduce marginal cost pricing (Treasury 1967) or 'verité des prix' (Dubois 1975: 31–2) are undermined by simultaneous government concern with inflation and hence with holding down public enterprise prices (and there are problems in principle with the application of marginal cost pricing[6]).

Second, the formal objectives themselves are liable to abrupt change. In the words of a former chairman of a British nationalized industry, when the economy fluctuates, 'ministers find it difficult to resist varying the targets or borrowing limits of the industries, frequently at very short notice, and these imposed fluctuations in general management direction produce severe strains on the efficient operation of the industry' (Tombs 1980: 5). Programme contracts have also been extremely vulnerable to alterations in political priorities and objectives. As the French experience following the oil shocks of 1973 and 1979 indicates, the commitments in programme contracts may be rendered meaningless by major changes in the economic forecasting parameters upon which they are based (Shirley 1983: 77−80).

Third, many political objectives may remain unquantified and even unacknowledged, and this makes it even harder to tell exogenous from endogenous reasons for failure to meet targets (e.g. NEDO 1976: 40). Many authorities have advocated the practice of setting clear political objectives and compensating the enterprise for the resulting financial detriment.[7] But as Tivey (1973: 196−200) argues, political and economic considerations do not impinge occasionally on nationalized industries but are continuous and pervasive features. The changeability of political concerns and priorities means that governments are unwilling to make long-term commitments to compensate enterprises for carrying out public service objectives (NEDO 1976: 28, 43). Moreover, political authorities are often unwilling to define or take public responsibility for objectives that are not seen to be politically 'legitimate'. For example, considerations of short-term electoral advantage may dictate an interest in the nature of price and pay policy in public enterprises (e.g. Foster 1971: 114).

Thus state enterprises are not faced with clear guidelines as to the balance between commercial objectives relating to the economic performance of the enterprise, and the political objectives concerning, for example, regional policy or employment. Such problems have led to the characteristic phenomenon in which *de facto* priorities have been established by *ad hoc* political intervention over such matters as pay and prices, purchasing policy, import substitution, investment location and closure decisions.[8] This breaching of the formally 'arm's-length' or contractual relationship has tended to undermine the supposed managerial independence of the enterprise; in the graphic words of Johnson (1978: 128), there were 'grounds for suspecting that the public corporations were becoming something like tenants in the great ramshackle mansion of central government administration'. This type of informal intervention in turn increased confusion over the weight to be attached to the enterprise's different objectives, and made it harder to co-ordinate political goals and express them in a coherent manner.

Even were objectives to stay relatively stable, a fundamental problem of control would remain: the acquisition by the controllers of the knowledge upon which to base targets and evaluate performance. Enterprises have considerable incentives to manipulate data. Corporate planning, for example, becomes a vehicle for obtaining political support, rather than internal managerial commitment (see below). The specialist managerial expertise involved in running complex public utilities ensures that public enterprises are able to control the data upon which assessments are made. Opportunities are therefore 'legion for bluffing, evasion and selective reporting in the course of the actual performance' (Chambers 1984: 128). The necessary expertise is scarce in the controlling agencies such as the sponsoring ministry and state auditing bodies, and studies suggest that enterprises attempt to control access to their own expertise. For example, the post-war British Electricity Authority tried to insist on the protocol of official contact through the board secretary rather than allowing civil servants to make contact directly with specialist personnel (Hannah 1982: 44).

Dunleavy (1982: 190−7), using the example of the British civil nuclear industry, argues that the 'professional' ethos of public enterprise specialists may strengthen their links with their professional colleagues outside the state and hence make them less susceptible to control by state agencies. If this is true, it would further increase the problems of control in countries such as Britain where the form of the public corporation relied on the notion of the 'professional ideal' of self-regulation, trust and responsibility to ensure that the 'national interest' was furthered (Burrage 1973).

Nor are these problems of control resolved by the activities of specialist state auditing agencies, such as the French Cour des Comptes and similar bodies such as the Tribunal de Cuentas in Spain or the proposed function of the comptroller and auditor general in Britain. Such forms of control suffer from many of the problems already detailed, particularly lack of specialist expertise.[9] The Spanish Tribunal de Cuentas was virtually inoperative during the 1960s (Fernández 1970) and control in general suffered from one of the characteristic features of the Spanish administration, an excessive concern for legal form and precedent rather than with the substance of performance (see Beltrán 1977: ch. 5; Medhurst 1973: 163). A more fundamental reason for the failure of these control bodies is suggested by the Spanish case: they can only operate effectively in a propitious political environment. Thus the clientelistic interplay of political interests within the Spanish state under Franco converted state enterprises into part of the political patronage system. There was also a nexus of interests between state managers and private capital in the firms controlled by INI which made supervision difficult (Medhurst 1973: 164). In short, there was an apparent absence of political will to ensure that formal control mechanisms functioned in practice.

The problems of measurement exacerbate a further fundamental problem of control, the difficulty in imposing sanctions for poor performance. Public enterprises run little risk of bankruptcy, and if targets are not met, governments usually step in to cover deficits. Even the supposedly rigid 'external financing limits' imposed by the post-1979 Conservative government in Britain have proved to be flexible in practice (Heald and Steel 1981), with targets being adjusted when it became apparent that they would not be met.

The major formal sanction in the hands of the government is the power of appointment and dismissal over boards and (normally) chief executives of public enterprises. A proposal for the reform of the Italian railway network advocated the dismissal of the board if it failed for two years running to achieve performance targets (Santoro 1985), and the Spanish Socialist government has similarly toyed with the idea of sacking unsuccessful chairmen (Tamames 1983: 371). But a number of writers have suggested that the sanction is often not effective in practice (Tivey 1982; Foster 1971: 70; Dudley and Richardson 1984). Partly this is because, where political objectives such as employment are given high priority, enterprise management will be judged on the basis of its ability to maintain or expand the workforce rather than on its financial performance (e.g. Grassini 1981: 84). In addition, as argued above, there are great difficulties in assessing the performance of public enterprises.

A major reason for the ineffectiveness of the sanction of appointment and dismissal is that politicians are as likely to wish to get rid of appointees for political reasons as on the grounds of poor performance. The Spanish public sector, for example, has long been characterized by the politicization of public appointments (see ch. 2). Senior management posts in nationalized industries were used under Franco to reward politicians and military men for services rendered to the regime (Medhurst 1973: 164). The use of state posts as a source of patronage and control was reflected in the hypertrophy of the state enterprise bureaucracy. It is claimed that about half of the almost 4,000 senior management posts in companies controlled directly or indirectly by INI were 'superfluous sinecures' (Graham 1985: 97), available for distribution as political favours. The practice continued when democracy was restored. In 1982, for example, among the chairmen of INI firms were 16 ex-ministers, 10 members of parliament and about 20 senior civil servants linked with the governing party UCD and with the Francoist regime (*El Socialista*, 15—21 September 1982). Nor did the Socialists abandon political appointments; indeed, the growing number of party activists occupying senior management posts in public enterprises (see *Diario 16*, 30 January 1985) illustrated the government's belief that the introduction of its policies of commercialism was an operation demanding political rather than purely managerial skill.

Relative Power and Bargaining Between Public Enterprises and Political Authorities

The issue of measurement and control presupposes a clear differentiation and distancing between the controller and the object of control. But in practice, there is often a process of 'co-option' of, or at least accommodation with, agencies whose nominal function is to control the public enterprise. Cassese (1981: 149) and Feigenbaum (1985: 75—6, 95—6) argue that the officials of the French Cour des Comptes acted more as advocates and defenders of the enterprises than their controllers, while Hannah (1982: 44) describes how civil servants in the sponsor ministry became 'valuable allies' of the electricity authority, translating 'known needs into appropriate Whitehall language, according to the changing fashions dictated by public opinion or cabinet preoccupations'.

The root of these accommodations is the bargaining power possessed by state enterprises. We have already discussed the leverage deriving from control over expertise. In addition, enterprises may take advantage of the characteristic fragmentation of political authority and inter-agency conflicts of the type described earlier. Thus Hannah (1982: 45) suggests that management in the electricity industry made common cause with civil servants against the demands of the Treasury. A state enterprise may be able to manoeuvre among the diverse pressures on it, playing one off against the other (Levy 1987); what Feigenbaum (1982: 113) refers to as 'corporate manipulation of the state'. The bargaining power of enterprises is enhanced by their strategic role within their own sectors and governments' dependence on them for implementation of policy.

Increasingly, state enterprises have been able to function as an organized political lobby, despite their differences of interest (e.g. Dudley and Richardson 1984; Tivey 1982; Vernon 1984: 10). As well as becoming proficient in the techniques of lobbying such as public campaigning and the use of the media, enterprises have frequently formed alliances with private interest groups, and (as we shall see below), with their own workforces, in pursuit of their political goals. The fragmentation of the state political authority thus 'allows an unpredictable mechanism of alliances and counter-alliances' to develop (Burgi 1985: 140), or as Smith Ring and Perry (1985: 281) call it, 'a process of coalition building involving diverse and ofttimes competing interests'.

The 'counter-power' of the state enterprise in relation to the controlling authorities has major consequences for the way in which control is exerted. As the foregoing arguments have suggested, control is not imposed so much as negotiated or bargained between parties who both have considerable power resources (cf. Aharoni 1981a: 1342). Enterprises have the capacity to thwart external assessment of their performance and to steer between the conflicting, multifarious pressures on them; while the political authorities can grant or withhold economic resources and more fundamentally, general political support. As a result, relations are characterized by *political exchanges* between the parties. For example, enterprises may agree to refrain from raising prices prior to an election or from publicly criticizing a policy with which they disagree in return for approval for expenditure. Thus Hannah (1982: 46 – 7) cites the case of government relaxations in the investment controls on the British electricity authority in 1951 in return for its silence on the policy of cutting rural electrification. In exchange for support from civil servants in resisting the cuts of the Treasury or in presenting its investment programme sympathetically to the government, an enterprise might refrain from padding out its capital applications; again the electricity industry provides an example (Hannah 1982: 44).

The Implications of the Logic of Control and Autonomy for State Enterprise Management Behaviour

A number of writers have argued that the peculiarities of the environment in which the public enterprise operates create distinctive managerial processes. With goals that are complex, conflicting, vague and set at least partially by external agencies, the planning process is much more of a political act than in private corporations (e.g. Grieve Smith 1981; Smith Ring and Perry 1985). Because plans set performance standards and create expectations in the political controllers, they are used to manipulate the external environment as much as to generate internal management commitment. As Grieve Smith says, enterprises are led to 'present a plan which shows a sufficiently favourable financial forecast to justify further investment or financial support' (1984b: 58). Although in some cases enterprises have tried to develop realistic 'performative' plans (Wernham 1985: 633), their incentives to do so are limited by the fact that plans are still subject to external political appraisal which may alter their content and assumptions and thus undermine managerial commitment. As argued above, the nature of state enterprise planning encourages the manipulation and concealment of data so that the enterprise may control the terms upon which its performance will be judged.

The limitations of performance evaluation lead to a concern with visible and politically acceptable results. State enterprises have to reconcile the needs of long-term planning horizons of a quarter of a century or more, especially in highly capital intensive sectors such as railways, telecommunications or energy, with short-term political pressures (Harris and Davies 1979: 50; 1981). The short life cycle of political control, conditioned by the frequency of elections and ministerial changes, means, in the words of Mazzolini (1981: 22–3) that politicians tend 'to impose a high discount rate on expected outcomes'. This leads enterprise management to place stress on the achievement of short 'pay back periods', particularly when the formal control devices themselves measure performance over short periods. A style of management is evolved that emphasizes visible outcomes; that is, oriented to 'managing public support in the political markets', as Zif (1981: 1326) puts it. One constituent of this is the pursuit of 'symbolic' goals with a high political 'payback', even to the detriment of more 'commercial' business objectives. Roig (1981: 14), for example, has noted that strategic changes in the public enterprise are often more 'rhetorical' than 'effective'. This reflects the fact that politics often involves the exchange of symbolic resources rather than substantive ones, since these are important in the mobilization of political action (see ch. 8). For example, it may be more important for a government that a public sector pay settlement appear to be within the limits of pay policy, than for it actually to be so.

This orientation to the political sphere conditions internal management organization and culture. The nature of the political environment confuses the normal distinction between strategic and minor issues, since what may be minor in operational or commercial terms may have important symbolic political impact. For example, a state enterprise may be subject to close parliamentary scrutiny by elected representatives, and this may have a major impact on the public image and hence the political vulnerability or strength of the enterprise. This need to deal with a tricky political environment has often led to managerial centralization of decisions that may have political overtones, and a consensual style of leadership based around committee structures (e.g. Batstone et al. 1984: ch. 2; Hannah 1982: 15, 47). An alternative strategy, developed into a model by Aharoni (1981b), is for enterprises to aim to maximize business objectives such as profits and cash flow in order to minimize their dependence on government. However, studies suggest that a major source of enterprise autonomy is the ability of management to manipulate the conflicting political pressures on it and to negotiate successfully with the fragmented political authorities in the central state administration (see, e.g., Hannah 1982: ch. 5; Feigenbaum 1985). Moreover, the ability of state enterprises to maximize business objectives depends on the nature of the political pressures on them, and indeed, a greater 'business' rather than 'political' orientation (Zif 1981) may flow from clear directives of the political authorities; in other words the dominant political objective may be for the enterprise to behave in a 'commercial' manner, so that the maximization of business objectives may be a reflection of *greater* dependence on political authorities.

The introduction of 'commercial' objectives has been a response to growing fiscal crisis, and generates its own tensions. For example, pressures to commercialism may lead management to replace blurred and ambiguous strategic objectives with clear and concise ones. But this clarity may make it more difficult to play off political demands against each other, and to handle the conflicting and diffuse political pressures that inevitably persist. Again, commercialism may lead to the pursuit of indicators, such as current balance sheet results, chosen more to convince the government that commercial goals are being successfully achieved than for their relevance to the economic objectives of the enterprise.

A further consequence of commercialism is the pressure for management to legitimate politically determined goals by clothing them in the language of managerial decision-making. The use of 'objective' business techniques of accounting to justify closures and rationalization reflecting political decisions has been extensively documented in the case of the British mining industry (O'Donnell 1985) and the nationalized steel corporation (Bryer *et al.* 1982; Manwaring 1981).

A corrective is needed, however, to the impression that state enterprise management is entirely conditioned by the political forces that impinge upon it. On the contrary, since the enterprise is an organization with a complex internal structure and of necessity relatively autonomous from political control, it is capable of developing its own internal interests and agenda (cf. Levy 1987). When political conditions permit, for example when the commercial orientation is more prominent, the internal agenda may come to the fore and inform the objectives of the corporation. Indeed, the logic of commercialism may lead the enterprise to pursue activities at odds with other government objectives. In that case, corporate interests may find themselves in conflict with their political controllers.

The Logic of State Enterprise and Industrial Relations

It was suggested in chapter 1 that the conventional accounts of industrial relations in the public enterprise sector have been too static and *ad hoc*. In this section it will be argued that, since industrial relations form part of the overall texture of state enterprise activity, the logic of public enterprises provides a starting point for understanding their industrial relations. The section will therefore draw out some general implications for industrial relations of the dynamic of political control and managerial autonomy within the context of growing fiscal crisis.

'Crystallized' Interests and Industrial Relations Institutions in State Enterprises

It was argued earlier that the role of state enterprises partly reflects the interests of social classes and groups and the way they are represented within the polity. The same is true of the use of nationalization as a form of state intervention. It is commonly argued that nationalization takes place in order to socialize the losses of sectors of capital where capitalist relations have broken down (e.g. Fine and O'Donnell 1981) or to resolve an immediate crisis in a sector of the economy, as with the creation of the Italian state holding company IRI by Mussolini in response to the impending collapse of the banking system (Maraffi 1980). But this is a partial explanation; as Urry (1981: 93) points out, not all industries taken over by the state are necessarily unprofitable in private hands;

a striking recent example would be the nationalization of some of the leading French banks and industrial conglomerates by the Mitterand government in 1982 (Durupty 1986a: 77–119). Furthermore, nationalization is only one form of achieving state policies of intervention. Whether it is adopted or not will depend on 'the strength, organisation and cohesiveness of the various social classes struggling in that particular society' (Urry 1981: 94). Although Urry (134) reasonably cautions against a 'politicist' account that sees nationalization as largely reflecting the ambitions of the labour movement and its political representatives, these ambitions have had a major impact on nationalization. For example, the aspirations of the labour movement have influenced the timing and form of nationalization, and the content of industrial relations in state enterprises, particularly forms of worker representation and managerial control.

In Britain, by the 1890s the TUC was calling for the nationalization of the 'whole of the means of production, distribution and exchange' (Weiner 1960: 4). The labour movement's demands stressed the democratic control of industry by employees' representatives. Similar currents flowed strongly through the ideology and programmes of the French union movement after the First World War (Dubois 1975: ch. 3). In Italy, too, the interests of sections of the labour movement, in alliance with factions in the Christian Democrats, were a force behind post-war nationalizations (Maraffi 1980: 514–21; Martinelli 1981: 94).

In both Britain and France, aspirations were greatly watered down by events. During the 1930s and 1940s the British labour movement accepted Morrisonian ideas of non-political administration of public enterprises (Weiner 1960: ch. 3), while the shape of early nationalizations in France was conditioned by the needs of approaching war rather than the political demands of the working class. Moreover, many actual nationalizations were indeed objectively functional for the restructuring of parts of the economy 'no longer organised as capital' as Fine and O'Donnell (1981) put it; and the British Conservatives only attempted to reverse the post-war Labour government's efforts 'where we believed that a measure of nationalisation was a real hindrance to our island life (Winston Churchill, cited in Weiner 1960: 80).

Nonetheless, nationalization still bore the mark of long struggles by the labour movement to further working class interests. This was most evident in the statutory requirements concerning industrial relations that were universal in the British nationalization acts, and the creation of complex machinery for consultation and negotiation with staff (see Chester 1975: ch. 8; Clegg 1951: ch. 3). In France, the post-war nationalizations set up a tripartite scheme of management with representation of users, public authorities and employees (Dubois 1975: 161–3; Holter 1982). Although in France changes in the balance of class relations permitted a whittling away of forms of labour representation in the state enterprises, in Britain they have been much more resistant to change, until recent years at least. In both countries, the class relations that gave rise to nationalization have been reflected in the continuing ethos of 'progressive' public sector industrial relations and the notion of the 'good employer', manifested in relatively good sick pay and pensions, 'humane' handling of redundancy, and so on.[10] In a number of countries, state enterprises were in the forefront of 'progressive' developments in industrial relations. Renault, for example, pioneered extension of annual holiday rights in France (Anastassopoulos 1981: 109−11), while state industries were among the first to introduce 'contrattazione articolata aziendale' (i.e. formal plant level bargaining) in Italy in the early 1960s (Martinelli 1981: 94).

Thus the pattern of current relationships in a nationalized industry may partly reflect events that happened in the past, even the distant past. As Therborn (1979: 35) says, 'in the historical course of the class struggle, the state apparatuses come to crystallize determinate social relations and thus assume a material existence, efficacy and inertia which are to a certain extent independent of current state policies and class relations'. In short, the inertial properties of ideologies and institutional arrangements allow them to colour industrial relations long after the constellation of political forces has changed.

In Spain, in contrast to Britain, the emergence and form of public enterprise owed little to the aspirations of the labour movement, and much to the state's own organizational interests. Public ownership was perceived as a means whereby the state elites could direct the Francoist strategy of economic autarchy launched in the 1940s, which in turn owed much to concerns with national security. The nationalization of the railways, the creation of the state holding company INI, the acquisition of a major state shareholding in the telephone company, were carried out by a repressive authoritarian regime which had crushed organized labour. The institutions of industrial relations in state enterprises were those of the Francoist state — vertical 'syndicates' and strictly controlled, docile company councils ('jurados'). It was only when democracy was restored in Spain that this legacy truly began to break down and the form of state enterprises changed to accommodate the interests of organized labour.

Fragmented Authority, Multiple Goals and Intervention in Industrial Relations

The fragmentation of political authority, and the existence of multiple, changing and politically defined goals, have led to continuous *ad hoc* intervention by the political controllers of public enterprises in their decision-making. This intervention has the effect both of undermining managerial autonomy and of weakening the coherence of political control by blurring objectives. It has been a particularly marked feature of industrial relations in state enterprises, since the conduct of industrial relations influences the achievement of a variety of state objectives. The pay of employees has been a traditional and frequent object of intervention, as have a wide range of other industrial relations issues such as closure and redundancy, working practices and dispute settlement.

Short-term political considerations have led governments (or parts of the central state organization) to put pressure on supposedly autonomous managements to grant concessions to the unions. Sometimes the government has wished to avoid the politically damaging disruption of vital public services; for example, Hannah, describes how, in the 1960 wage negotiations at the Central Electricity Generating Board, the settlement was made 'after management consultation with the Ministry had indicated that they should settle, as the Cabinet were not willing to force matters to a strike' (1982: 223). The phenomenon is vividly described by a former chairman of the British Prices and Incomes Board:

On the first appearance of a wage claim, [the government] whispers to the nationalised undertaking to stand firm — even though the undertaking may think that some concession may be reasonable. The fact that the undertaking is not speaking with its own voice but is merely the echo of another's soon becomes known. The indignation of the trade union mounts; there is the threat of a strike; Government, which fears a strike more than the nationalised undertaking, sounds the call for retreat; and amid paeans of praise for everybody's wisdom in choosing the path of peace the claim is settled — more generously than it could have been in the first place (Aubrey Jones, cited in Bell 1975: 10).

On other occasions a high settlement has been desired as part of a strategy of political alliances. Grassini (1981: 82—3), for example, cites the case of the Italian state enterprise bargaining body Intersind which in 1960 was pressed into making a settlement favourable to the unions because the Christian Democrats were contemplating a coalition with the Socialist Party. Such intervention has often had to be exerted through covert pressure, since it conflicts not only with the formality of managerial autonomy, but also with the achievement of other formally defined goals such as financial performance targets and even policies on controlling public sector wages. Even when intervention is compatible with official pay restraint policy, it may still be covert since politicians may not wish to take public responsibility for influencing the outcome of a specific case and prefer to see the opprobrium attached to management. An example, again from Hannah's study of the British electricity industry, is provided by the 1961 pay negotiations. Although the Macmillan cabinet pressed management to delay a settlement, ministers were not prepared to take responsibility for a breakdown in negotiations; when the industry settled, the Prime Minister publicly rebuked management for capitulating to the unions and breaching the pay pause (1982: 225—6).

Finally, intervention in industrial relations often expresses the tensions between long-term government strategy, for example to promote industrial restructuring, and short-term political considerations, such as electoral advantage. In a Spanish case in 1984, the PSOE government intervened in the restructuring programme of the state-owned steel firm Aceriales, forcing it to modify its plans for severe cuts in the workforce. The intervention was the result of the governing party's worries about the effects of job losses on its chances in elections to the Basque regional parliament (Ariño 1985: 59—60).

Such interventions have tended to undermine the autonomy of the state enterprises' internal industrial relations institutions, especially where governments have funded concessions to the workforce beyond what management was prepared to consider (cf. Kelf-Cohen 1973: 176), and have encouraged complex bargaining relations extending beyond the boundary of the enterprise to encompass the political authorities themselves (see below).

Fiscal Crisis and State Enterprise Industrial Relations

The growing political preoccupation with controlling public expenditure and limiting the role of the state has had far-reaching, if ambiguous, consequences for state enterprise industrial relations. First, political attention has been focused

on public sector pay as a major element in the growth of state expenditure and
of the deteriorating financial performance of state enterprises (see, e.g., Dubois
1975: ch. 2). This has heightened the importance of anti-inflationary policies of
wage restraint, in which the highly 'visible' state enterprises have often been expected to play an exemplary role, because of concern for the impact of their actions on other employers. It has also encouraged the use of new financial control
mechanisms such as external financing limits, which in Britain since 1979 have
been used as a covert pay policy (Heald and Steel 1981: 15).

Second, commercialism in the form of tighter financial constraints and increasing competition has created pressures on state enterprise management to cut
labour costs and increase flexibility. A major issue for research is how these
pressures become incorporated in the policies of strategic management and how
they are then propagated down through the management organization, changing
the environment in which middle and lower levels of management operate, and
altering the constraints on their handling of industrial relations questions.

The Role of the Unions and Political Exchange
Unions in state enterprises operate in an environment in which corporate objectives are subject to continuous renegotiation and intervention by fragmented
political authorities outside the corporation. As we have seen, this applies to industrial relations issues such as pay determination, and to matters having a major
bearing on industrial relations, such as restructuring and rationalization plans.
The government does not merely confine itself to setting the 'rules of the game',
but is in a sense a participant in industrial relations to the extent that it chooses
to intervene. Intervention varies according to factors such as the degree of commercial autonomy of the state enterprise, although as we have seen, commercialism is no deterrent to intervention and may indeed promote it.

The consequence of this logic of action is that the management of the state
enterprise ceases to be the unions' sole potential bargaining partner. Formal or
informal bargaining may take place across the boundaries of the corporation between unions and political authorities – ministries, governments and local or
regional authorities. The possibility of government intervention on pay, by putting pressure on management to settle or even by funding additional increases,
encourages the unions to try to deal with 'the organ grinder, not the monkey'
as the chairman of a British public corporation told the House of Commons
Select Committee on Nationalised Industry (SCNI 1968: 190). But such union–
government bargaining has taken place on a wide range of issues; for example,
over new investment in poorer regions (e.g. Eisenhammer 1985: 42–4), rescue
bids for ailing private sector companies (e.g. Grassini 1981: 82), extension of
union participation in management (e.g. Batstone et al. 1983: ch. 2; Holter
1982), and plant closures or service rationalizations (Ariño 1985: 59–60).
Much bargaining is tacit and informal, but at times it may become formalized
into tripartite arrangements involving government, unions and enterprise
management; a rare example in the British context was the drawing up of the
1974 'Plan for Coal' (Burgi 1985).

As the words of Aubrey Jones cited above suggest, bargaining is based on the
unions' threat to disrupt the state enterprise's activities. Because of the strategic

nature of the services and products provided by the major state enterprises, and because of their monopoly position, industrial conflict may cause widespread disruption and lead to severe political embarrassment for the government. This may take the form of pressure from third parties affected by disruption, aimed at influencing the outcome of management—union negotiations (Thomson and Beaumont 1978: 132—5).[11] The political damage that may be done to governments by industrial conflict may be illustrated by the fall of the Heath government in the course of the 1973—4 British miners' strike. The capacity of the unions to disrupt can be expected to vary according to factors such as the internal unity and organization of the unions. But it also varies, as we shall see in the case studies in later chapters, according to the resources that the government has at hand to defuse the political consequences of disruption.

The bargaining relations between state enterprise unions and the political authorities may be seen in terms of Pizzorno's well-known concept of 'political exchange'. He drew attention to the difference between exchanges in the market and in the political sphere. In the labour market, the commodity being bought and sold is labour power; in the political market, the union is trading on the power to prevent disruption. In Pizzorno's words, an 'actor (generally the government) which has goods to give is ready to trade them in exchange for social consensus with an actor who can threaten to withdraw that consensus' (1978: 279). Exchange could also take place on the basis of ideological support, commitment or obligation, as has often been the case between public enterprise unions and social democratic governments.

An important consequence of the orientation of state enterprise unions to the political sphere is that industrial disputes and strikes may be aimed at putting political pressure on government as much as economic pressure on the enterprise's management (cf. Thomson and Beaumont 1978: 146—51). This may affect the form of conflict, favouring, for example, the short, widely publicized demonstration strike. It may mean also that strikes are openly directed against state policy as much as against management's negotiating position, as with the French public sector strike in the mid-1960s against government fixing of the total wage bill (Dubois 1975: 114—15), or the wave of public sector conflicts over the Spanish government's wage control and restructuring policies in early 1987.

The scope for political exchange complicates the nature of bargaining in state enterprise industrial relations. In addition to the conventional bilateral union-management negotiations of the private sector, both parties may be engaged in simultaneous bilateral negotiations with the political authorities. This might be called 'triangular' bargaining, i.e. negotiations in which each of three parties deals bilaterally with the other two. At times, triangular bargaining may be replaced or supplemented by 'tripartite' bargaining, that is where the three parties negotiate jointly.

There are two further complications that the logic of state enterprise suggests are likely to occur. First, the fragmentation of the political authorities means that the unions may be negotiating separately with a number of different state agencies: for example, with the sponsoring ministry and the ministry for labour or employment. Second, the political bargaining that accompanies the definition of state enterprise objectives provides opportunities for alliances between groups within the state and outside it. In such cases, management may seek alliances with its own unions in order to pursue courses of mutual interest within the state machinery. Dudley and Richardson (1984), for example, describe joint campaigns involving several British nationalized industries to ease financial constraints, and to defeat attempts to introduce parliamentary auditing. In the British coal industry, management and unions have fought for changes in energy policy (Robens 1972: chs. 9, 10) and more recently, a successful alliance of interests prevented the separate privatization of the gas corporation's retail showrooms (Tivey 1982: 46).

Conclusions: Some Elements of a Framework of Comparative Analysis for Industrial Relations in State Enterprises

This chapter has laid out some general elements for an understanding of the 'logic' of state enterprises in an era of increased commercialism. The implications of that logic for industrial relations issues have been discussed. These arguments together with those of chapter 2 on the role of the state provide a framework for understanding the consequences for industrial relations of the current economic crisis in the advanced capitalist countries, and suggest some dimensions of variation that may account for differences between different national systems.

In chapter 2 it was suggested that political responses to economic crisis were lagged and variable. The same is true of political projects responding to the specific problems of the public sector and state enterprises, such as those that have emerged in Britain and Spain in recent years. There have been general pressures towards greater 'commercialism' as a way of restructuring the public enterprise sector and of easing the problems of fiscal crisis. Yet the extensive range of state objectives, their mutual contradictions and the way in which they are determined within a fractured state organization, leave ample scope for variation in both the content and timing of projects to 'reform' the role of state enterprises and to change the balance between political control and enterprise autonomy.

It has been argued that forms of control over state enterprises are inherently problematic. This raises the issue of how political objectives are *transmitted* into the enterprise. The British and Spanish cases will be examined in terms of the nature of *transmission mechanisms*. These, on the arguments that have been put forward above, would be likely to vary according to the nature of the relationship of the state enterprise to other state agencies. The effectiveness of formal control devices such as financial targets coupled with monitoring of performance is likely to be affected by institutional variables such as the quality of information produced and the arrangements made by controlling agencies to gain access to it. But given the limitations on control devices discussed above, given the fragmentation of the state and the diversity of objectives, political bargaining or 'exchange' between enterprise actors and the state is likely to be a major method of transmitting state objectives to the public enterprise. Variables such as the degree of 'distance' between state enterprises and central state agencies, the internal coherence of management and unions, the ability to inflict costs on government, and conversely of government to bear the political costs of disruption, will affect the way objectives are transmitted; as will wider relationships between social classes and the state.

Transmission mechanisms are concerned with changing the way in which actors within the enterprise perceive the costs and benefits and calculate the balance of relative advantage associated with different courses of action. But the issue is not simply one of 'cross-boundary' transmission from the state to the enterprise, but also of 'intra-organizational' transmission. For example, once strategic management has assimilated new objectives on the basis of a changed perception of costs and benefits, these objectives have to be promulgated within the organization. This process will be influenced by variations in internal forms of planning and control. On the other hand, transmission mechanisms may work by changing the perceptions of costs and benefits made at the 'working level' of management, and this in turn may create upward pressures in the organization for strategic management to bring its policies into line. In certain circumstances, both downwards and upwards pressures may be at work at the same time. Similar pressures apply to the relationship within the workforce between top level representatives, local activists and the 'rank and file' (cf. Batstone *et al*. 1984: part III; Terry and Ferner 1986). Variations in intra-organizational transmission will reflect the internal composition of enterprise actors, their relationships with each other, and also the external relations of each with other parts of the state.

The industrial relations consequences associated with the reform of state enterprises are therefore doubly ambiguous. First, there is scope for variation in the precise composition of the government's political strategy, granted the general pressure for cutbacks in labour costs and increased flexibility. Second, once a strategy has been formulated, its impact on industrial relations in the enterprise depends on how it is transmitted into and down through the organization. Indeed, its transmission is likely to be profoundly dependent on existing industrial relations practices and processes, since negotiation between management and workforce is central to the transmission and internalization of political objectives. In the following chapters, these will form the principal themes in the examination of industrial relations in British and Spanish railways.

Notes

1 On the role of INI in 'socializing' losses, and its mounting problems, see, e.g., Croissier 1985; Cordero 1985; Graham 1985: 96−7.
2 This decline could be expected to continue, with the privatization of British Airways at the beginning of 1987 and the planned sale of the electricity and water industries. A significant part of the fall was due to shrinking of the remaining state industries. For example, employment in British Coal fell by 41,000 between 1985 and 1986.

 The figures given are for 'public corporations'. Almost all the nationalized industries in Britain are public corporations, which are 'the public sector equivalent of public limited companies' (Curwen 1986: 1); the government is their sole shareholder. However, a small number of companies in the state-owned sector, such as British Leyland, are ordinary public companies and thus are not included in these figures. The public corporations also include organizations which do not obtain the bulk of their revenue direct from the sale of goods and services to the public. This category includes major bodies such as the British Broadcasting Corporation, as well as an assortment of organizations such as development agencies (for a complete list see CSO 1987: 121). These qualifications will cause some distortion to the figures presented but they do not affect the overall picture. Pryke (1981: 2) provides figures for 1977 which include all and only the trading enterprises in the state sector. These show nationalized industries producing 13 per cent of GDP, employing 2.3 million people, and being responsible for 23 per cent of gross domestic fixed capital formation (excluding housing).

3   For examples from these countries, see Ariño 1985: 59; Grassini 1981: 76−81; Eisenhammer 1985: 40−44; Mazzolini 1981: 24−7; Anastassopoulos 1981: 108−9; McEachern 1980: 153.

4   On Britain, see, e.g., Tivey 1973: 142−5, Heald 1983: 155−7; on Spain, e.g., García 1985; on France, Delion and Durupty 1982: 177−86; on Italy, Martinelli 1981: 92−3.

5   These are summarized, for example, in Curwen 1986; Likierman 1986.

6   Marginal cost pricing, for example, is dogged by problems of definition of the marginal unit especially where there are indivisibilities in output (e.g. Littlechild 1979: 7−14). Rates of return on investment may be inappropriate guides to decision-making where the investment forms part of a network that public policy has decreed should be maintained at a certain size, as has been the case with the rail network in Britain (NEDO 1976: 32), or where political considerations dictate the need for regional investment regardless of the rate of return (e.g. Eisenhammer 1985: 42−4).

7   See, e.g., in the British context, SCNI 1968: 34−5, 150−62; Likierman 1984: 160−61; Tombs 1980: 7−8; on Spain, see Boada 1985.

8   See, e.g., Johnson 1978; NEDO 1976; Anastassopoulos 1981: 100−2; Mazzolini 1981; Ariño 1985.

9   On Spain, see, e.g., Bolúfer 1985; on France and Italy, Cassese 1981; on Britain, Normanton 1981: 159−62; Dudley and Richardson 1984: 118−19.

10   On Britain see, e.g., Pryke 1971: 100−01; Thomson and Beaumont 1978: 83−6; Kelf-Cohen 1973: 166−7; on France see, e.g., Dubois 1975: 132−6.

11   An extensive literature on the industrial relations of the public sector in the United States deals with questions such as these. A major concern is with the effects of electoral accountability on the behaviour of the employer side. See, for example, Lewin et al. 1977.

4

The Railways in Britain and Spain:
An Overview

Introduction

This chapter applies the framework of chapter 3 to the specific case of the railways. It provides an overview of British Rail and RENFE and the issues confronting them. The first section outlines the main features of the British and Spanish networks. The rest of the chapter explores broader issues of the historical development of the railway system in the two countries. It briefly examines the legacy of private development during the nineteenth and earlier twentieth century and the nature of the pressures for taking the railways into state ownership, which are likely to influence the subsequent development of industrial relations. It then considers the patterns of state—railway relationships since nationalization, particularly the conflicts between state control and enterprise autonomy, and the consequences of growing pressures for 'commercial' management of the railways.

The Railway Systems Compared

The Networks
The distinctive features of railway activities affect organization and management—workforce relations independently of the fact that in most countries of the world the major railway networks are owned and run by the state, and everywhere without exception they are subject to close state regulation. The nature of railway transport, with heavy trains travelling at speed along fixed tracks between stations and terminals, dictates within broad limits the organization of railway work and creates requirements for specialized control systems. In the words of Dunlop (1958: 20), the technological context of 'railroads has many distinctive features affecting the relations of managers and workers: the

train operating divisions use small crews working together and in movement far from close and immediate supervision; complex and expensive equipment is utilized with a high ratio of capital to worker; ... the costs of accidents can be consequential; the hours of operations for equipment may be around the clock, and they do not conform to normal factory schedules ...', Similarly, Fontgalland (1984: 131) maintains that the 'parameters influencing the internal organisation of a railway are continuity of operations; co-ordination of this with the management of an infrastructure used concurrently to supply two totally independent markets, passengers and goods; the large number and geographical dispersion of installations; and individual staff discipline in the matter of safety.'

Thus certain features of railway organization are universal. For example, every railway has complex safety regulations containing an injunction to the effect that 'every member of staff, whatever his rank, owes complete obedience to the signals' (Fontgalland 1984: 52). The nature of railway operation gives rise to standard tasks and categories of work that are to be found in any railway administration: the staffing of trains; the control of their movement between points of the network; the running of stations, yards and other terminals; maintenance of the traction, rolling stock, and the permanent way.

BR and RENFE are both among the major West European railways, although West Germany and France have considerably larger networks, higher traffic and more employees. The main differences between BR and RENFE are summarized in table 4.1. BR has a somewhat longer network, employs more than twice as many railway staff and carries considerably more passenger traffic than does RENFE. Most of the British network is double track, while in Spain, four fifths of the network is single track. However, the percentage of electrification in the Spanish system is much higher than in Britain and will remain so even after the completion of BR's current major electrification project on the East Coast Main Line. In both networks, operations are organized on a geographical basis. BR

TABLE 4.1
BR and RENFE: Network Comparison 1984

	BR	RENFE
Route kilometres	16,961	13,464
Percentage electrification	22.6	45.8
Percentage double track	70.6[c]	18.3
Number of railway employees	147,219	65,612
Freight ton kilometres	12,028	14,693
Passenger kilometres	29,767	15,574
Percentage land passenger transport	6.4[a]	7.8[b]
Percentage freight transport	15.6[a]	9.5[c]
State support as percentage of all receipts	36.2	59.3
Deficit[d] as percentage of GDP	0.37	0.92

Notes: [a] 1980; [b] 1981; [c] 1982; [d] deficit = state subsidy + operating loss.
Sources: BR *Report and Accounts*, RENFE, *Memorias*, IETC *Memoria* (1983), Serpell (1983: 13).

has five regions, subdivided into 'areas', responsible for providing the rail services 'contracted' by the different business 'sectors' (see below). RENFE's operations are organized by seven geographical 'zones' which are in turn subdivided on a functional and geographical basis.

The Legacy of Historical Development

Both networks, and in particular the Spanish one, suffer the legacy of the age of private railway building during the nineteenth century. The price of competitive development was overbuilding, which in other countries had been controlled by government regulation. This was one cause of the severe financial problems of the railways in later years which led to increasing state intervention even before nationalization. In Spain, linear state subsidies for building led to meandering lines (Carr 1982: 266) with the result that today, railway routes are often appreciably longer than the competing road route. Increasing problems of indebtedness meant that railway development could not keep pace with changing population patterns. In Spain this was particularly serious since the age of major railway building in the mid-nineteenth century preceded industrialization and the massive shifts in population and traffic that it was to bring, especially from the 1940s. In Britain, by contrast, the 'Railway Age' occurred when the demographic patterns of the industrial revolution were already becoming clear and the main industrial centres well established. In addition, one effect of the civil war of 1936−9 in Spain was considerable internal migration. As a result, the major coastal population centres are now ill-served by what is still a predominantly radial network with lines emanating from Madrid in the centre of the country.

A further legacy of the financial difficulties of the Spanish companies was the failure to adapt the network to changing technological requirements. Meandering of lines was compounded by steep gradients and curves (RENFE 1984a: 22), since tunnelling and bridging were costly. The radial Spanish trunk network had to contend with one of the most difficult geographies in Europe, which means that most routes from Madrid to the coast have to cross at least one mountain range, while in Britain the major centres are connected across relatively easy terrain. International connection is hampered by the use of a non-standard gauge of 1.67 metres (compared with normal international width of 1.44 metres).[1] The combined effect of these problems is currently felt in the Spanish railways' extremely low commercial speeds which greatly hamper competition with road and air transport. For example, the main trunk services from Madrid to Bilbao, Barcelona and Seville have fastest average speeds of 80, 91 and 94 km per hour respectively, and in the early 1980s, the fastest long distance route, from Madrid to Valencia, achieved only 102 km per hour (RENFE 1984a: 24). By contrast, BR's Intercity services attain much higher commercial speeds and, where High Speed Trains are used, average speeds may be over 160 km per hour.

Nationalization and Competition

In Britain and Spain the underlying financial weakness of the private railway companies, caused by lack of demand and later by increasing road competition, led first to increasing state intervention and then to nationalization.[2] RENFE came into being in 1941. BR's forerunner, the British Transport Commission (BTC), which ran the newly nationalized road haulage industry as well as the railways, began operations at the beginning of 1948. In both countries the following decades were to be dominated by the issue of how to put the railways on a sound financial footing. Once it was realized that financial self-sufficiency was no longer possible, the focus moved to forms of state control of the railway and the need for state resources to fund its deficit.

The main problem facing the railways was the inexorable growth of road competition. Road haulage overtook rail as a carrier of freight in 1959 in Spain and in 1957 in Britain (by which time BTC no longer ran the road haulage industry). Road passenger traffic exceeded rail traffic by the beginning of the 1950s in Britain, and by 1957 in Spain. Thereafter, as in all other European railways, the share of railways in surface transport steadily declined, especially with the massive road building programmes of the 1950s and 1960s. In 1969, nearly one third of Spain's freight and almost a quarter of Britain's still went by rail. But, as table 4.1 shows, by the early 1980s the railways' share of passenger traffic was well below 10 per cent in both countries, their share of freight traffic not that much higher. And in Britain, freight's decline was absolute as well as relative.

Part of the growth of road transport reflected the political tolerance of what unions and rail pressure groups regarded as unfair competition. In Britain, heavier lorries failed to pay an equitable share of the infrastructural costs of the road network while passenger transport was favoured by tax incentives for company cars equivalent to far more than the value of the annual rail subsidy (TEST 1984a; Potter and Cousins 1983; Bagwell 1984; ch. 1).[3] In Spain, a competitive framework that formally favoured rail was systematically infringed in practice as even the pro-deregulation 1962 World Bank report conceded (IBRD 1963: 173; El País, 18 September 1983, 10 October 1983).

The growth of competition put paid to repeated attempts by the railways and the political authorities to establish a financially viable railway. During the 1950s, both railways hoped that major investment plans (BTC 1955; RENFE 1950; 1957m: ix) would allow them to modernize, reduce costs and attract sufficient traffic to break even. Even in the mid-1960s, RENFE's revised statute (Decree Law 23−VII−64) embodied an expectation that the company would be able to dispense with state support: there were provisions for RENFE to pay back a portion of its gross income to the treasury. But by the 1960s the emphasis was on the need to restore financial self-sufficiency through drastic pruning of the network. In Britain, the Beeching Report on 'Reshaping the Railways' (BRB 1963) led to a programme of closures and cutbacks that by 1968 had halved the number of stations, closed 8,000 km of route, halved the number of goods wagons and sharply reduced passenger services; by 1970, railway employment was less than half what it had been in 1963.

In Spain, however, the pressure of the World Bank on RENFE and the Spanish government to reduce the loss-making portions of the network (IBRD 1963: esp. 188) was largely ineffective, and at the beginning of the 1980s, the length of the network was slightly greater than it had been in 1964, despite proposals in the interim (usually tied to credit agreements with the World Bank) to consider for closure several thousand kilometres of route.

However, RENFE, like BR, did greatly reduce staff from the 1960s, largely as a result of technological modernization (see ch. 5). Between 1962 and 1970, numbers were cut by a third, from 127,000 to 83,000. This contributed to a temporary operating surplus between 1970 and 1974, though it was far from being able to fund investment and interest payments.

State Subsidy of the Railways
The long-term problem of the railways and the failure of earlier strategies to stem the tide of losses led to political awareness of the need for permanent state support and to steps, earlier in Britain than in Spain, to formalize the financial relationship between railways and the state.

In Britain, the Transport Act 1968 introduced subsidies for loss-making passenger services which the minister judged to be socially or economically desirable. The system was unwieldy, since grant applications had to be submitted for some three hundred individual services, and there were problems in the calculations of costs and hence of the appropriate subsidy (Joy 1973: 127—31; Parker 1978: 7).

The Railway Act 1974 replaced the service-by-service approach with a block grant on the EEC model for 'public service obligation' (PSO); support for metropolitan area rail services was also to be provided by the Passenger Transport Executives of the large metropolitan authorities. According to a government minister at the time, the act recognized that the railways 'are not a normal nationalized industry but a unique type of public corporation which exists to service social and environmental purposes as well as the economic needs' (Hansard, 24 June 1974). Originally the 'social railway' encompassed the whole of the passenger service. In 1977, however, it was decided that inter-city (as well as freight) rail services should not in principle be subsidized (Department of Transport 1977: chs. 6, 7), although in practice they continued to be.

In Spain, the principle of state financing of operating deficits was established in a 1954 law and enshrined in RENFE's 1964 statute, and a portion of RENFE's investment programme was financed directly through the general state budget. RENFE repeatedly complained that deficit financing weakened management 'which has not been motivated by economic or commercial considerations but purely by technical ones' (RENFE 1971m: 49). Later, the company submitted provisional accounts showing forecast losses so that these could be included in the state budget. But the budgetary credits finally approved tended to be substantially lower than those requested, and the state lagged increasingly behind in the settlement of the company's deficits. In the words of a report of the ministry of economics and finance (cited in *El País*, 6 July 1983), 'the losses that occur in practice tend to be higher even than those originally forecast because, among other reasons, of the increase in financial charges implied by the need to finance the lags in financial flows caused by insufficient budgetary provision'. By 1982, the state's accumulated 'debt' with RENFE was rather more than the annual operating revenue (RENFE 1984a: 45). RENFE's deficit, for reasons discussed in other chapters, exploded during the 1970s and the first half of the 1980s. In real terms, it expanded by more than twelve times between 1973 and 1984, increasing from a low point of 0.16 per cent of GDP to 0.90 per cent.

It was only in 1984, with the entry of Spain into the EEC looming, that the principle of PSO grants calculated in advance was properly implemented for Spanish railways. The grant was broken down for individual lines, as with the pre-1974 British system (RENFE 1984a: 55−7, 82). Yet even the new system brought criticism that the budgeted grants were not in fact paid by the government (*El País*, 6 November 1985).

The Railway Deficit and State Control

As concern over state expenditure mounted, governments have looked for ways of cutting back the volume of support for the railways. This process, characteristic of the whole of the public enterprise sector, occurred earlier in Britain than in Spain for reasons explained in previous chapters. In both countries, optimistic expansion strategies fell victim to the harsher financial climate of the mid-1970s onwards. BR's 1973 'Interim Rail Strategy', which had initially received government approval, had proposed a doubling of the rate of investment up to 1981, and its impact was to be seen in the rise in staff numbers by nearly 6,000 during 1974−5, after years of virtually continuous decline. In Spain, the concern with the public sector deficit put paid to the extremely ambitious 'general railways plan' of 1980. The plan (see Guitart 1981; RENFE 1980m: 53−67) was expected to create 50,000 permanent new jobs and aimed to put RENFE on a par with the best European railways within a dozen years. It failed to win government and parliamentary approval. Perhaps surprisingly, the PSOE gave its approval in 1987 to another massive investment plan, the 'railway transport plan' (PTF) (*Trenes Hoy*, May 1987). It proposed expenditure of 2,100 billion pesetas (about £10 billion) by the end of the century on the modernization of the Spanish network. But it differed from the earlier plan in its concentration on the inter-city and suburban commuter services for which there was high demand, and it was to be achieved with a falling labour force rather than an expanding one. Moreover, by this time, a more rigorous framework of control was in place (see below). There were also special political factors at work: in 1992 Spain was to host both the Olympic Games and celebrations for the 500th anniversary of the 'discovery' of the Americas, and an improved rail transport system was seen as essential. But it remained to be seen whether the ambitious plan would withstand the impact of possible future austerity measures.

Both governments also attempted to control the financial demands of the railways by strengthening the framework of financial targets and constraints. In Britain, successive revisions of the grant system had not brought financial stability and during the early 1970s BR showed major losses even after payment of the grant. This led to the introduction of new controls. Cash limits were imposed for the value of the PSO, external financing limits and total investment spending (MMC 1980: ch. 3). In 1976, the government pegged the grant for future years to the 1975 level in real terms, while expecting a comparable service to be maintained. The political priorities of the post-1979 Conservative government, focusing attention even more directly on the public enterprise sector and on BR, intensified the financial pressures. In 1983 BR, which was planning a gradual reduction in its PSO requirement, was asked by the transport minister to reduce it by a quarter within three years. In 1986 the minister set BR the target of a further 25 per cent reduction by 1990. The government also laid down target rates of return for the commercial sectors, that is freight, parcels and Intercity. These objectives, however, proved vulnerable to external events, especially the disruption caused by the miners' strike of 1984−5, and the government was forced to revise them downwards. In 1987 the target for the commercial sectors was a 2.7 per cent operating profit on net assets by 1990.[4]

In Spain, RENFE has been set targets under the various modernization plans and international credit agreements to eliminate its operating deficit, and subsequently cover its depreciation costs and interest charges. But it was only with the election of the PSOE in 1982 that a programme for braking the rise in RENFE's deficits was seriously implemented. The condition of RENFE was seen by the new government as one of the most pressing problems that it had to face. It found that the company's true deficit for 1982 was some 200 billion (CEFE 1984: 22), a sum equal to roughly 1 per cent of GDP, and that, unless it was checked, it could reach 400 billion pesetas or even higher by 1986. The government's first priority was to impose discipline and reform RENFE's finances. For the first time, detailed financial targets were set, under the 1984 programme contract between RENFE and the state (RENFE 1984a). The contract consisted of a set of mutual commitments tied to precise targets over a three-year period. It clearly defined the PSO payments, and committed the state to settling its accumulated debt with the company. The contract included limits for external financing which had not been subject to overall control previously, and set RENFE a variety of financial objectives including a reduction in its call on state funds. It also covered objectives on a wide range of physical and quality of service indicators, such as volume of traffic, physical productivity, and commercial speeds. Programme contracts were also to govern the implementation of the 1987 rail transport plan.

These increasingly stringent financial targets, together with the need to finance investment largely from internal sources, have made the railway administrations look for ways to cut costs and increase efficiency. At the same time, severe economic problems in both countries in recent years added to cost-cutting pressures by reducing traffic and revenues. In BR's case at least, these pressures have been accompanied by government efforts to strengthen the competitive forces facing the railways.[5] The framework of regulation for the transport sector has been significantly loosened, especially by Conservative policy since 1979. Increased maximum weights for 'juggernaut' lorries, competition from deregulated bus and coach services and the opening of new motorways, especially the London orbital M25, have posed major threats to BR's freight and long distance passenger traffic. One indicator of the competitive climate was the loss of the Post Office's important parcels contract to road transport in the spring of 1986, and the subsequent loss of major newspaper contracts.

Since labour costs account for around 60 per cent of operating costs in BR and RENFE, these pressures for financial stringency and cost cutting have naturally had a major impact on industrial relations in the two enterprises as later chapters will show. But, as the arguments of chapter 3 suggest, the passage from government policies for reducing the deficit to concrete cost-cutting measures within the railway enterprises is complex and often beset with contradictions. First, the relative autonomy of railway management means that the assessment of its performance by outside authorities is problematic. This is compounded, second, by cross-cutting political objectives that conflict with the achievement of clear financial targets and make it difficult to hold management to account for its actions. Third, even where priorities are clear and performance is relatively unambiguous, what sanctions are available in the event of 'poor' performance? This raises a fourth question. The railway organizations have complex internal structures that may impede the implementation of the state's objectives; transformations must take place in the strategies, organization and relationships of groups within the railway enterprises − both management and workforce − in order for external pressures to become effective. In short, how is the cost-cutting imperative to be transmitted to and down through the railway organizations? These issues are dealt with in the subsections that follow, though some of them naturally can only be dealt with fully in later chapters concerned with the details of industrial relations on the railways.

Ministerial Power, Managerial Autonomy and Control of Knowledge

The railways in both Britain and Spain are in theory governed by the principle of the autonomy of public enterprise management from the sources of political authority that formulate their objectives. The alternative, of close integration of the railways into the central machinery of the state, has not proved suitable for the efficient conduct of complex productive activities; a Spanish experiment with direct ministerial control during the late 1950s (RENFE 1957m: vii, ix; IBRD 1963: 192−3) was shortlived, and the disadvantages of direct control have recently led the Italian government, for example, to remove the state railway from under the direct control of the transport ministry and endow it with an autonomous corporate structure (*Railway Gazette International*, December 1985: 926−7).

In both Britain and Spain the minister has statutory powers to approve budgets, plans and investment programmes, annual reports and accounts, overall price increases, and rail closures; to set the level of state support for the railways; and to make or confirm appointments to the board, including the chairman.[6]

The British minister is also empowered to issue 'general directions' in the national interest, although this has rarely been used, or specific directions to the British Railways Board: for example in the interests of 'national defence', or to 'discontinue any of their activities, dispose of any part of their undertaking, dispose of any assets held by them . . .' (Transport Act 1962: section 27). In Spain, the power of the government is represented, as in the French model, by ministerial delegates to the RENFE board, one for the treasury and one for the ministry of transport (before 1977 for the ministry of public works).[7]

Managerial autonomy has been fostered by the growth of public sector commercialism based on the principle of allowing managements to operate freely within the framework of targets set for them by the state, and on the promotion of an 'entrepreneurial' approach to the management of the railways. Yet the strengthening of autonomy creates practical and conceptual difficulties of control and the transmission of state objectives. The setting of targets and the control of performance depend on the political authorities having access to the relevant knowledge: the costs of services, the basis of investment appraisals and so on. As was argued in chapter 3, this is problematic, and in the cáse of the railways it is especially so.

The central problem for the government is to determine the value of the subsidy to the 'social' railway, that is the services that would not exist or would be extremely highly priced without state support, and to set appropriate targets for the 'commercial' railway. There is, however, no simple way of fully dividing up total costs among the different parts of the railway, such as the provincial or suburban sectors in BR. This is because only about 40 per cent of total costs are 'specific' to particular sectors; the rest represents facilities, such as track, signalling and administration, that are shared by the different sectors. These costs vary only indirectly or not at all with changes in the level of traffic. In recent years BR has been developing techniques for giving each of the business sectors responsibility for part of the network's infrastructure costs. One sector is designated 'prime user' of a section of track, for example, and the other sectors only contribute to the extent that they cause additional 'avoidable' costs.[8] However, this system was devised primarily as a means of internal management control over the business sectors, rather than as a guide to the allocation of the PSO grant. An alternative approach, used on continental railways such as SNCF and RENFE, and on BR prior to 1974, is to allocate costs fully by 'analytical', that is arithmetical, accounting techniques based on traffic shares. But 'allocations to sectors based on measures of use have only the most tenuous relationship with cost generation' (MMC 1980: 27) and are essentially arbitrary. The problem is compounded when attempts are made to find out the costs of individual services when subsidies are paid line-by-line, rather than for whole sectors; yet this is what RENFE's 1984 programme contract with the state claimed to achieve (RENFE 1984a: 80).

As a result there are areas of ambiguity in determining the value of state support for the railways. It is not uncommon for the allocation of costs to be recalculated. Ambiguities appear to be resolved through negotiation between railway management and the sponsor ministry. In the days when BR's grant was allocated to over 300 individual services, a participant observed attempts to load some of the costs of main line services onto subsidized ones. BR managers resisted probing by ministry officials of why a particular service operated in a particular way. There was considerable leeway in deciding which services should be subsidized and the 'right' allocation would be determined by 'talking it over between the railway managers and the official' (Joy 1973: 127–31).

Managerial control over information allows the railways to manipulate the public presentation of results to political effect. For example, ministry officials and union leaders alike believed that RENFE deliberately gave overpessimistic forecasts so that actual results would be seen in a favourable light (Sánchez 1984; *El País*, 5 June 1984). Constant changes in accounting criteria, for example in the allocation of items between operating and investment accounts, made it difficult for external controllers to calculate the true size of the deficit.

Observers believed that RENFE sometimes loaded items onto the capital account in order to reduce the apparent deficit, and sometimes did the reverse, boosting current costs in order to be able to get a higher grant from the state. Yet the political authority was to an extent dependent on the company's sources of information, however suspect or inadequate they were seen to be; according to one civil servant interviewed, the PSO requirement was 'basically calculated by taking on trust the figures which RENFE gave'.

The 1982 PSOE government tried to alleviate the problem of knowledge by placing senior government officials on the board of RENFE. But the danger was that this would either interfere with managerial autonomy, or be ineffectual given the many other commitments of the appointees and the limited role of the board in decision-making. Government appraisal of RENFE's investment proposals was similarly affected by the limitations of the information made available. Under the 1977 law of the budget, state enterprises were required to submit an 'action plan on investment and financing' to an inter-ministerial committee on public investments. But the action plan was merely a listing of the planned investments and control was little more than a bureaucratic formality, because of the notion that state enterprise management was autonomous.

In Britain too there was criticism of the ineffectiveness of ministerial checks on BR's investment projects, especially during the 1950s and 1960s (e.g. Joy 1973: 19; SCNI 1960: lxxxvii−viii). The alternative to 'taking things on trust' was an excessive ministerial involvement in the detail of costing and investment appraisal (SCNI 1968: 177−8) and a subversion of managerial autonomy. The Serpell committee argued that:

> The Department has been deeply involved in the detailed examination of such projects as the programmes for the construction of new sleeper cars, electrical multiple units, and HST [High Speed Train] sets ... [I]t cannot be satisfactory for the Department to have to substitute its commercial judgment for the Board's in this way. It blurs the lines of accountability and draws the Department deep into matters with which the industry should be competent to deal (Serpell 1983: 52).

Thus both the setting and the monitoring of performance of the railways in relation to the PSO grant, to investment programmes and to planning, are beset with problems of information. In recent years governments, particularly the Conservatives in Britain, have tried to cut the Gordian knot by imposing cuts in state support and forcing the railways to adapt. But unrealistic targets may be met by 'creative accounting': some railway managers have reported desperate attempts to stay within annual targets by, for example, cancelling trains to save overtime costs. Moreover, efforts by the railways to make their internal planning more realistic may be thwarted, since plans are liable to arbitrary ministerial reduction.

But a further problem looms for control of the railways: what happens if targets are not met? It will be argued below that management is provided with an alibi for poor performance by constant *ad hoc* ministerial interference. Even if the case can be 'proven', however, the sanctions available to politicians when things go wrong may be limited. The threat of bankruptcy and takeover is absent. In theory, ministerial powers of appointment and dismissal can be used to discipline management, but in practice the powers are not as great as they might seem. As chapter 3 suggested, nationalized industry chairmen in Britain, on the rare occasions that they lose their positions, do so for political disagreements with ministers rather than through incompetent performance. In Spain, turnover of chairmen of RENFE has been extremely rapid. Since nationalization there have been 19, and their average period in office has been less than two-and-a-half years, half that of their British counterparts. But this has nothing to do with the use of ministerial sanctions; it largely reflects the use of RENFE (as of other state enterprises) by aspiring politicians as a springboard to ministerial or other high office.

But the political authorities still of course have considerable power to control the railways. At a fundamental level, they define the broad nature of the economic task that the railways must perform. They also possess more subtle powers of political pressure and the use of persuasion. Railways are politically very exposed because the service attracts so much public attention and because of the size of the state subsidy (e.g. SCNI 1968: 432). Select committees in both countries frequently scrutinize the railways' behaviour and performance and hundreds of questions are asked in parliament about BR and RENFE: in 1966, for example, 550 questions were tabled in the British parliament and MPs addressed some 1,100 letters to the BRB chairman (BRB 1968: 160). BR and RENFE are faced with powerful road lobbies with good access to the transport ministries, and with the pressures of user groups. In the words of one politician, 'given that the major public utilities are under constant political attack, it is in the interests of the chairmen to have the minister broadly defending the industry and not letting it be known in the ways the minister has at his disposal that he basically agrees with the critics' (fieldnotes).

Railway management is dependent on the minister 'fighting its corner' in battles in cabinet, especially over public expenditure, and in defending it before select committees. Where major investment decisions, such as BR's electrification plan or RENFE's new investment plan, are pending, the minister may be in a strong bargaining position and be able to extract concessions from railway management in return for mustering support in cabinet.

While the power of dismissal may be of limited use, where the government has been able to appoint a new rail chairman, it has the opportunity to shape a management team more in tune with its thinking. In BR, for example, the new chairman appointed by the transport minister in 1983 was considered to be more sympathetic than his predecessor to the government's objective of reducing financial support for the railways.

Ministers may also use committees of inquiry to place the railways under public scrutiny and help them to push through changes. In Britain, BR has been investigated by the Monopolies and Mergers Commission and by special inquiries such as the Serpell committee. RENFE, according to one estimate, had seen some forty study commissions by the early 1980s (*Nueva Empresa*, no. 193, 15 October 1983), and a major commission of inquiry set up by the government reported in 1984 (CEFE 1984). However, the railways are not passive recipients of such political pressure, but political actors and manipulators in their own right. BR has defused critical scrutiny by skilful use of the media; for example, it was able to undermine criticisms in the Serpell report by focusing public attention on the politically unacceptable options for a much reduced network. In 1973, the board used the public outcry over leaked reports of proposed cuts in the network 'to press for a higher level of investment, which they now thought they had a chance of being granted' (Pryke and Dodgson 1975: 23). BR used press campaigns in the early 1980s to put the arguments for higher state support, basing its case on the higher subsidies of other European railways as a percentage of GNP. It has also been adept at gaining support, for example for its electrification programme, by lobbying in parliament among MPs known to be interested in the rail sector, including the group of railway union-sponsored members. In Spain, RENFE too keeps in touch with 'opinion formers'; the chairman will, for example, arrange meetings with the heads of major financial institutions to discuss the company's results.

Thus both sides have power resources which they may mobilize. Government control depends on bargaining, rather than on formal sanctions that are generally ineffective. Ministerial power is somewhat counterbalanced by railway management's control of internal information and by its own political resources. In recent years, the Conservative government in Britain has increasingly been able to impose its agenda on the nationalized industries, including the railways. This reflects complex changes in the relative power resources of government and enterprises that are described in later chapters. Despite the growing assimilation by management of the new 'rules of the game', however, the distance between government objectives and enterprise behaviour remains.

Complex and Conflicting Objectives

Even with the advent of clear financial targets and greater 'commercialism', the continuing acknowledgement that the railway contains a major, if not predominant, 'social' element requiring continuous state support poses difficulties for state control. The problem of establishing coherent, explicit and stable objectives for state enterprises applies with particular force to the railways. Many of the 'social' or non-commercial objectives imposed on the railways by the state remain unacknowledged; they are not incorporated into calculations of state financial compensation and state control has thus been weakened since railway management has been given reasonable pretexts for failing to meet targets. Moreover, the railways in both countries have served as instruments of broader macroeconomic goals such as price and wage control, employment stability and the health of the supplier industries.

In Britain prior to the 1968 Transport Act BR was, according to Joy (1973: 84–5), 'working to a whole range of sub-goals, some imposed by the Government, others voluntarily assumed by BR, and all of which were in conflict with the basic break-even objective laid down by Parliament'. The lack of clarity in government objectives meant that the criteria of government decisions often remained unclear to management. This was particularly true of government approval of corporate plans during the 1970s. Harris and Williams (1980: 129), writing with an insider's perspective, argue that no particular pattern was discernible in the rejection of proposals by government officials; rejection or acceptance seemed 'very often to rely more on temporary political expediency than on any thought out policy'. Thus planning became a 'political patchwork based on the "art of the possible"'.

These problems remained, even after objectives had been partially clarified and formalized through grant financing and stringent financial controls. Objectives were still too diffuse to be encompassed within the scope of financial targets. On the other hand, the growing emphasis on the achievement of targets could divert attention from the more substantive concerns of railway management with running a service to 'meet the needs of industry and the public', as BR's aims and objectives put it (BRB 1980r: 5). Indeed, tighter financial targets increasingly conflicted with the consensual political decision to maintain a certain size of railway system. BR complained that the result was likely to be deteriorating services, especially since there was simultaneous pressure to keep down tariffs, while BR's costs themselves were rising faster than the retail price index. The corporation, and outside bodies such as the MMC, suggested that the government should define more closely the level and quality of rail services to be provided (BR 1979r: 5; MMC 1980). In recent years, this particular conflict has become even sharper with government instructions to BR to reduce the PSO requirement drastically. Cash limits have also led to underspending on investment ceilings (MMC 1980: 16−17), and real investment was falling sharply from 1980 (TEST 1984a: 32−5).[9] This affected BR's plans to reduce costs and increase traffic by renewing its ageing fleet and investing in modern High Speed Trains (see, e.g., SCT 1983: xvi), and was seen as making difficult the maintenance of even existing railway services.

The government (and the Serpell committee inquiry into railway finances) clearly believed that the circle could be squared by increases in efficiency. As the Secretary of State for Transport told the chairman of BR in October 1983, 'your guiding objective should be to run an efficient railway, providing good value for money. Service to your customers should be reliable, attractive and punctual, at acceptable fares and charges; and the cost to the taxpayer should be reduced' (reprinted in MMC 1987: 257). But the claims of the user organizations and of the trade unions were of declining standards and cuts in services 'by stealth'. The official railway 'watchdog authority', the Central Transport Consultative Committee, claimed to have amassed 'a considerable amount of evidence of a direct link between a decline in some aspects of quality of service provided for passengers, and major reductions in government subsidy' (*Financial Times (FT)* 4 August 1987).[10]

RENFE has experienced similar conflicts between maintaining the service, reducing its call upon state finances, and keeping prices low (e.g. CEFE 1983: 18). (This has been intensified by the relative weakness of the financial framework of control until recently.) For example, between 1973 and 1982 the retail price index rose 14 per cent more than freight tariffs and 32 per cent more than passenger fares; while short-term efforts to restrain the deficit, such as the 1984 programme contract, led, as in BR, to restraints on capital expenditure, jeopardizing longer-term possibilities of reducing the deficit by means of cost-saving and revenue-attracting investments.

Like BR, RENFE has been used to serve macroeconomic objectives, affecting the achievement of its own immediate goals in a manner not amenable to simple quantification. Its view of itself as an instrument − and interpreter − of public policy (e.g. RENFE 1981m: 31) was reminiscent of BR's outlook until the 1960s. Indeed, in the absence of clear definitions of its obligations and objectives, the company interpreted its public service task in a broad manner. An internal management circular of 1980 talks of its role as an 'element promoting Spanish development and stimulating employment'. Its grandiose modernization plan of the early 1980s was presented as its contribution to the 'struggle against unemployment' (RENFE 1982m: 9), and when in 1981 it negotiated with the unions an increase in staff of 7,000, the chairman defended the agreement as 'an appropriate response to [RENFE's] public service task' (quoted in *El País*, 12 December 1981).

Its 'public service' role went well beyond that of BR's in two other respects. First, RENFE was a strategic element in defence planning and, more importantly, in the military's contingencies for controlling the population and assuring internal 'security'. The transport of military equipment and troops had absolute priority on the railway network, and the military were determined opponents of programmes of line closures.

Second, RENFE in effect subsidized other sectors of the economy directly through so-called political prices, special low tariffs that were supposed to be compensated by the state but in practice were frequently not. RENFE received compensation for some political prices, such as those used to support the Asturian coal mining industry. But in addition government departments, notably the ministry of defence, enjoyed subsidized tariffs for their rail transport, and in some cases had large unpaid bills with RENFE amounting to many billions of pesetas; for many years RENFE carried the mail of the Spanish Post Office entirely without charge (IBRD 1963: 196).

Many commentators have urged governments to 'define priorities among the ultimate objectives, frequently incompatible among themselves, that must govern the activity of public enterprises in general and of railway enterprises in particular' (CEFE 1984: 37). This assumes that governments are willing to make all their objectives explicit, that they can specify them precisely, and that they are stable over time. In fact, as we have argued, governments may have hidden agendas and their priorities may fluctuate according to political cycles. Short-term electoral considerations such as the likely fate of marginal constituencies may determine decisions on issues such as line closures, for example (see Marsh 1978). Government commitments, such as the 1984 programme contract with RENFE, may be very vulnerable to changes in the political and economic context.

The nature of representative politics may affect the continuity of policy. Adversarial British economic policy-making (see Gamble and Walkland 1984) reduces the continuity of transport policies as governments change. This pattern, which has also been a feature of aspects of Spanish policy-making since the return to democracy, contrasts with the relatively high degree of continuity, particularly on railway investment policy, of other countries. As the TEST report on the European railways (1984a: 4) puts it, 'it is interesting to see how apolitical continental European railway decisions often are. The TGV system was introduced, and then authorised, within the Giscard presidency. ... West Germany is also right of centre yet its rail investment plans are undiminished'.

The effect of adversary politics in Britain is intensified by the rapid turnover of government personnel. Although there have been only five changes of governing party in Britain since nationalization in 1948, there have been 21 transport ministers during that time, an average of one less than every two years. In the unions' view, this is an indication of the low status attached to transport matters and hence to the transport portfolio within the government. As well as reducing continuity, the rapid turnover also disrupts the bargaining relationship and understandings between the minister and the railway chairman; in the words of one respondent, each new minister had to be 'taught in' by railway management.

The clear definition of objectives is also impeded by the fragmentation of political authority that was discussed in chapter 3. Policies that directly or indirectly impinge upon the objectives of the railways are formulated at a number of different sites within the state administration, and co-ordination between them is not always assured. The independent agenda of the Spanish defence establishment, sometimes at odds with the policy objectives of the treasury and transport ministry, has been mentioned above. While in theory the costs of the ministry of defence's demands on the railway system could be charged directly to it, in fact relations between parts of the state machine are governed by considerations of bargaining and relative power, rather than accounting clarity. In Britain, the role of fragmented political authority in muddying the formation of objectives is illustrated by conflicts within the present Conservative government over BR's electrification plans, with close advisers of the Prime Minister, and according to some accounts the Treasury, undermining the efforts of the Department of Transport to secure cabinet approval. This led the government, in the words of one senior manager, repeatedly to 'move the goalposts', in other words to change the criteria that BR had to meet for electrification schemes to be approved.

More generally, British transport policy itself is more fragmented and less co-ordinated than in other European countries, such as West Germany and France, which stress 'intermodal' planning. For example, railway investments are not evaluated using the same cost−benefit techniques that are used in road planning, despite recommendations that this should be done (see, e.g., Leitch 1977). This is likely to provide a further obstacle to clear and stable objectives for rail transport. Fragmentation has also been a feature of Spanish transport policy, although the PSOE has been attempting to co-ordinate planning, establish a consistent competitive framework and draw up standardized criteria for investment in different modes.

Ad Hoc Government Intervention

The difficulty in defining coherent and stable goals has meant that in practice priorities among competing demands on the railways have frequently been established by *ad hoc* government intervention. But these priorities have been predominantly short-term and fluctuating and often in open contradiction with the formal longer-term objectives of the railways. Intervention also occurs because of the difficulty for the controlling authorities in finding out what is going on within the company and ensuring that policies are implemented in practice.

In the early 1960s, the World Bank report on Spain referred to the 'constant interference by the State in the detailed administration of the railway system'

(IBRD 1963: 192). Indeed, as mentioned above, the railways were for some years under the direct control of the sponsor ministry (at that time the ministry of public works). Two decades after the World Bank report, another commission of inquiry was complaining that the state 'interferes excessively in the running of the [railway] companies, without that resulting in the clarification of the objectives that they should pursue or in exercise of effective control over them' (CEFE 1984: 33).

In Britain, too, observers have noted instances of direct government interference in the day-to-day running of the railways stretching back to the early days of nationalization. Indeed, some participants have seen this interference as legitimate and necessary. As a former transport minister, Barbara Castle, expressed it,

> One's relationship with the nationalised transport industries must be a very close one because there is a continuing interaction between one's economic and social purposes and their own operating requirements and policies ... Transport has so many social implications of one kind or another that there can never be an arm's length relationship ...

The minister could never say to the board, 'right, now you have a logical remit, go away and fulfil it and so long as your rate of return is what it ought to be, we will not interfere' (SCNI 1968: 431, 434–6). There was of necessity a 'grey area', and in this zone, BR and the sponsor ministry were habitually unable to agree 'where the dividing line lies between each other's responsibilities' (NEDO 1976: 38).

In both countries, the concern with the political and economic effects of price increases has led governments to intervene on tariffs. The intervention has taken the form of more or less open ministerial arm-twisting rather than the invoking of statutory powers. One case in the mid-1950s prompted a student of British nationalized industries to comment that it was a 'particularly flagrant example of ministerial intervention because the Minister overrode the statutory duty of the Transport Commission to pay their way ...' (Robson 1962: 154).

But, from the perspective of this study the most significant area of state intervention is industrial relations. Industrial relations in the railways have an impact on central macroeconomic policy issues such as inflation, pay policy and employment, and on a wide range of other pressing political concerns such as industrial peace and the continuity of public transport services. It is this combination of factors that has led to a stream of government interventions over pay determination, productivity and working practices, investment and closure decisions, and industrial conflict. Even where they are not directly linked to major matters of public policy, industrial relations may have a political resonance far beyond their apparent importance, entering the terrain of political symbolism: as exemplified perhaps by the gesture of Franco in intervening to prevent the closure of a railway workshop in Andalucía (*Sur*, 30 March 1968).

Cost-Cutting Pressures and Internal Organization

Government objectives, we have argued, are transmitted to the railways through bargaining relationships between the political controllers and railway management, rather than being directly and automatically imposed. Transmission depends not only on the external relations of the railway administrations with the government, but also on their internal structure.

New and more stringent financial constraints and other commercial pressures on management required appropriate organizational channels through which to take effect. Both BR and RENFE, in common with railways elsewhere (Bouley 1985), have stressed the new 'reality of competition' and the need 'to shift the emphasis from "running a railway" to providing a value for money service to the customer' (BRB 1985r: 5); in these conditions, it was 'the market that has to give the orders' (RENFE chairman, cited in *El Nuevo Lunes*, 16 December 1985). But traditionally neither has had an organization capable of responding to commercial pressures.

In BR, commercialism has led to radical organizational change. The old system consisted of functional responsibilities, for activities such as engineering, superimposed on a geographical structure of regions, divisions (until the early 1980s) and areas. According to the BR chairman, it

> was production led and cost conscious, but not motivated to bring income, expenditure and price into an optimum relationship ... perhaps most significant of all, it was difficult to respond to government pressure to improve business performance without being able to identify the source and scope of costs incurred in providing uneconomic passenger services for which a revenue support public service obligation (PSO) grant is paid (Reid 1984: 258).

From 1982, a new structure was put into place, based on five 'business sectors'. Three of these, freight, parcels and Intercity, were the commercial services of the railway. The other two, making up the subsidized 'social' railway, were the commuter services in the south east of England, centred on the metropolis (Network South East), and rural and local services (the Provincial sector). Each sector was made responsible for its net revenue results; previously, there had been no responsibility for overall profit and loss below the level of the chief executive.

BR's corporate planning was reformed to fit in with the new structure by devolving responsibility for planning largely to the five businesses and by developing 'action plans' to commit lower level management to business objectives (Heath 1984: 221). But the nature of the relationship between railway and government made internal reform of this kind problematic. Planning in the railways has traditionally had an important political dimension that has sometimes been at odds with its use as an internal business tool. Its role has been 'to provide reassurance to the government, to give support to policies which BR wish to pursue, to provide briefing material for Department of Transport Ministers in argument and negotiations with ministerial colleagues, and to provide an atmosphere of professionalism and control over the business which governments — and the public — expect' (Heath 1984: 221). The recent technical improvements in BR planning (Allen and Williams 1985: 92—6) are unlikely to eliminate political influences; indeed, as already noted, the effectiveness of action plans may be undermined by subsequent government alteration of planning objectives. Moreover, the reform process itself is part of the currency of political debate. Ministers are enabled to defend BR's interests by arguing that its planning is now more 'realistic' and 'professional', rather than 'over-optimistic' (see, e.g., Serpell 1983: 51), and the entrepreneurial language of the 'bottom line' and 'value-for-money' enters the processes of political exchange and bargaining between politicians, civil servants and corporate actors.

RENFE, like BR, had, in the words of a Spanish government official, 'not been at all concerned with capturing customers and markets, it was more a question of waiting for people to come and request its service' (fieldnotes). It had traditionally lacked a commercial ideology. Managerial pronouncements contrast sharply with those of their British counterparts in the late 1970s and early 1980s. Justifying the railway deficit in 1980, for example, the chairman maintained that 'no one would think of talking of the deficit of the armed forces or of the fact that our state educational establishments show a deficit ...' (*Cinco Días*, 19 December 1980). The company's structure was very hierarchical, centralized and dominated by the functional departments, on the French model. Unlike BR, RENFE management was also politicized to a considerable degree. Under the dictatorship, senior managers often had close connections with Francoist notables, while many technical and professional staff, as well as blue-collar railway workers, had fought in the civil war on the nationalist side against the Republic. The influence of the Opus Dei lay catholic movement, whose members dominated Francoist economic policy for a time from the late 1950s, was particularly strong in RENFE. When democracy returned, the chairmanship was used to reward political services and to advance careers. In the words of the new Socialist minister of transport, RENFE was 'at the same time a breeding ground and nursery for training ministers who then went into the government, and an elephant's graveyard for those leaving the government' (quoted in *El Nuevo Lunes*, 24–30 January 1983).

From 1985 RENFE planned to introduce a new structure more suited to the demands government was making on it, based on what they saw as the 'Anglo-Saxon' model. The commercial function had previously been subordinate to operations, and according to a manager involved, its philosophy was 'to sell what the operating departments produced'. The commercial function now became the focus of the organization. It was organized into twelve different product groups, four for passenger services and eight for freight, each with responsibility for its results and control over pricing, planning and investment decisions. However, at the time of writing it is not clear how the new structure will work in practice, especially since RENFE's systems for determining costs of services appear to be less advanced than those used by BR.

Moreover, many in RENFE were profoundly sceptical of organizational reform. Each new chairman, as the PSOE's transport policy document complained, brought with him a 'cascade of appointments and political reorganisations' in the company (PSOE 1981: 62), so that superficially at least RENFE was in constant upheaval. This 'affected primarily the redistribution of personnel at higher levels without reaching the heart of the problems ... and ... often resulted in incoherencies, contradictions and duplications' (CEFE 1984: 59). A company of RENFE's size was, moreover, incapable of assimilating successive reorganizations. As a result, a state of flux coexisted with 'an excessive rigidity, a pronounced level of centralisation, a very numerous senior management group and a bureaucratised mode of operation ...' (59). By contrast, the relative stability of organization in BR allowed major changes to be digested and implemented throughout the organization.

A further complication in RENFE was the continuing politicization of appointments under the PSOE. The PSOE government at first tried to break the pattern by appointing a 'professional' businessman to the chairmanship in 1983, and by purging those who had come to RENFE as a result of their political connections with earlier governments (see *Diario 16*, 4, 5 February 1983); about twenty people who had held senior posts in the previous UCD administration were on RENFE's pay roll when the PSOE came to power (*Cinco Días*, 2 November 1983). However, securing organizational change and a move to more entrepreneurial strategies demanded more than ever political skills and access to political resources, and this led to a reversion to earlier patterns with the appointment in 1985 of a chairman closely linked to the PSOE. As in the past, he filled some key managerial positions with 'hombres de su confianza', men who had his confidence and trust and who were also holders of PSOE membership cards (see, e.g., *El País*, 22 November 1985).

Conclusions

This chapter has explored the consequences of the railways' 'relative autonomy' within the state at a time of economic crisis and increased political concern with public expenditure. Two broad tendencies are at work. The first, linked to the fiscal crisis of the state, is the growing effort of governments to control the railways' demands on the public exchequer by encouraging more commercial behaviour and imposing a framework of financial targets and constraints. But this tendency, which increases managerial autonomy within prescribed limits, intermeshes with a second, more constant characteristic of the relationship between railways and the state: the tension between autonomy and control. Objectives remain complex, diffuse, changing. Priorities are not always easy to ascertain, even when government objectives are relatively clear. This leads to *ad hoc* government intervention which in turn may undermine the consistency and stability of objectives still further. In practice, priorities have to be established on a shifting, provisional basis through constant political bargaining between enterprise management, civil servants and politicians.

Even with greater commercialism and managerial autonomy, government intervention persists, partly because the drive to greater efficiency and economy in the public sector is a *political* process. Governments may intervene in the railways in a way that undermines managerial autonomy and responsibility, but which makes sense from the point of view of political symbols and messages about productivity and efficiency; this will become clearer from the case studies in later chapters.

The processes that we have described were broadly similar in BR and RENFE. In both cases, political programmes crystallized around the idea of rationalization, cost cutting and improved use of resources on the railways. This contrasted with the more expansionary programmes of France, West Germany and Italy; programmes which have been modified but not extinguished by the economic recession and the concern with state expenditure. In these three countries, for example, major new high speed passenger lines are being constructed,[11] and the level of state support as a percentage of GNP is considerably higher than in Britain or Spain (BRB/Leeds 1980; Nash 1985a). In both countries, the nature of managerial autonomy and the existence of an internal organizational structure and interests poses problems of transmission which the state has attempted to solve by a variety of overlapping mechanisms: statutory and financial frameworks, the invocation of market forces, the creation of political pressures, political bargaining and exchange, and direct intervention. Their aim has been to alter the way in which management perceives its interests, calculates costs and benefits, and establishes objectives.

The timing of the political programme was significantly different in Britain and Spain, however, reflecting the different ways in which economic forces have become translated into political strategies and ideologies in the two countries. Most notably, the Spanish strategy was being implemented by a modernizing, socially reformist government, while in Britain the increasing pressures on the railways in recent years have come from a radical Conservative government hostile to the public sector in principle. The Spanish railway 'crisis' was considerably more acute than the British, reflecting the interconnected factors of the lag in forming a political response to economic crisis, and the forces unleashed by Spain's transition to democracy. The relative tardiness of the political response to the railway question in Spain meant that the formal framework of relationships was less developed than in Britain and thus the general problem of unclear objectives was more severe.

The bargaining relationship between the railways and the state could be expected to show different patterns in the two countries. In Britain, the ethos of professional, arm's-length management of nationalized industries, including the railways, meant that politicization primarily affected the boundary between the board and the political authority. In RENFE, by contrast, political manoeuvring was internalized within the organization, so that the management process itself was politicized.

The difference in the political context meant that the formulation and transmission of government objectives took on different forms and involved different actors in the two cases, most notably where the unions were concerned, as we shall see. And the different dynamics of RENFE and BR as organizations, reflecting, for example, the very different ways in which each internalized political pressure, affected the way in which government objectives were construed and implemented within them. The following chapters will illustrate these processes as they affected − and were affected by − the characteristic industrial relations of the two railway administrations.

Notes

1 The 1.44 metres was not yet standard at the time the choice was made (Sanz 1978). Unlike other countries, Spain was unable subsequently to rectify the gauge owing to lack of investment funds and the gauge difference remains an impediment to

Spain's integration into the European rail network. There was also a significant network of one metre track, used predominantly in coastal routes filling in the gaps in the radial network; today the 1,360 km of narrow gauge line are exploited by a separate state company, FEVE (Ferrocarriles de Vía Estrecha).

2   On the nationalization of Spanish railways see Wais 1974. On Britain, see, e.g., Barker and Savage 1974: ch. 3; Gourvish 1986: part I; Chester 1975.

3   According to the NUR, unfair competition was intensified by the relaxation of drivers' hours and speed limits on lorries, and by the Department of Transport's instructions to police authorities not to prosecute the owners of 38-tonne lorries overloaded by less than 10 per cent.

4   The targets are mostly laid down in letters from the minister to BR's chairman setting out the corporation's objectives. The letters are reprinted in MMC 1987, Appendix 3.

5   In Spain, the traditional unenforceability of the regulatory framework and the systematic flouting of traffic and health and safety regulations by road transport, meant that recent efforts to ensure 'fair' intermodal competition would if anything favour the railway by ending anomalies. On the new transport bill, see *Diario 16*, 27 August—3 September 1984, *El País*, 22 October 1985.

6   In the case of RENFE, there was a 'double tutelage' according to the Statute, with the treasury having a supervisory role on financial matters (Decree 23—VII—64: art. 32). Moreover, in some cases, such as powers of appointment and dismissal, the powers were those of the cabinet (council of ministers) as a whole rather than of the sponsoring minister.

7   There was also a 'delegate of the government', but this role was later assumed by the chairman.

8   For discussions of costing conventions and problems, see Nash 1985b, especially p. 38; Allen and Williams 1985; Harris and Williams 1980: ch. 3.

9   The examination of investment expenditure is complicated by the classification of investment as 'capital investment' (mainly traction and rolling stock), or 'revenue investment' (mainly signalling renewal and track rationalization), and by reclassification (for example, of continuous welded track renewal as 'other revenue investment' from 1980) (see Serpell 1983: 42).

10   See also *FT*, 1 August 1985, 2 November 1985, *Transport Review*, 21 September 1984: 1, 9 November 1984: 2.

11   For example, on West Germany, see *Modern Railways*, June 1985: 293—308; on Italy, see *Railway Gazette International*, December 1985: 925—35; and on France see TEST 1984a: 35—6 and 1984b: 69—74. As the TEST report (1984a: 33) notes, 'Britain's investment in its railway is shown to be small in itself and to have declined over the time period. France with a similar population, shows about twice the investment while Germany, with a slightly larger population, shows about three times as much as Britain'.

5

Industrial Relations in BR and RENFE – Institutions and Actors

Introduction

The growing pressures on the railways for cost-cutting and rationalization have had profound consequences for industrial relations. Railway managements have devised new labour strategies, and at the same time, other organizational changes in response to commercialism have had their own specific impact on industrial relations. The ensuing changes have not taken place in a vacuum, but have had to take account of existing industrial relations institutions and practices. For example, the formal machinery of collective bargaining, and the 'culture' of industrial relations that builds up around it, acts as a filter through which external pressures for change must pass. The same is true of the organization, strategies, and interrelationships of the railway unions. In this chapter, therefore, the existing patterns and institutions of industrial relations in BR and RENFE are examined, beginning with a description of the workforce and the unions in the two companies.

The Workforce and Patterns of Employment

Over the last three or four decades, BR and RENFE have had, in common with other major railways (with the notable exception of Italy), a steadily declining workforce (see table 5.1). This fall largely reflects the technical modernization of the network, particularly the replacement of steam locomotives by diesel and electric, the introduction of power signalling and automatic level crossings, and mechanization of work on the permanent way. In the British case, the fall has been compounded by cutbacks in the network of rural and provincial services from the 1960s under the Beeching strategy for 'reshaping the railways' (BRB 1963). This led to an especially sharp decline during the 1960s, from over half a million to well under 300,000. The rationalization of remaining services, for example, the withdrawal from wagonload freight traffic and the related reduction in marshalling yards, has permitted a continuing steady fall in numbers. In RENFE the pruning of little-used rural services has only just begun. As a result, the fall in numbers has been slower, though still considerable: from a high point of nearly 140,000 during the 1950s, the workforce had fallen to 74,000 in 1984. Unlike BR, where the decline has been virtually continuous, numbers in RENFE were more or less static between the mid-1970s and 1984. This pause in the decline was a reflection of the influences of the transition to democracy in RENFE, especially the rapid reduction of the working week from 48 hours in 1976 to 40 hours in 1984. Thereafter numbers fell sharply, showing the impact of the programme contract between RENFE and the government. In three years, the workforce was cut by about 11,000.

These changes have led to significant increases in labour productivity on the railways, despite the falling tendency of rail traffic. The major increases took

TABLE 5.1
Employment in BR and RENFE 1950–1987

	BR[a]	*BR (incl BREL)*[b]	*RENFE*[c]
1950	606,000	—	133,000
1955	563,000	—	135,000
1960	515,000	—	129,000
1965	365,000	—	111,000
1970	213,000	251,000	83,000
1975	190,000	225,000	72,000
1980	178,000	215,000	71,000
1981	170,000	205,000	72,000
1982	161,000	193,000	74,000
1983	155,000	183,000	75,000
1984	[d]	[d]	70,000
1985	147,000	173,000	66,000
1986	143,000	166,000	64,000
1987	140,000	159,000	n.a.

Notes: [a] The figures for BR exclude the board's shipping, hotels and catering activities.

[b] The numbers in this column include those employed in BR's manufacturing and repair subsidiary, British Rail Engineering Limited (BREL) which was set up under the Transport Act 1968 to run the main workshops at Derby, Swindon, Crewe, etc. Prior to that date, all workshop employees are included in the general BR total. The workshops do not have an exact equivalent in RENFE, since they are major manufacturers for BR and other railways. In addition, they carry out much of the heavy maintenance and repair work that in RENFE is subcontracted to private companies. Of BREL's total turnover, about half comes from repairs and less than a quarter from 'new build'. In November 1987 the government announced that BREL was to be privatized.

[c] The RENFE figures include the 2–3,000 'militares en prácticas' or military trainees who undergo their training for jobs in RENFE in specialist regiments.

[d] In 1984, BR's accounts were converted from a calendar year to a financial year basis. From 1985 on, the figures are for 31 March of each year.

Source: BTC and BRB *Annual Reports*; RENFE *Memorias, RENFE en 1986.*

place during the 1960s, but especially in BR with its steady job losses, the trend has continued (see table 5.2).[1]

The nature of railway operations, revolving round the movement of passenger and freight trains along a network of tracks between stations and terminals, gives rise to the characteristic categories of railway work: the upkeep of the permanent way and its associated bridges, embankments, tunnels, overhead line equipment and so on; the maintenance of rolling stock and locomotives; the crewing of trains; the control of their movements by signalling etc.; the staffing of stations, depots and terminals. The breakdown of these main categories of staff, together with administrative and other groups, is given in table 5.3.

Railway work is governed by complex rules and regulations stemming from the safety and technical requirements of operating the railway network. It has also generated a wide variety of specific, untransferable skills among train crews, signalling staff, maintenance workers and so on. Railway employment has, for the individual, been marked by great stability − it has traditionally been 'a job for life'. Compulsory redundancies have been rare (a major exception being the recent closures and cutbacks in the BR workshops subsidiary, British Rail Engineering Ltd). An indication of this is the high average length of service of BR and RENFE employees. In 1983, for example, the average length of service of RENFE workers was over 20 years. Thirty-eight per cent of the workforce had been in the company for 32 years or more and 55 per cent of them were 50 years old or over (RENFE 1984b: 160−1). These characteristics have engendered an 'enclosed order of railwaymen' (Gourvish 1986: 577), with a strong loyalty, discipline and dedication to the railway among all groups of employees.

TABLE 5.2
BR and RENFE: Traffic Units (Passenger Kilometres + Freight Ton Kilometres) per Railway Employee 1960−87 (000's)

	BR	*RENFE*
1960	126[a]	98
1970	256	271
1975	269	317
1980	277	346
1981	283	351
1982	267	347
1983	303	343
1984	b	388
1985	284	419
1986	324	420
1987	338	n.a.

Notes: [a] The figure is deflated by the presence in staff numbers of employees in the construction workshops. See table 5.1, note *b*.
[b] See note *d*, table 5.1.
Source: BRB *Report and Accounts*, RENFE *Memorias*, RENFE 1984a: 18.

TABLE 5.3
BR and RENFE: Breakdown of Employment by Categories 1986

	BR		RENFE	
	Number of Employees	%	[a]Number of Employees	%
Administrative, technical and clerical	39,600	27.7	7,300	11.6
Train crew	31,100	21.8	10,500	16.8
Station, yard, terminal and signalling	26,000	18.3	15,300	24.5
Permanent way, S & T	24,700	17.3	11,100	17.8
Workshop	[b]18,000	12.6	10,300	16.5
Miscellaneous	3,300	2.3	8,000	12.8
Total	142,700	100.0	62,500	100.0

Notes:[a] RENFE figures exclude *militares en prácticas* − see table 5.1 note *c*. The different proportional breakdown of staff in the two companies appears partly to reflect differences in definition, and partly the greater extent of subcontracting by RENFE of maintenance of rolling stock and permanent way, and other work.
[b] BR workshop staff figures exclude BREL.
Source: BRB *Report and Accounts* 1986; *RENFE en 1986*.

As Murdoch (1986: 25−6) notes, the railway labour market in Britain corresponds closely to Burawoy's (1979) description of the 'pure' internal labour market; the same point applies equally to Spanish railways. Thus priority is given to existing employees in the allocation of individuals to posts, and entry points to the system are at the lowest level of any particular hierarchy. In the case of a totally sealed labour market, new employees would only be drawn from the families of existing staff, and efforts would be made to ensure that individuals did not seek places outside the firm. Although the ra ways do not approach this extreme position, there is a strong element of family recruitment in both BR and RENFE. According to a survey carried out in RENFE in 1984, for example, some 64 per cent of respondents claimed to be children of employees and 14 per cent to be grandchildren of railway workers (Encinas 1986: 53). In BR, Robbins (1986) found that vacancies for the entry grade to the train drivers' ('footplate') line of promotion were still advertised only through internal channels. The different occupational categories of railway worker have, to a greater or lesser extent, occupational hierarchies up which they proceed, during a lifetime's work on the railways, by a combination of aptitude and seniority, with the latter predominating. Transfer between hierarchies is a complex procedure, often raising tricky questions concerning the loss or preservation of seniority rights. In the extreme case of train drivers, there is no transfer into the hierarchy above the entry grade.[2] In both British and Spanish railways, these features of the occupational structure, closely guarded by the trade unions (see below), have meant that despite equal opportunities legislation, there is still a virtual absence of female employees among groups of workers such as train drivers, permanent way, workshop or signalling staff (on BR, see Robbins 1986).

Workforce Representation: The Unions in BR and RENFE

There are a number of important differences in the organization of trade unions in BR and RENFE. The origins of British railway unions go back more than a century (Bagwell 1963; McKillop 1950; Murphy 1980), although it was only in 1911 that the unions won recognition, with the help of government intervention, from the railway companies. As will be seen below, the unions' long and uninterrupted development contrasts with the fractured history of the Spanish railway unions.

There are currently three main unions in BR. The largest is the National Union of Railwaymen (NUR) with about 90,000 members in BR. It was formed in 1913 out of the Amalgamated Society of Railway Servants, together with the General Railway Workers' Union and the United Pointsmen's and Signalmen's Society (Bagwell 1963). Given its origins, the NUR saw itself as an industrial union; originally it organized most groups of BR workers, and it continues to be recognized by BR as representing all grades of staff other than management. But it has become increasingly confined to manual staff other than footplate, and there has been a trend towards sectional, occupationally-based unionism in BR (Streeck *et al.* 1981).

The principal union for train drivers and other footplate staff is the Associated Society of Locomotive Engineers and Firemen (ASLEF). ASLEF started life as a breakaway from the Amalgamated Society of Railway Servants in the 1880s and it retained its autonomy during the process of amalgamations that led to the formation of the NUR. ASLEF now has a membership of about 20,000 in the railways, and the overwhelming majority of footplate staff are members of it. Although the NUR still has some members among drivers, it agreed in 1983 that it would stop recruiting them.

The main white-collar union is the Transport Salaried Staffs' Association (TSSA), formerly the Railway Clerks' Association, with about 32,000 members in BR. It competes with the NUR for the recruitment of clerical and supervisory staff, and now also includes many managerial staff. A small union, the British Transport Officers Guild (BTOG), has joint recognition with TSSA for management grades. In the mid-1980s it became part of the electricians' union the EEPTU. Finally, the Confederation of Shipbuilding and Engineering Unions has joint recognition with railway unions for workshops engineering activities.

Breakaway unions have occasionally arisen, notably the Union of Railway Signalmen from the 1920s. More recently, the Federation of Professional Railway Staff, created in the wake of the national strikes of 1982, was estimated to have some 1,600 members in 1987 (MMC 1987: 69). But these unions have not been recognised by BR for negotiating purposes and their impact has been limited.

Although the activities of the three major BR unions are not confined to the railways, railway employees form the large majority of their membership. Thus 78 per cent of the NUR's membership, 91 per cent of ASLEF, and 65 per cent of TSSA are in BR (Pendleton 1986: 91). Their membership in sectors such as hotels, shipping, ports, buses and road haulage, usually reflects the historical association of these sectors with British Rail and before that with the British

Transport Commission. They also have substantial membership in London Regional Transport.

BR's unions, in common with those of many British public sector organizations, have a very high membership rate. Even during the 1920s and 1930s, density never fell below 50 per cent. Since nationalization, it has been at least 80 per cent (Bain and Price 1983). After 1970, the operation of union membership agreements pushed overall membership consistently above 90 per cent, and for some grades such as train drivers, unionization has been virtually total. Since 1980, the membership agreements have been weakened by the Conservative government's trade union legislation. In 1985, BR announced that it was withdrawing from existing agreements with the unions, although it seemed unlikely that this would seriously reduce the level of unionization.

The BR unions share the relative ideological homogeneity of the British labour movement as a whole. All three major rail unions are affiliated to the Trades Union Congress and the Labour party, and the NUR in particular has a long tradition of sponsoring Labour MPs (Bagwell 1982: ch. 12), 'equalled only by the miners' union' (Eaton and Gill 1981: 41). Thus the ideological conflicts of the kind that have characterized the union movement in Spain (see below) and elsewhere in Europe are almost entirely absent. Instead, inter-union conflict in BR has been restricted to issues of occupational interests and representation (Bagwell 1982: ch. 12). In recent years, the major underlying conflict, stoked up by personality clashes between union leaders, has been between the industrial union ethos of the NUR and the continuing craft aspirations of ASLEF. This has repeatedly led to clashes over such questions as differentials, with ASLEF attempting to protect the elite status of its members. Declining membership and the prospect of further job losses have raised the question of ASLEF's financial viability, and its future as a separate organization. Moreover, changes in technology, notably the end of steam traction and more sophisticated technical aids for drivers, have called into question the exclusive craft character of drivers' skills. The NUR has traditionally advocated a single union for railway workers, but this has been strongly resisted by ASLEF. With improved personal relationships, however, steps have been taken in the last few years towards closer links. In 1983, the two unions finally established a loose 'railway federation' (which TSSA declined to join), and they subsequently worked in close co-ordination in areas such as the presentation of annual pay claims and a programme of opposition to cuts in services.

RENFE's unions differ in three main ways from those of BR. In the first place, the two major railway unions[3] are part of wider union federations and confederations, the Unión General de Trabajadores (UGT) and the Comisiones Obreras (CCOO), respectively. The Spanish unions are profoundly divided along ideological lines. The UGT confederation is a socialist union with close historical and organizational ties to the PSOE that go back about a century. The early railway unions that emerged during the 1890s were generally socialist in orientation, although in a few cases they were anarcho-syndicalist. During the 1930s the UGT railway union was in the vanguard of the Spanish labour movement and had some 49,000 members.[4] Waged members of the PSOE are required to contribute a proportion of their income to the union. A number of individuals are prominent members of the governing bodies of both the union and the party, and some 40 union leaders, including the confederation's general secretary, were members of parliament in 1985. Following the PSOE victory in the 1986 general elections, a senior member of the union, the confederal secretary for information, became Minister of Labour and Social Security.

The CCOO by contrast is closely associated with the Spanish Communist Party. It emerged as a spontaneous, semi-clandestine, workplace-based movement in the early 1960s, often working through the existing Francoist vertical union and works council system. In its early days it attracted support from a wide range of anti-Francoist groups, including Catholic workers' organizations, but subsequently it came increasingly under the control of the communist party. In RENFE, the severity of the repression under the dictatorship largely stifled the emergence of an independent union organization. But communist and other militants were active, especially in the railway workshops, and during the 1960s they managed to organize industrial action, put up their own candidates for elections within the vertical union framework, and published a sporadic newssheet (Martino de Jugo 1980; Bulnes 1967). The CCOO railway union was formally established in 1977.

On the restoration of democracy and of union rights, the CCOO went through a process of institutionalization, establishing a federal and confederal structure similar to that of the UGT. With the re-emergence of the UGT from its period of relative inactivity during Francoism (it had refused to participate in the vertical union system), the ideological divisions between the two unions became an important feature of the post-1975 Spanish labour movement. These differences, which have largely supplanted the historical division between the socialist and anarcho-syndicalist traditions, were fully reflected at the level of the CCOO and UGT railway unions in RENFE.

The Spanish rail unions are members of their respective transport federations within the wider confederations. This may affect their autonomy at least in terms of overall policy. In the case of the UGT, for example, there appears to be a tendency towards greater federal control of the member unions. The general secretary of the railway union is elected by the federal congress rather than by the railway delegates alone, and there is a growing concern to concentrate policy-making at federal level. Both UGT and CCOO in RENFE generally respond to the broad political and strategic line of their respective federations and confederations. In negotiations, the railway unions will often look to their federations and confederations to support their demands and to put additional pressure on management or on the administration. Equally, however, the railway unions may be subject to pressure from higher levels to moderate their demands if these are seen to conflict with the union's national negotiating strategy. In the words of one UGT leader,

> on the one hand the transport federation and the confederation support the demands of the railway sector at the negotiating table, and on the other hand, let us say, they also call for prudence and moderation when they realise that these demands may not be achievable, and rather than lead people over the precipice and into more strikes that will not have positive

outcomes, they recommend the adoption of an approach based on increased dialogue and the moderation of demands.[5]

The second major difference between RENFE's unions and those in BR is that the Spanish unions are not grade-based but compete across the board for membership. There is no separate union for white-collar and management staff, and both unions organize well up the employment hierarchy. The UGT includes relatively senior managers among its activists. One of the major demands of the RENFE unions, achieved in 1984, was the inclusion of the 1,500 or so higher management staff within the scope of annual collective agreements. Union competition for membership reflects the relatively unstable condition of union organization in Spain, which has been in a state of flux and development since the restoration of trade union rights. The unions are still engaged in a struggle to establish themselves in the available 'space', a struggle that has very largely been resolved in the case of the BR unions where it was in any case mainly confined to representation of the footplate grades. Nonetheless, CCOO has become the dominant union among certain occupational groups. For example, in the mid-1980s it represented almost two-thirds of unionized traincrew staff, and the same proportion of staff in the workshops and on the permanent way. The UGT, together with a smaller union, the Sindicato Libre Ferroviario (SLF) that merged with it in 1984, was predominant only among 'movement' staff (that is signalling and station staff handling the control and movement of trains), and among the scarcely unionized technical and managerial staff (Encinas 1986: 182).

However, in late 1986 a challenge emerged to the predominant pattern of unionization in the shape of a new grade-based union, the Sindicato Español de Maquinistas y Ayudantes Ferroviarios (SEMAF – Spanish Union of Train Drivers and Drivers' Assistants). The union won 7 per cent of delegates in the 1986 union elections. By late 1987 it claimed 3,200 of the 7,000 train driving staff, and was confident enough to launch paralysing one-day strikes in support of its demands.

The two major unions' struggle to establish themselves, together with the ideological differences between them, has led to repeated conflict, both at confederal level and within the railways. Conflict has arisen over the unit of representation and forms of election to joint union committees within companies (see below), often reflecting national debates about union organization. There have been frequent disagreements over the use of industrial action to bolster annual negotiations. The UGT has on several occasions accused the CCOO of calling politically motivated strikes, aimed at disrupting the government's economic policy. Conflict has also led to the UGT pursuing its own parallel negotiations with management, at times outside the formal negotiating structure.

The third major difference between BR and RENFE is that union density in the latter is very low by British standards, though high in the Spanish context where only an estimated 20 per cent of the wage-earning workforce were members of unions (Rijnen 1985: 235). Total union membership in RENFE appears to be about 46 per cent of the workforce.[6] CCOO has about 17,000 members or 26 per cent of the workforce, and SLF-UGT 12–13,000 (of which something under 2,000 were brought into the union by the SLF). A small vestigial union, the Unión Sindical Obrera (USO), most of whose members had joined UGT in an earlier merger, had 700 members in the mid-1980s. In 1986 the rump of USO also joined the UGT.[7]

Industrial Relations in BR and RENFE: The Formal Machinery of Collective Bargaining

It is important to consider the institutional framework regulating relationships between employer and unions, since this will influence the way in which external political pressures for change are carried into the corporation. The pre-existing structures of industrial relations shape and channel managerial response to external influences; and for that reason also themselves become the object of management's initiatives for reform. This section will therefore describe the formal machinery of collective bargaining in BR and RENFE.

BR

Like other public corporations in Britain, BR has an elaborate formal machinery of consultation and negotiation. The nationalization acts creating public corporations usually made it a statutory requirement for such machinery to be set up, although the form and details were left to the parties. In the case of BR, the act merely sanctioned a lengthy historical tradition of formal industrial relations in the old private railway companies. The Central and National Wages Boards, the precursors of the national level of the current machinery, were set up in 1920 and given statutory status in the Railways Act 1921. The current machinery for the main railway grades was agreed in 1956. Separate machineries exist for workshops, professional and technical staff, and for managerial staff. The following description covers the main railway machinery, which applies to the great majority of railway employees in BR.

Negotiation BR's arrangements[8] make a clear formal distinction between negotiation and consultation. The machinery of negotiation consists of a hierarchy of joint committees at workplace, regional and national levels. The committees are composed of management and workforce representatives. At the workplace level, that is in stations, depots, offices and so on, there are some 1600 'Local Departmental Committees' (LDCs) concerned with the details of local working and holiday arrangements, rosters, local seniority questions, health and safety and so on. In footplate LDCs, one of the main activities has traditionally been the 'scrutiny' of alterations to work programmes or 'diagrams' to ensure that they comply with agreements concerning continuous driving time, meal breaks, and so on. According to the MMC (1980: 95), most of the drivers' LDCs on Southern Region spent almost all day every Thursday scrutinizing proposed alterations for the coming week. This activity in the region amounted to a total of 6,000 paid days off in 1985–6 (MMC 1987: 70). However, under the 1986 agreement on single manning of locomotives, footplate LDCs lost the right to scrutinize diagrams. The staff representatives here as at other levels of the machinery must be members of the signatories to the 1956 agreement, that is NUR, ASLEF and TSSA; union branches play no formal part in the LDCs, but in practice there are often close informal ties and overlapping membership (Edwards and Lloyd 1981).

In each of the five BR regions, there are four Sectional Councils covering broad occupational groups: footplate; 'traffic' (i.e. guards, signalling, station and depot staff); other manual staff (permanent way, signals and telecommunications and overhead line staff); and salaried non-manual staff. The Sectional Councils may reach agreements on matters affecting the region, and also, through a system of subcommittees, review a large volume of individual claims that have not been resolved at LDC level. The great bulk of these items concern questions of grading, seniority and payments for rest day working (Anderson 1976).

At national level, there are two main tiers to the machinery. It is in these that all agreements on pay, conditions of employment and working conditions are reached. This highly centralized system reflects the view that the railways form an integrated network for which localized differences in terms and conditions would be inappropriate. The Railway Staff Joint Council (RSJC) is organized, as at sectional council, according to occupational groups, with separate sections for footplate staff, other 'conciliation' grades (the term refers to the manual grades included in the original machinery established in the 1920s), and salaried staff. A fourth section of the RSJC deals with general questions of interest to all three groups. The RSJC has a dual function. It is the final stage of machinery for 'minor' issues that have worked their way up the machinery from other levels, and the first stage for 'major' issues such as proposed new staffing arrangements or working conditions affecting broad groups of staff throughout the railways. The union side at this level is composed of senior officers and lay negotiators from the unions' national executive committees. Management's team is made up of senior headquarters and regional industrial relations managers, together with functional specialists (for example representing 'traction and train crew'). The higher tier of the national level is the Railway Staff National Council (RSNC). It deals with major negotiating items that have not been settled at the RSJC and in recent years has been the forum in which the unions present their annual pay claims.

The machinery also has a stage for voluntary arbitration through the Railway Staff National Tribunal (RSNT), composed of an agreed independent chairman and two other outside members, nominated by the unions and the BR board respectively. The tribunal's main job is to give judgements (virtually always non-binding) on the interpretation of existing agreements, and on major items of negotiation not settled at the RSNC. Reference to the tribunal has usually come from the unions, rather than from BR management. Since 1948, there have been over 90 'decisions' of the tribunal on questions such as annual pay claims, the length of the working week, bonus schemes and payments, and in recent years, changes in working practices. Recourse has also been made to other external bodies outside the formal machinery of negotiation. Such bodies as ACAS, the TUC, or *ad hoc* commissions of inquiry have intervened at the request of the parties or of government to avoid the breakdown of negotiations, or to resolve existing disputes.

Consultation   The 1947 Transport Act refers to the promotion of measures on safety, health and welfare 'and the discussion of other matters of mutual interest ... including efficiency in the operation of the [British Transport] Commission's services'. An elaborate structure of consultation has subsequently developed, in which major management decisions with implications for the staff, for example closure plans, service reductions or administrative reorganizations, are discussed at national level and then in greater detail in the regions and areas affected. Unlike negotiation, consultation procedures do not generally allow disagreements to be referred up to higher levels of the machinery; once the formal consultation has taken place, management may implement its measures with or without agreement.[9]

At national level, BRB and senior union leaders discussed corporate plans, business forecasts, financial performance, pricing, and major investment proposals at the British Railways Joint Consultative Council. The Council's role was largely superseded by a new top level consultative body, the Rail Council, created in 1979 in response to the Labour government's promotion of industrial democracy in the nationalized industries. The BR board chairman and his senior colleagues meet with union leaders to discuss a wide range of policy issues at an early stage. BR hoped that the council would serve as a way of by-passing the cumbersome formal machinery and speed up new initiatives at a time of management efforts to increase productivity. As will be seen later, it was used by management and unions in 1981 to make a joint approach to the Secretary of State for Transport to get more government support for the railways.

At regional and local level, consultation takes place within the Sectional Council and LDC structure. Consultation items are placed on formally separate agendas, but in practice the distinction between consultation and negotiation is blurred and the relative strengths of the unions and management may determine the agenda on which a particular item is placed, especially at LDC level (see Edwards and Lloyd 1981: 21—5). Consultation covers the way in which national programmes are to be introduced at these levels, and matters such as the efficiency of working arrangements, closure plans, staffing arrangements and relations with the public.

The machinery of negotiation and consultation in BR is striking in its extent and in the volume of business that it handles. At LDC level, an extrapolation of the figures provided by Edwards and Lloyd (1981) suggests that there are something in the order of 14,000 local-level formal meetings a year. The Monopolies and Mergers Commission (MMC) (1980) found that in 1979 120,000 days were recorded as spent in negotiation and consultation by the staff side alone. At sectional council, Anderson's study (1976) of one region reveals a workload of several hundred items a year. Many items are small individual claims not settled at LDC. Minor items may spend many years at the various stages before being settled. At high levels of the machinery, the complexity of the structure creates lengthy delays in the processing of negotiating items, and the opportunities for procrastination (for example, in arranging meetings) are exploited by both management and unions to suit their purposes. This complexity is partly the result of the 'entrenched multi-unionism' (Pendleton 1986: ch. 4) which characterizes the machinery. While the NUR represents less than 2 per cent of footplatemen, it is entitled to sit on the locomotive section of the RSJC.

Moreover, 'a number of supervisors, footplate supervisors in particular, retain their original membership on promotion from wage grades, with the result that all three unions attend the salaried section (the RSJC (Salaried))' (1986: 93). Management have consequently found it difficult to process new working practices and productivity measures through the machinery, while it in turn has sometimes delayed items to postpone their reaching the arbitration stage at the RSNT.

Alongside the formal structures, a network of informal relationships has grown up at all levels of the organization. This helps to ensure the smooth working of the machinery by settling issues informally and clearly establishing areas of agreement and disagreement. At national level, informal contacts have been important in maintaining long-term bargaining relationships, for example by 'clarifying' the signals sent out by union conferences, and indeed have been sometimes used in progressing major negotiating issues. However, there is also a certain suspicion of informal bargaining, especially in ASLEF which has tended to advocate a strict constitutionalism with regard to the machinery.

RENFE

Unlike the BR machinery with its long historical roots, the RENFE system of negotiation is a recent development. When the nationalists came to power in 1939, union organization in RENFE was systematically destroyed and republican supporters among the workforce were purged. Thousands of workers lost their jobs, and the railways' staffing needs were met by an influx of combatants who had fought on the nationalist side in the civil war; a war that was commonly referred to by the victors, and indeed in RENFE documents of this period, as the 'war of national liberation'.

Under the dictatorship, a hierarchical, authoritarian system of 'vertical' unions or 'syndicates', influenced by Fascist corporativist ideas, was established in Spain.[10] Each sector of economic activity had its own union to which all employees and employers belonged. The movement as a whole, the 'Organización Sindical', remained under the control of a minister belonging to the Falangist tendency within the Francoist political coalition. Senior union leaders, often powerful figures in the Francoist political system, were nominated from above, or chosen in elections under ministerial control. Subsequently, a system of company councils and of union representatives was established as a vehicle for consultation and participation within the vertical system.

From the late 1950s, the pressures of economic development led to the 'controlled liberalisation' (Fina and Hawkesworth 1984) of the system. Elections for company councils were 'democratized' and a measure of collective bargaining was introduced. Previously, collective bargaining had been prohibited, and wages and conditions had been determined by regulations issued by the ministry of labour. The reforms were intended to contain developments such as the growth of wage drift in larger companies. The introduction of bargaining and the capacity to negotiate collective agreements or 'convenios', although still closely controlled, gave the company councils a genuine industrial relations function for the first time and encouraged the workers' commissions' strategy of working through the official system and putting forward candidates to company council elections. The success of this strategy led, despite a more repressive turn from the later part of the 1960s, to the undermining from within of the formal Francoist system of labour regulation.

In RENFE, however, the developments of the 1960s had less impact. Although some public enterprises, such as the state airline Iberia, were permitted to negotiate convenios from the mid-1960s, the pay and conditions of RENFE workers continued to be determined by ministry of labour directives. Extremely detailed ordinances covered every aspect of remuneration, working hours, staffing, recruitment, promotion, transfer and discipline. The absence of even the controlled liberalization evident in other sectors of the economy appears to reflect RENFE's strategic position. Military planning relied heavily on the rail network both for national defence and for maintaining internal control over the population in the event of civil unrest. There were close links between the railway and the military, and military personnel played a role in RENFE management in the company's early years (Wais 1974: 664) (as indeed was the case in the British Transport Commission). The links predated the Francoist regime; the army had long been responsible for the training of footplate, traffic and other staff who entered RENFE through military service (as they continued to do after the restoration of democracy). Staff were thus subject to military law and discipline (Sartorius 1976) and the threat of militarization hung over them, although it was not actually used during the Franco period. Discipline was enforced by the feared railways police, the so-called Railway Investigation Group of the guardia civil (Martino de Jugo 1980).

This climate severely limited the ability of opposition groups to mobilize within the existing vertical structure, although they did have some success in getting their candidates elected as workplace representatives and as members of the company council. The council showed signs of being influenced by opposition demands, but it remained firmly in the hands of 'officialist' candidates. On the whole, therefore, the machinery of collective bargaining was virtually nonexistent in RENFE under Franco.

The death of Franco brought about a radical change in the institutions of industrial relations, in RENFE as in Spain as a whole. In the immediate transition, industrial relations were in a state of flux as new forms of workforce representation emerged in a spontaneous way, with the semi-clandestine activists of the Francoist period playing a major role. Until the abolition of the company council system, there was a sort of dual power structure in RENFE. Management acknowledged the *de facto* authority of the so-called general plenum of representatives set up by opposition groups among the workforce (Martino de Jugo 1980: 202–4, *El País*, 3 November 1976). The plenum won a labour amnesty for employees sacked by the nationalists after the civil war, and took the lead in negotiating the first collective agreement in 1976.

Thereafter, a formal machinery of collective bargaining was gradually set up. The current machinery broadly follows the framework of collective bargaining laid down in the 1980 Workers' Statute. Unlike BR with its three-tier system, RENFE has a two-tier structure. The lower tier work centre committees operate at a level intermediate between workplace and zone (the RENFE equivalent of the BR region). Each committee covers a major section of work within a geographical area, linked to the activities of a broad management function, for example 'transport' (i.e. train crew, stations, signalboxes, etc.), 'works and installations' (i.e. permanent way activities), offices and workshops. The committees thus cover a far wider geographical and functional area than the LDC in BR. There were 134 committees in 1984, composed of nearly 1,947 workforce representatives.[11] As with the LDCs, the committees are concerned with such issues as local establishments, rosters, overtime and holiday arrangements. They are made up of representatives of the RENFE unions in proportion to the results obtained in the periodic union elections in which the whole workforce is entitled to participate. The trend of the three elections that took place between 1978 and 1982 was for UGT to narrow the gap between itself and CCOO. But the tendency was reversed in the 1986 elections which gave CCOO a clear majority of the votes (see table 5.4). As in BR, there are fairly close, although informal, links between the local union branch or 'section', and the work centre committee.

At national level, negotiations are carried out between representatives of management and those of the joint union committee, the 'comité general intercentros' (CGI). The CGI nominates a negotiating committee to negotiate the annual (or bi-annual) convenios covering pay and a wide variety of conditions. Between 1976 and 1987, there were seven collective agreements. Between major negotiating rounds, a standing body of the CGI handles relations with management.

In addition to the major annual negotiations covering pay and conditions for the workforce as a whole, there are national negotiations for different occupational groups such as drivers or station staff. Agreements reached for these groups are incorporated into the convenio. There are also a number of other national joint committees, covering appeals against disciplinary sanctions, health and safety and 'social policy'. Unlike BR, there is no provision within the machinery for independent arbitration. In the event of deadlock in negotiations, there is a procedure for conciliation by the ministry of labour. On two occasions, in 1980 and 1981, the failure of conciliation led the ministry to impose a binding settlement on the parties. However, other less drastic methods of resolving

TABLE 5.4

Results in Union Elections in RENFE, 1978–86 – Percentage of Votes

	1978	*1980*	*1982*	*1986*
CCOO	53.0	51.6	47.7	59.0
UGT	35.2	35.6	42.1	30.6
USO	4.3	3.7	3.4	[a]—
SLF	—	—	5.9	[b]—
Others	7.4	9.0	0.9	10.3

Notes:[a] USO merged with SLF-UGT in 1986, but a rump of USO candidates received 1.5 per cent of the vote. This is included under 'Others' for 1986.
[b] SLF merged with UGT in 1984.
Sources: RENFE 1984: 187; *El País*, 18 December 1986.

disagreements are available. In 1984, for example, an external mediator was appointed following the breakdown of negotiations, and agreement reached under his auspices.

Traditional Patterns of Industrial Relations: Joint Regulation, Centralization and Conflict Avoidance

In both railways, the machinery has been the means by which the unions have come to exert a profound influence over the conduct of railway activities. In BR especially, it has been the vehicle for the comprehensive internal regulation of railway affairs and for the resolution of both collective and individual conflicts. This highlights perhaps the major difference between BR and RENFE in the way the machinery is used and the culture of industrial relations that has grown up around it: the handling of individual grievances. In BR they are characteristically processed through the various stages of the machinery, in some cases up to RSJC level. Despite the growing role of legal intervention in industrial relations as a result of the Conservative government's legislation, the recourse to legal remedies for individual grievances remains rare in Britain outside cases of unfair dismissal, redundancy, and racial and sexual discrimination. By contrast, the pursuit of grievances through the legal route had traditionally been almost a way of life in RENFE. The corporation's workforce is renowned for the phenomenon of 'pleitismo' which could be translated as litigiousness. This was seen by critics (e.g. CEFE 1983: 27–33; 1984: 73) as a vestige of the Francoist past when the 'objective' protection of the law was important for the workforce in the absence of the 'subjective' protection afforded by strong trade unions and collective bargaining.

An internal management machinery for the handling of individual grievances exists in RENFE (the procedure of 'reclamación previa', or prior claim, characteristic of the public administration), but time limits for application to the courts mean that many grievances are the subject of concurrent actions by employees in the labour courts. There are thousands of such cases annually (the figure for 1983 was over 12,000), covering grading, overtime payments, and allowances for transfer, detachment and replacement at higher grade: the 'classic and traditional subjects of litigation on the railways', according to one industrial relations manager. In recent years, by far the most important item has been individual demands for back payment of overtime earnings following court decisions on the method of calculating the hourly overtime rate.

The complexity, and at times the ambiguity, of the norms, regulations and negotiated agreements gives plenty of scope for legal action. Indeed, one of the main sources of growth of the small SLF union following its foundation in 1981 was its willingness to take up the individual grievances of the workforce, very much in the tradition of the vertical union of the Franco era.

The law has also been used to pursue collective issues. 'Collective conflicts' under Spanish law are legal disputes over the interpretation of legal norms or clauses of collective agreements. The use of legal paths of dispute settlement reflects the much greater role of legal regulation of labour relations in the

Spanish system than in Britain. Substantive matters such as hours of work, over-time and shift working are covered by complex legislation that gives rise to legal battles over interpretation. One of the most important areas of legal dispute in RENFE has been the calculation of overtime earnings, with matters taking several years to progress through the courts. Such disputes in BR would most probably be settled by ultimate recourse to the Railway Staff National Tribunal. RENFE management has also occasionally used the path of collective conflict, particularly to break a stalemate in negotiations. In 1980, the procedure was a prelude to the obligatory pay award of the ministry of labour. It is worth noting, too, that recent British labour legislation has led to an increasing use of the law in industrial disputes by BR management: notably to claim damages for in-dustrial action carried out without a workforce ballot, and to obtain injunctions to prevent the NUR from blacking new equipment.

Beyond this difference in the scope and use of the machinery in the two com-panies, the pattern of industrial relations has shown some striking similarities. In RENFE since 1976 and in BR over a far longer period, a wide range of agreements have been reached through the machinery, giving the unions in-fluence over the determination of virtually all aspects of conditions of employ-ment and work organization. BR's conditions of service for conciliation staff run to some four hundred pages covering duties, hours, allowances, manning of trains, training, health and safety, and travel concessions. The conditions are made up of a myriad of separate agreements, some going back to the 1920s. A separate, major agreement regulates promotion, transfer between jobs and geographical areas, and redundancy arrangements. The 'PT&R Arrangements' give the unions considerable control over the operation of BR's internal labour market. The arrangements for train drivers, for example,

> contain minute and complex detail of when, how and where a driver can be promoted, moved between depots or made redundant . . . The system of advancement through the grades was (and is) tightly controlled, and was (and is) done strictly on the basis of seniority, and a driver is penalised if he breaks the chain: if his name is top of the list for promotion to a cer-tain level, he is allowed to refuse such promotion twice (Murdoch 1986: 44; 30).

Thereafter a refusal will lead to the individual being expelled from the footplate line of promotion. In RENFE, collective bargaining over the past decade or so has basically been a process of dismantling the framework of Francoist labour regulation and replacing it with a series of negotiated agreements. The unions have thus been able to extend their influence over a comprehensive range of working arrangements, and to reduce the areas of sole managerial prerogative. A number of the gains made by the unions are the direct result of changes in the labour legislation; for example, as noted above, the regular working week was reduced in stages from 48 hours to 40 hours. But much of the collective bargaining went beyond legal minima. Areas where the workforce extended their influence were in the procedures for promotion, where the power of managerial prerogative was weakened and increasing weight was given to seniority and skill tests; in joint determination of rosters for footplate and train staff; in the ending of split shifts; and in the reform of the authoritarian disciplinary system.

In this respect, RENFE benefited from its special status as a symbolic embodiment of the processes of democratization in the years following the death of Franco. It was the 'empresa modélica', the model or pattern for other companies to follow in restoring trade union rights. Its success in coming to collective agreements and avoiding industrial strife was seen as a gauge of the wider success of the national compacts between employers and unions (see, e.g., *Pueblo*, 3 March 1982). Moreover, a collective managerial guilt was at work, attempting to 'compensate for the forty years of Francoism suffered by the mass of the workforce'. In the words of a senior industrial relations manager,

> The UCD [Union of the Democratic Centre under the leadership of Adolfo Suárez] government consented to things which were not totally justified but which were necessary so that the mass of the workers could see that the country had changed and that dialogue was beginning. ... RENFE avoided all confrontations with the workforce, in the attempt to ensure that people no longer talked in terms of fascists and non-fascists but at the most in terms of left-wing and right-wing, in other words the company managed to dilute or avoid social and political tensions resulting from the transition (fieldnotes).

Thus RENFE unions achieved a position of influence over the day-to-day organization of railway work comparable to that exerted by the unions in BR.

While much of this consensual pattern in RENFE had its roots in the peculiar circumstances of the transition, a similar ethos of conflict avoidance has also been a feature of industrial relations in BR. Union leaders and senior managers were traditionally involved in a '"tacit alliance" based on common, and often shared, perceptions of problems and objectives' (Pendleton 1986: 67). The underlying basis of this consensus was a common appreciation of the political pressures facing the railway: the parties recognised 'that they both walked a political tightrope, and that if either party fell off the other would be likely to follow' (68). In particular, disruption of the network as a result of conflict was a matter of great political sensitivity, making the railways vulnerable to the sort of external attack that both unions and management were constantly concerned to deflect. This consensual relationship was revealed in the remarkable absence of overt conflict and the high degree of union co-operation in the major changes in employment and working practices that have taken place on the railways over the past decades (Hyman and Elger 1981). Co-operation was underpinned by the willingness of BR management to avoid compulsory redundancies and to find alternative work for those displaced by schemes for change.

The ethos of conflict avoidance has also promoted a propensity on the part of both management and unions, and encouraged by the political concerns of governments, to avoid major industrial action. As a result, strikes have been limited, either in number as in BR, or in duration as in RENFE (see below). But there has been an additional weight put on the avoidance of strikes in Spain, reflecting a deep concern with social consensus as a prerequisite for the consolidation of democracy. In both countries, the nature of railway work provides the workforce with a number of weapons short of strike action, notably bans on overtime and rest day working, and the work-to-rule. The latter is particularly appropriate to the railways with their highly bureaucratic, rule-bound organization and their emphasis on safety embodied in complex systems of regulations such as the 'Rules for the Observance of Employees' in BR or the 'Reglamento de Seguridad en la Circulación' (Safety Regulations for Railway Traffic) in RENFE. In RENFE, work-to-rules have often taken the form of safety campaigns. For example, in May 1984, CCOO recommended to its train drivers the 'exhaustive examination of all the equipment of the vehicle, noting all anomalous situations in the incident book . . . (and) in the event of atmospheric conditions (fog, snow, rain, etc.), a considerable reduction in the speed of the train'. The delays caused by such action can have considerable impact on services because the integrated railway timetable is very susceptible to disruption.

There are nevertheless significant differences in the patterns of industrial action in the two companies, reflecting differences in the legal framework in Britain and Spain, and in the political context in which the two railways have operated. In BR there has been a strong tradition of resolving disputes peacefully by negotiation through the various stages of the machinery. According to the 1956 agreement on the machinery, industrial action should only be contemplated when all the relevant stages have been exhausted. Similarly management would be expected to exhaust the machinery before attempting to implement changes without agreement with the unions. As a result, large-scale 'official' industrial action has been rare in BR. Official strikes have fallen into two broad categories. The first is the one-day national or regional stoppage over some aspect of management policy such as closures, or over support for another group of workers. Examples are token strikes in 1962 over the Beeching plan for cutting the network, and in 1984 in support of the miners. The second category is the national stoppage resulting from the breakdown of negotiations and the exhaustion of the bargaining machinery. The only important examples are the two-week stoppage over differentials by ASLEF in 1955, and the same union's two-week strike in the summer of 1982 (following a series of short strikes in January and February) over flexible rostering.

Strikes in RENFE have followed a different pattern. From the resumption of collective bargaining in 1976 until 1986, there were over 30 national strikes, but almost without exception they lasted for 24 hours or less, often for only 4 hours. This reflects their rather different function in the context of RENFE's industrial relations. They have regularly been used to put pressure on management during major negotiations, and could be said to be part of the ritual of collective bargaining. That is, they are a step on the way towards a negotiated solution, rather than a reflection of the exhaustion of negotiation as in BR.

The strike weapon is relatively weak in RENFE for two reasons. First, union organization is weak compared with BR, and the majority of employees are unrepresented by unions. Moreover, ideological divisions have frequently led to union rivalries which can undermine strike action, especially since the unions compete for the same grades of employees; in BR a single union can in most cases bring out most or all members of a grade. Second, strikes have been seriously restricted since 1980 by a government decree (also applying to other public services such as the airlines) allowing management to maintain a minimum level of service during strikes. As mentioned earlier, the state also has powers to militarize railway staff in the event of industrial disputes, and militarization occurred in 1976. Nonetheless, it is possible to exaggerate the extent of these limitations. First, a strike by even a proportion of core workers such as train drivers or signalmen can paralyse the network. Second, it is questionable how far militarization remains a serious check on industrial action now that democracy has become more securely established in Spain. Third, since 1984, unions in RENFE have won the right to negotiate over the level of minimum service, and management has not normally run services in excess of that level even if resources were available. As a result it could be argued that, in a context of relatively low unionization, the imposition of minimum service levels provides the unions with a guaranteed degree of success with strike action.

The concern with consensus, and the desire of national railway management and union leaders to control industrial action, has reinforced the tendency towards centralization in collective bargaining. Both management and unions tend to keep a tight grip on local activity to ensure that it keeps to national agreements and to avoid the embarrassment and disruption of uncontrolled local initiatives. Nonetheless, in both companies there has been scope for local initiative on the margin of national agreements, and at times in violation of them. BR's LDCs have considerable influence over issues such as the allocation of work between depots, and have strongly resisted changes to the established pattern of working, since this determines earnings levels. Informal arrangements in contravention of a national agreement or against stated union or management policy have been noted in areas such as the use of overtime and rest day working. On parts of the Southern region where the 'round-the-houses' short-haul commuter work is unpopular, for example, high overtime opportunities were provided in order to retain staff and avoid high training costs. The MMC (1980: 97) found that in some guards' depots, twelve-hour days were routinely worked, and that, apparently, 'those staff who wish to work their Sundays mostly have the opportunity to do so every other Sunday without strict regard to the numbers actually required to operate train services'.

In RENFE, centralized bargaining could not prevent national agreements, and even statutory provisions, on hours of work and overtime maxima from being regularly flouted. The regulations on transfers and replacements at higher grade were also frequently infringed in practice (see IGAE 1984: 19, 42; *Carril*, September 1985: 13). This was partly the result of the practical difficulties of running the railway with the resources available. But it also reflected the problems of headquarters managers and union leaders in monitoring and controlling activities at lower levels of the organization, and in ensuring that national agreements and regulations were respected. As one industrial relations manager in RENFE commented, 'control is very difficult, and it is the responsibility of the head of a workplace to get the service out, which he is going to do however he can, as long as he doesn't overrun his budget' (fieldnotes). An example of this was higher management's belief that overtime was often paid for although not worked. For example, 'in the case of shunting, the work should be covered by a foreman and three "station specialists". But if there are only two, they will divide up the work of the third in overtime hours, but will they actually be present at work during that period?' (fieldnotes). Thus in RENFE, as in BR, there is scope for local action on the fringes of the nationally agreed framework.

Despite the extent of union influence and the predominantly co-operative patterns of industrial relations, collective bargaining has not brought BR and RENFE workers great financial rewards, even as a *quid pro quo* for job loss and changing working practices. From the beginning of the period of rapid employment reductions in BR in the early 1960s up to the present, manual employees' earnings have scarcely reached average levels for industry as a whole. Only briefly at the end of the 1960s and again in the mid-1970s did average earnings rise significantly above the all-industry average. The BRB/Leeds (1980: 15) comparative study of productivity in ten European railways concluded that 'mean earnings per hour for rail employees in Britain are substantially below those of all the other study countries, and also that British railwaymen fare worse in gross earnings terms in comparison with their continental colleagues than do all British manufacturing industry employees'.

The situation in RENFE appears somewhat different at first sight. Collective bargaining brought a rapid growth of real wages as RENFE workers attempted to compensate for their position during the Franco years. Earnings per employee rose over four times between 1975 and 1982, while the cost of living index rose only three times. Nonetheless, this was a continuation of a growth that had begun during the mid-1960s, reflecting the transmission to RENFE of pressures for wage increases elsewhere in the economy. Between 1966 and 1975, real earnings per employee rose by nearly 90 per cent in RENFE, although they were starting from a very low base in absolute terms (Ferner and Fina 1988). Moreover, by the 1980s earnings still remained lower than average, and pay rates were in the bottom quartile, especially for non-skilled manual and clerical workers (RENFE 1984b: 169–71; 1984a: 38).

Railway workers in both countries have had to work exceedingly long hours even for these comparatively modest rewards. In 1984, manual grades in BR worked an average of ten hours overtime per week, compared with an average of about five hours per week for all industries (Department of Employment *Gazette*). The hours worked in the late 1970s were between a third and a quarter longer than those in all the other railways studied by the BR/Leeds team (1980: 15). RENFE workers' overtime levels have also been high, though somewhat less than in BR where overtime and shift earnings are virtually the only way of supplementing basic pay. In RENFE, basic pay has been supplemented by a plethora of bonuses and allowances (in 1983, there were well over 100 separate remunerative headings in addition to basic pay), and in contrast to BR, employees receive age-related increments at four-yearly intervals. In 1977, RENFE manual staff worked an average of about seven hours per week overtime, but the figure had fallen to about 4–5 hours per week by 1983 (based on IGAE 1984: 14), and total overtime hours were some 15 million for the year (compared with around 60 million – including Sunday working – in BR).

Government Intervention and Industrial Relations in BR and RENFE

Industrial relations and collective bargaining in BR and RENFE have been profoundly conditioned by the railways' status as a major state-controlled public service. Two different and sometimes incompatible impulses have been at work.

First, pay bargaining has been influenced by the state's concern with public expenditure and with macroeconomic policies such as wage control. Second, governments have desired to avoid the politically damaging disruption of the network by industrial action. As a result there has been repeated political intervention in the bargaining strategies of railway management, with the government even orchestrating the negotiations in detail, as Gourvish convincingly documents for BR (1986: chapters 7, 12). The conflicting motives for intervention have sometimes led in practice to the government oscillating 'wildly between stubborn resistance and instantaneous surrender' (560). A typical pattern is described by a former minister of transport and subsequent chairman of BR: 'Over and over again we could have settled much more cheaply by settling more quickly but, at each stage, we were told that we must not settle quickly because the Government really were going to fight this one to the bitter end. . . . The end result was an undignified collapse in the last few days' (Marsh 1978: 176).

Governments have been particularly concerned with the application of pay norms and incomes policies in the railways because of the industry's size and political salience. In Spain, governments have been keenly aware of RENFE's position as the model whose pay and conditions were likely to have major repercussions for other firms throughout the economy. Moreover, loss-making Spanish public enterprises have been subject to specific pay bands lower than those for profitable companies. These bands are laid down in the state budget, and a committee of ministerial under-secretaries vets nationalized industries' collective agreements to make sure that they conform to pay limits. The government's concern has led it to exert fairly direct, although informal, control over the pay bargaining process. According to one senior management informant in RENFE, 'the company could not in general make an offer for increased wages and salaries without first getting very direct approval from the government'; labour relations managers recalled urgent telephone calls from the minister in the early hours of the morning to determine the wage offer.

In Britain in recent years, pay determination in BR and other nationalized industries has been severely constrained in practice by the more indirect method of tight external financing limits (see ch. 4). At other times, direct intervention has also been used to discourage management from accepting pay demands. In the 1972 pay negotiations, for example, the government ignored BR's advice for appeasement and 'demanded a hawkish response', invoking the powers of the Industrial Relations Act 1971 to force a compulsory strike ballot (Gourvish 1986: 559–60; Bagwell 1982: 250–67).

The second impulse – the desire to avoid disruption – has frequently brought direct pressure on the parties from senior politicians, often in the face of imminent industrial action. In 1979, the Spanish government bent its own guidelines on pay increases in deficit public corporations. This followed the intervention of the finance minister, who defended his actions with the Spanish refrain that 'the letter kills, and the spirit gives life' (*El País*, 17 January 1979). In Britain, 'whisky diplomacy' was repeatedly used to resolve conflicts, and pressure was brought to bear by means of appeals to the parties from the Prime Minister, for example by Harold Wilson in 1966 (see Bagwell 1982: 168–71).

A notable example among many of government intervention to avoid strike action occurred in the 1954 pay negotiations. It is interesting for the way it captures the conflicting impulses for restraining public expenditure and avoiding disruption. According to Rab Butler, then Chancellor of the Exchequer, Churchill

> said to me, 'We cannot have a railway strike, it would be so disturbing to all of us'. . . . I said at the time that it was rather important from the point of view of the economy that we should not have wage increases which we could not afford. Winston, typical of his more human side, firmly backed Walter [Monckton, Minister of Labour] in his efforts to avoid a railway strike which would have paralysed the country over Christmas. . . . I had an interesting experience. I was rung up about midnight by Winston Churchill who said, 'Walter and I settled the railway strike so you won't be troubled any more'. I said, 'On what terms have you settled it?' and Winston answered me, 'Theirs old cock! We did not like to keep you up'. I was up nearly every night until one o'clock doing my boxes. Of course I could have been present (Butler 1982: 137).

The episode ended with the appointment of a committee of inquiry, a device several times used by governments as a way of legitimating particular criteria of pay determination and hence avoiding industrial conflict. In this case, the 1955 Cameron inquiry established the principle that, having willed the objective of a national rail system, 'the Nation must will the means' of providing it. This implied 'that employees of such a national service should receive a fair and adequate wage, and that, in broad terms, the railwayman should be in no worse case than his colleague in a comparable industry' (Cameron 1955: 6).

Where the desire of governments to avoid disruption conflicts with other priorities, such as the need to be seen to control public sector pay or working practices, intervention may well be secretive. In 1984, leaked Department of Transport letters revealed that the Conservative government had put pressure on BR management during pay negotiations. Similar intervention apparently occurred in RENFE in the 1985 bargaining round when an improved offer was made following a meeting between confederal leaders of the UGT and the minister of transport (see ch. 7).

The possibility of such interventions may undermine management's negotiating position and has sometimes meant that the autonomy of the bargaining machinery is more apparent than real: the government rather than management becomes the interlocutor in the last instance. At times when the government has been responsive to union calls for intervention, appeal to the minister has become a *de facto* final stage of the machinery. An example is the 1975 pay award in BR, which had already been through the RSNT when the Prime Minister Harold Wilson intervened to press management to resume negotiations and make a higher offer (see ch. 9). Similarly, RENFE management's negotiating strategy in 1985 was effectively nullified by the political deal between the government and UGT leaders. For the unions, the nature of state intervention in railway industrial relations emphasizes the importance of political contacts and the ability to engage in political exchange. This theme will be taken up in more detail in later chapters.

Conclusions

There are several important similarities in the patterns of industrial relations of BR and RENFE. These are partly the result of the nature of railway work and the way in which it has developed in recent decades. Thus both networks have seen large falls in the number of employees, and changes in the pattern of work with the advent of new forms of traction and other technological innovation. A very bureaucratic, highly regulated organizational form has grown up to meet the operational and safety requirements of the railway system and this has had its own industrial relations consequences: for example, wide scope for inter-pretation of complex regulations; reliance on a variety of forms of shift, roster and overtime working with their attendant rules and regulations and financial compensations; or the use of the work-to-rule as a weapon of industrial conflict. The need for a stable workforce trained in specific skills appropriate for and often unique to the railways has encouraged a pattern of long-term employment with strict rules for determining movement up occupational hierarchies and mobility between them.

The regulation of a wide range of such matters by negotiation, rather than managerial prerogative, has encouraged the development of extensive formal collective bargaining machinery. But in the British case, the machinery reflects a long and continuous tradition of bargaining between management and very well-organized unions. In RENFE, the machinery has had to be built up more or less from scratch in the last decade, and the union side is less well established as well as more ideologically heterogeneous. Moreover, the scope of the RENFE machinery is reduced by the continuing recourse to labour courts to resolve a wide range of individual grievances that in BR would be settled intern-ally and indeed constitute a large part of the business of the lower levels of the machinery.

The nature of the machinery, the organization of the unions, and the framework of law also determine a rather different pattern of industrial conflict. The emphasis in RENFE is on the symbolic use of industrial action in the course of negotiations, compared with the resort to action in BR on the exhaustion of the machinery. But the differences in the use of industrial action mask a deeper similarity, reflecting the railways' position as state-owned public services. The political dimension of disruptions to the network is a constant consideration in relationships between management and unions, and has traditionally been a major source of direct government intervention, often in the context of disputes over pay settlements.

The avoidance of conflict has been only one government objective, and the state's concern with the control and reduction of public expenditure has also greatly influenced the conduct of collective bargaining on the railways in both countries. Bargaining has generally taken place within a more or less explicit framework of pay norms, financial criteria and so on. Incompatible government objectives have often led to the characteristic *ad hoc*, even secretive, interventions that signal a divergence between publicly proclaimed policies and immediate priorities. At times the unions have been able to mobilize their political links in order to take advantage of this dilemma of politicians.

One conclusion is that the introduction of new industrial relations strategies on the railways will partly depend on the shifting balance between conflicting state objectives. For example, if the political costs of disruption are lowered, and hence the value attached by government to its avoidance is diminished, the leverage of the unions in bargaining with management may in turn be reduced. Bargaining leverage may also depend on the unions' ability to continue to engage in political exchange. Thus the transmission of new state objectives is conditioned by features of industrial relations which are at least in part subject to external government manipulation. As we shall see in later chapters, these factors varied considerably between Britain and Spain.

Beyond that, however, the industrial relations in BR and RENFE have their own relative autonomy. This chapter has shown that a complicated set of traditional institutions and relationships form the terrain on which new political projects for the railways have to be introduced. As we have seen, the machinery of collective bargaining is the means through which the workforce has exerted a pervasive influence over the organization of railway work. Such influence is not just a fact of railway industrial relations, but a positive value and premiss, reflecting and mobilizing the skill, knowledge and commitment of the workforce, and helping to ensure the stability and predictability of the railways' activities. By the same token, however, the patterns of industrial relations represent a formidable, inertial weight of established practice. As a result, the introduction of new industrial relations strategies is not simply a question of adapting the system to the needs of commercialism, efficiency and flexibility. Rather, as will be seen in subsequent chapters, there is a complex process in which the new strategies challenge, and at the same time adapt to and even work through, the existing realities.

Notes

1 The comparison of productivity in BR and RENFE should be treated with caution. BR's employment figures may be relatively inflated, since it carries out some workshop, track maintenance and other activities which in RENFE would be contracted out. A further problem is that the input figures are expressed in terms of employees rather than labour hours. Factors such as differences in the amount of overtime worked or changes in the working week will therefore distort the figures. The output in terms of traffic units will be affected by geographical and other factors: for example, the average length of haul of freight trains is much lower in Britain than in Spain, for geographical reasons. This will affect labour productivity, since some labour costs (such as assembling trains) do not vary with the length of haul. (On the problems of international productivity comparisons, see Nash 1985a.)

2 This characteristic of train drivers' work is not universal. In the West German Bundesbahn, for example, the concept of a 'footplate line of promotion' does not exist and there is much greater occupational flexibility than in British or Spanish railways (see Seglow *et al.* 1982).

3   The unions are the Sindicato Ferroviario de la Unión General de Trabajadores [Rail Union of the General Workers' Union] (SF de UGT), or UGT Ferroviaria, and the Sindicato Ferroviario de Comisiones Obreras (SF de CCOO) [Rail Union of Workers' Commissions]. In 1984 SF de UGT merged with a much smaller, independent union, the Sindicato Libre Ferroviario, and the union is now known as SLF-UGT.

4   Encinas (1986: 111–15) summarizes the historical development of the railway unions. Other, scattered, information is available in Tuñon de Lara's (1972) work on the development of the Spanish labour movement. See also Castillo (1975) on the growth of the Catholic company unions in the early decades of the century. A useful general account of the Spanish unions is Almendros *et al*. 1978.

5   I am indebted to Eduardo Encinas for access to primary research data on this point.

6   Exact figures are hard to obtain since payment by check-off has only become universal in RENFE in recent years and some earlier members still pay by 'coupons' at their union branch.

7   The move by the smaller unions in RENFE to merge with the UGT reflected the impact of the new law of trade union liberties, which made it hard for unions below a certain size to have any effective participation in collective bargaining.

8   A more detailed description of the machinery in BR is given in Ferner, 1987c.

9   But under the Worthing Understanding of 1984, an extra tier of consultation was introduced for route, track or depot closures, allowing for further discussion between union head offices and regional headquarters in the event of failure to agree at sectional council.

10   For detailed descriptions, see ILO 1969; Amsden 1972. A summary may be found in Carr and Fusi 1981: ch. 7 and in Fina and Hawkesworth 1984. See also Balfour 1984.

11   In 1986 the committee system was reorganized. There is now one committee for each of Spain's mainland provinces except for Madrid which has four and Barcelona two, making a total of 51 committees. This led to a reduction in the number of representatives to 1,139 in the 1986 union elections.

6

New Management Strategies for Industrial Relations in BR and RENFE

Introduction

This chapter examines the broad changes in industrial relations in BR and RENFE in recent years. It concentrates on the changing style and content of management strategies.

In both BR and RENFE there appears to have been a critical period in which a new set of industrial relations policies crystallized. 'New' strategies are not necessarily neat labelled packages clearly distinguishable from older ones. The strategies introduced in BR and RENFE had important elements of continuity, rather than being radical departures from existing policies. But under the pressure of external circumstances a significant shift of emphasis took place. The focus of strategy changed from one set of policies to another, and in addition, the style of industrial relations management began to undergo a transformation. As would be expected from the discussion of earlier chapters, the changes have advanced further and become clearer in BR. In RENFE they were still often embryonic in the mid-1980s and the danger of over-estimating their real importance was consequently greater. In many cases, policies had been enunciated but not put into practice.

This raises the general question of what is meant by strategy and strategic change. It can be argued that a change of strategy implies not only the formulation of distinct policy objectives, but their implementation. The first may occur without the second, and as Pendleton (1986: ch. 2), for example, argues in his study of BR, this cannot be considered to amount to strategic change. With management constantly formulating and reformulating its ideas about personnel and industrial relations policy, company history is littered with abandoned plans and strategies. In some cases, strategies may lie 'dormant' for long periods before meeting the appropriate circumstances in which they can be activated and put into practice. Conversely, changes in patterns of policy may occur without formal or explicit recognition of strategic objectives. This may reflect a desire to withhold information from competitors or from trade unions. Or it may be that strategies have not been consciously formulated. Managers may merely be responding in a systematic way to changes in the external environment and these responses may only with hindsight reveal a strategic pattern (cf. Mintzberg 1978; Batstone *et al*. 1984: 5—6).[1] Thus strategic changes may be taking place without being formally signalled by management.

The following sections describe the 'critical period' of strategic change in personnel and industrial relations policy in BR and RENFE. Then the differences in the contents of the new strategies in the two companies are analysed. They are explained as much in terms of the different political circumstances as in terms of the internal organization and technology of the two railways.

'Critical Periods' in the Formation of New Personnel and Industrial Relations Strategies in BR and RENFE

BR: The Pursuit of 'Productivity in its Broadest Sense'

The watershed in BR's industrial relations strategy can be located in the events of 1981—2. The new strategy did not mean a completely new set of policies so much as a change in management attitudes towards implementing existing proposals. Focusing on working practices, flexibility and labour productivity, its essential element was the abandonment of the implicit assumption that the consent of unions and workforce was necessary for introducing change. The critical period begins with the 'crystallization' of management's demands for change into the so-called 'six items' in the summer of 1981 and ends with the defeat of ASLEF's strike over the introduction of flexible rostering nearly a year later.

While 'productivity' has been a continual preoccupation of BR management, the mid-1970s saw a particular resurgence of interest in the issue. Increasing financial pressures on the railways coincided with the need for a major new cycle of investment to replace ageing assets from the previous investment peak in the late 1950s and early 1960s. So there was pressure on BR to cut costs and raise productivity.

But there were no longer 'easy technical or operational means of achieving quick and significant productivity improvements' (BRB 1976: 56). In the 1950s and 1960s, rapid technical innovation, particularly the change from steam to diesel and electric locomotives, and the large-scale closure of little-used sections of the network, had brought major increases in productivity. Subsequent technical change was less dramatic and, after the period of widespread closures during the 1960s, the size of the network stayed more or less the same.

Management realised that 'future improvements will result from detailed management reappraisals of the purpose and cost of every labour intensive activity in every department at all levels . . .' (BRB 1976: 56). In this it was stimulated by the outside influence of bodies such as the House of Commons Select Committee on Nationalised Industries (SCNI 1977: xxxiv—xl) and, later, the Monopolies and Mergers Commission (MMC 1980: chs 5—7). An influential analysis carried out by Pryke and Dodgson (1975), who also gave evidence to the Select Committee, argued that the workforce could be cut by 36 per cent in a decade with little reduction in traffic.

The board's 1976 document, 'Opportunity for Change', forecast job cuts of 40,000 between 1976 and 1981 (BRB 1976: 58—60). But only 3,500 of these were to come from new investment, mainly in the area of track and signalling. Reducing services in line with falling demand would cut another 10,000 jobs, and administrative reorganization a further 6—8,000. The remaining 17—19,000 were from 'productivity in its broadest sense', by which BR meant 'ways of do-ing the required work with significantly fewer staff where reductions are primarily dependent on vigorous management action, with a lesser dependence on selective investment and the application of proved technology' (58).

Nevertheless, the board remained cautious about the possibilities for major improvements, arguing that any programme of productivity changes could not 'be executed without the whole-hearted co-operation of unions, management and staff' (BRB 1976: 19). Indeed, it stressed that so-called 'overmanning' was often the result of lack of investment, and it defended existing work organization by arguing that 'in the matter of "restrictive practices" — more properly described as negotiated agreements on job content, rostering and manning — current BR operations compare favourably with that of most other railway administrations' (19).

Cost reductions and productivity improvements from the rationalization of services and from technical innovation continued during the 1970s and 1980s. The marshalling yards were run down following the withdrawal from traditional wagon load freight business, and BR pulled out of the unprofitable 'collect and delivery' parcels service. But increasingly management attention turned to 'pro-ductivity in the broadest sense'.

A new organizational structure for encouraging productivity improvement was put in place from the mid-1970s. In 1974, a Productivity Steering Group was formed by the board to co-ordinate progress on productivity and influence 'the ongoing dialogue with trade unions on this subject' (BRB 1976: 62). Later, a board member was given special responsibility for productivity. Until this point, 'productivity' had largely concerned the management of work study, together with organization and methods, and had provided relatively routine work for 'an army of clerks'. Under the direction of the board member, the Internal Con-sultancy Services Unit was used to 'light the fuse' of productivity, as one manager put it. The unit co-ordinated initiatives through productivity steering groups at BR board and in the regions (MMC 1980: 289). In addition, the analysis of productivity was refined through the development of physical and financial performance indicators (BRB 1982), which were introduced into the rail planning and budgeting process.

This new structure was not immediately accompanied by a radical change in the style of industrial relations management. In the late 1970s management still looked on productivity initiatives as a way of meeting the aspirations of the trade unions for better pay and conditions, particularly higher basic rates and shorter hours (BRB 1979r: 20). In the 1979 pay settlement, the unions agreed to talk 'positively' with BR about ways of increasing productivity. The NUR saw this as an opportunity to pursue matters of 'mutual benefit' to BR and the union

(Weighell 1983: 68). Both sides agreed to spell out their aspirations as a way of establishing common ground. The union proposed a 'Railwaymen's Charter' which called for a £288 million package of improvements including a new pay structure, with much higher levels of pay, better sick pay, a 35-hour basic week and four weeks' annual holiday. Management produced a document known as the 'Challenge of the '80s'. This listed areas of change that would 'reduce jobs through re-shaping traditional business activities' and bring in 'new manning concepts, revised production methods, technological developments and organisational streamlining' (BRB 1979: 2). Union co-operation in these changes would provide the savings to fund improvements in terms and conditions.

At the end of 1979, working parties were set up to develop productivity proposals for use in the 1980 pay negotiations. A 'very concentrated managerial exercise' produced thousands of ideas. They were boiled down to a list of 52 proposals that would cut staff by 29,000 and save £50 million (MMC 1980: 101). Many of the items concerned changing working practices and increasing flexibility in stations and terminals, in engineering work and among train crew. There were also measures to rationalize services and eliminate excess capacity, especially in freight and parcels, and proposals to reduce the number of tiers in the management hierarchy.

The productivity initiatives of the late 1970s were therefore linked to the unions' aspirations for improved pay and conditions for their members, and to the NUR's willingness to bargain pragmatically over working practices and other productivity issues in order to achieve these improvements.

By 1981 the board had achieved considerable concessions from the unions on the rationalization of freight and parcels, and the reduction of workload, but little progress had been made in the area of working practices, which normally required changes in national agreements. It was at this point that 'productivity in the broadest sense' became the central issue of industrial relations in the railways, and the style of industrial relations abruptly changed.

The 1980 pay agreement had granted the unions a reduction in the working week to 39 hours from the autumn of 1981, in exchange for the unions' commitment to 'discussions to minimize the cost' and agreement on a timetable for consultation and negotiation on the 52 items (MMC 1980: 88). In the summer of 1981, industrial action was threatened when BR management declined to implement the second stage of an 11 per cent pay award by the RSNT, on the grounds that it was not linked to a commitment by the unions to productivity changes.

The intervention of ACAS led management and unions to come to two 'Understandings' in August 1981. One, on pay, provided for the second stage of the 1981 pay award to be delayed until January 1982, together with the implementation of the shorter working week. The other, on productivity, committed the two sides to resume discussion of six central productivity proposals culled from the 52 items. These were the 'open station' concept which replaced ticket barriers with ticket inspection on trains; flexible rostering; the introduction of freight and passenger trains without guards or conductors, known as 'driver only' operation; an extension of single manning in the driver's cab of locomotives by removing second drivers or driver's assistants; and the 'train-man' concept, which broke the hermetic barriers between different lines of pro-motion by providing a career link between guards and footplate staff.

The agreement on productivity laid down a timetable for completing negotia-tions on four of the six items. One of the items, flexible rostering, was by now closely linked to the shorter working week, since management saw the former as a way of offsetting the cost of the reduction in the hours of train crew. Flexi-ble or 'variable day' rostering referred to variations in the number of hours worked in a day in accordance with the needs of the service. The main aim was to increase the relatively small proportion of drivers' time actually spent driving locomotives. It was, however, one of the most contentious of the six items, since ASLEF and its members regarded the 1919 agreement on the guaranteed eight-hour day as a sacrosanct pillar of the footplatemen's conditions of service (see McKillop 1950: chs 10, 11). Under the old agreement, drivers were rostered for eight hours a day and were paid for eight hours even if there was no work for them to do. If their turns lasted for more than eight hours, management had to pay overtime, and 'second men' (driver's assistants) had to be used.

BR's determination over the following months to negotiate the introduction of flexible rostering for footplate staff was to lead to one of the worst conflicts on the railways since nationalization. In the absence of an agreement on flexible rostering, the board threatened to withhold the second instalment of the 1981 pay agreement. This led ASLEF to call a series of one-day strikes in early 1982. After outside intervention, the question went back into the machinery of negotia-tion and in May 1982 the RSNT recommended the negotiation of a flexible rostering agreement for footplate staff similar to the one already implemented for guards. There would be daily variations of between seven and nine hours (and an alteration in existing manning agreements so that drivers could work for the whole of the nine hours without a driver's assistant in the cab). ASLEF re-jected the terms of the agreement. In the summer management posted new rosters unilaterally at some seventy depots. On 4 July, the union went on strike. The conflict lasted for two weeks until, facing defeat and the loss of TUC sup-port, the union was forced to accept the end of the eight-hour day.

Thus the period 1981−2 marks the watershed in management strategy. Atten-tion turned to raising productivity through the reform of working practices and the renegotiation of long-standing national agreements with the unions that this entailed. Management aspirations were condensed into a totemic list of six pro-posals. The first item, flexible rostering, was pursued with a quite unaccustomed zeal in the face of staunch union opposition.

The change in management strategy was therefore much to do with a change of style. The traditional emphasis on avoiding confrontation at all costs was replaced by the idea that 'management must manage, to use the old cliché, and management cannot do so if it is dictated to unreasonably by the workforce', as one traditionally-minded senior manager put it.

BR saw the six items as the first step, the thin end of a wedge of initiatives for pursuing 'productivity in its broadest sense'. Some managers saw other changes in working practices, such as flexible rostering and single manning of locomotives, primarily as ways of making feasible a major reorganization of BR's network of train depots. There were about 350 train crew depots scattered around the country, many of them small and close together, having been built to serve an earlier pattern of traffic and services. Management hoped to cut between two and three thousand footplate jobs by reducing the depot network and concentrating activities into a much smaller number of key depots.

Another, longer-term strategic aim was to challenge the union controls over recruitment, training, promotion and transfer. The easement of single manning would affect that 'treasured plank' of ASLEF's control over the job and the 'line of promotion', the PT&R arrangements: the elimination of driver's assistants would 'upset much in the PT&R arrangements about the eligibility for certain vacancies, and drastically [alter] the training arrangements'. For example, the existing rule that drivers could only be appointed after 500 'turns' (shifts) as driver's assistants would have to be changed (Murdoch 1986: 43, 51–2). Similarly, the trainman concept, by creating a single line of promotion for train crews, would have a radical effect on ASLEF's control of footplate work and the job structure. The type of training would change, promotion on the grounds of seniority would be undermined and the union's control over the entry grades would disappear since there would be a common training grade for driver's assistants and guards. In the words of a senior manager quoted by Murdoch (1986: 56), 'the trainman seems the most innocuous of all the productivity proposals but is in fact the most far-reaching, both because of bringing the guard and driver together, (and) because of the revision of PT&R and the reduction in the training period from several years to 12 or 13 months'.

Strategic change also extended to procedural reforms. Management's desire for greater flexibility, particularly under the impetus of business management, and its perception that the unions used the 1956 machinery to delay agreement on changes in working practices, rekindled its interest in revising the machinery of consultation and negotiation. The task was subsequently given added point by the report of the Monopolies and Mergers Commission (1987: ch. 8) which strongly criticized the length of time it took to negotiate major agreements. The Commission also recommended that the area, rather than the workplace should be the basis of the local level of the machinery, and that the staff should be represented by multi-grade groups representing all staff, rather than by occupational groups as in the existing LDC system. One of BR's major proposals for the machinery was for the abolition of the Railway Staff National Tribunal and its replacement by a system of binding arbitration carried out through ACAS. BR argued that the tribunal's decisions generally benefited the unions more than management (by no means a new complaint – see Gourvish 1986: 533), that it made recommendations for which it could not provide the finance, and that it interfered with managerial responsibilities by pronouncing on issues which management saw as its sole prerogative.

RENFE: The Vth Convenio and the Challenge to 'Acquired Rights'

As so often, the data on RENFE are less rich and detailed than might be hoped, largely owing to the shortage of published material and internal documents. The significance of recent developments is therefore less certain than in the case of

BR. Nevertheless, a critical period of change in industrial relations is equally discernible. In some respects it is more abrupt than in BR where, as we have seen, there were important continuities in the content of managerial strategy.

Until 1983, post-Franco industrial relations in RENFE were dominated by the construction of a democratic machinery of collective bargaining and the extension of union influence over wide areas of corporate life (see ch. 5). In these years RENFE had largely reacted to union claims. The strategic concern to be found in BR from the mid-1970s with 'productivity in its broadest sense' appears to have been almost entirely absent. A programme contract, drawn up in 1979 but never implemented, saw investment as the principal way of containing labour costs arising from concessions to the unions. Investment would release employees from their present work and allow them to be used to cover the increased holidays and rest allowances (RENFE 1979m: 79).

The same lack of emphasis on productivity was evident in the 'Objectives and Actions Plan' for 1982 (RENFE 1981m: 58—9) which was, among other things, 'oriented towards the generation of employment' (58). The labour relations content of the plan (referred to as 'social policy)' was overwhelmingly concerned with the achievement of consensual goals: managing the company according to 'participative and integrative criteria', maintaining the institutionalized dialogue with employees, providing the staff with adequate career opportunities. Productivity was mentioned in passing, in the same breath as plans for increasing the establishment by 6,000 in 1982.

The last gasp of this era was the 1983 collective agreement, the IVth convenio, negotiated too soon after the arrival of the new chairman appointed by PSOE to show a significant shift in industrial relations strategy. The convenio awarded a pay rise of 11 per cent, well above the government's intended upper limit for loss-making public sector companies. A job restructuring upgraded thousands of posts and was worth a further 2 per cent. The press called it a 'bad example' (*Cinco Días*, 12 March 1983). But the most striking clause in the agreement concerned recruitment. RENFE agreed to hire 6,000 staff in 1983 and the first quarter of 1984 — 2,300 to cover natural wastage, 1,700 to compensate for a statutory reduction in the working year, and 2,000 in advance of a 'scientific and rationally based study' of the corporation's establishment. The chairman defended the sharp increase in staff on the grounds that it was necessary to rejuvenate RENFE's ageing workforce (*Cambio 16*, 11 April 1983).

The negotiations did, however, reveal the germ of future developments when management presented a set of counter-proposals to the unions' claim. These included changes in working practices, especially for train crews, the reform of working time and holiday arrangements, greater management control over rostering, and measures to increase the geographical and occupational mobility of labour. These proposals were not pursued, but many of them were to reappear the following year during the negotiation of the Vth convenio, which revealed a marked change of emphasis: management arrived at the negotiating table in 1984 with a comprehensive and well-prepared 'platform' of its own.

The change in RENFE's approach to industrial relations can be traced back to the spring of 1983. In May, the new chairman took 30 of his senior managers out of Madrid and set them to work to prepare strategy studies in different areas including personnel policy. At this meeting it was concluded, in the words of an industrial relations manager, that 'there was a need to hit out at the union organisations, to take them on, to redo everything that has been badly done over the past seven years' (fieldnotes).

As part of an 'emergency action plan' devised as an interim response to RENFE's parlous financial situation, the company decided not to honour clauses of the 1983 agreement on recruitment and the reform of the grading structure, saving an estimated 2.1 billion pesetas. The emergency plan also called for a committee to be set up to prepare a so-called 'white paper on negotiation'. The committee, 'which all the main groups of the firm had a role in nominating, . . . brought together suggestions and came to a diagnosis of where the company wanted to go' (fieldnotes).

The resulting document was not a statement of broad policy or a set of general guidelines, but a list of scores of concrete measures on working hours, 'social' benefits and so on. According to one manager, 'the common element uniting them was a new harsh attitude' towards industrial relations questions. As its name implied, the document was intended to provide a continuing agenda for RENFE's future negotiations with the unions, and items from it formed the core of management's proposals in the 1984 negotiations.

These proposals concerned changes in working practices, measures to increase flexibility, and the reduction of social benefits. One area of flexibility concerned working time arrangements. Employees' rights to take part of their holidays in the summer months were to be curtailed. Split shifts, abolished after the re-establishment of collective bargaining, were to be reintroduced for grades such as ticket office staff in close contact with the public. (This reflected Spanish cultural habits, with the working day generally being broken by a very long lunch break of two or three hours: a continuous working day involved keeping offices open for long periods when custom was at a very low ebb, and required additional staff at times of heavy usage later in the day.) The traditional half-hour mid-morning break, or 'sandwich time' as it was called, was to be reduced to the legal minimum of 15 minutes, largely in order to reduce the costs of train crew and traffic staff who were compensated in cash for working their break.[2] Another measure aimed principally at train crews was the proposed reduction of preparation and disposal time for drivers. Management regarded the time allowances as excessive, a problem resulting, like so many of the issues addressed in RENFE's proposals, from the concessions granted under pressure from the unions in the period after the death of Franco.

Among the proposals were several measures for increasing the geographical and occupational mobility of the workforce. Management wanted to loosen the union controls that had grown up over promotion, transfers and retraining. For example, the company wanted to restrict the compensation paid to workers who were compulsorily transferred to other jobs, and to curtail the right of employees to seek voluntary transfers (by raising the minimum period they had to spend in one job before they could seek transfer). The rules governing promotion were to be changed to give much greater weight to managerial discretion and judgement, less to seniority, and the rules on recruitment and retraining altered to allow management greater room for manoeuvre.

An important proposal was to introduce multi-task grades or 'polyvalence' for some occupational groups, particularly for traffic staff where there existed 'a whole hierarchy of station staff from the station master, down through traffic clerks to pointsmen and workers doing the coupling and so on' (fieldnotes). One of the aims of the change was to increase the 'saturation' of the working day (i.e. the proportion of productive time) in small rural stations, reducing the staffing requirements of little-used parts of the network.

A final group of proposals aimed to reduce 'social' benefits such as housing allowances, free travel, subsidized canteens and company stores or 'economato'. The 'economato' was the epitome of Francoist paternalism. Created in RENFE in 1942 soon after the railways had been taken into state ownership, it had developed to the point where it employed nearly 1,000 people, had 48 sales outlets, and a turnover in 1983 of more than 7 billion pesetas (about £35 million at contemporary exchange rates) (IGAE 1984: 51–8).

Managers conceded that the savings from the proposals on these items were not great (although it was hoped to staunch the losses of the company stores that sometimes amounted to billions of pesetas, i.e. several million pounds). But, as a senior industrial relations manager said,

> RENFE is a company offering services . . . it is not a firm supplying food to its employees or running company stores. Its obligation towards its staff is to offer them a job of work, and the appropriate compensation in monetary terms. Having company stores . . . was suitable as a policy after the [civil] war in an era when it was difficult to get basic commodities (fieldnotes).

Thus the function of these proposals was more symbolic, expressing a change in the style of the firm. They represented a move away from what were seen as unjustified, extensive social benefits and 'acquired rights', and a challenge to what management saw as the 'dead weight' of union influence.

RENFE continued to pursue these and other issues from the 'white paper on negotiation'. Management was concerned with several broad, interlinked areas. They centred on the problem of controlling labour costs, which formed over 60 per cent of total cost and had risen from 76 per cent to 106 per cent of revenue between 1976 and 1982. The first area was the general pursuit of increased flexibility and mobility of labour. In order to achieve this, the radical reform of the 'labour norms' ('normativa') was deemed to be essential. The 'normativa' comprised the complex, vague and often contradictory structure of statutory regulations and collective agreements governing industrial relations in RENFE. It was for management 'the root of all the problems', making rational management impossible. Mobility was restricted by the regulations governing recruitment, transfer, promotion, temporary replacement and so on; regulations in which, in the words of the CEFE commission, considerations of 'the individual interest of the employee' predominated over 'the needs of the railway service' (CEFE 1984: 70). This led, from a managerial point of view, to a serious maldistribution of personnel by geographical areas and grades. It also caused severe blockages in the system, exacerbated by the antiquated, often manual procedures used in personnel management. For example, transfers entailed an extremely complicated procedure, 'long and iterative, with first a public "competition" [within the company] and then applications by employees, followed by provisional lists, appeals, counter-appeals, etc.' (fieldnotes). The process was supposed to be annual, but in 1986 it had not been done for four years, and a backlog of thousands of applications for transfers had built up.

These considerations prompted personnel and industrial relations management to begin a minutely detailed study of existing norms with the aim of producing a much reduced and simplified version that would be less of an impediment to management aims.

Like BR, increasing concern with flexibility and rationalizing industrial relations led RENFE to look at the procedures and machinery of collective bargaining. Management were especially worried by the ability of occupational groups to extract concessions outside the framework of the annual (or, as in 1985—6, bi-annual) general collective agreement. For example, in 1985, bonuses increased by around 30 per cent, compared with a rise of 7—8 per cent in overall pay, partly reflecting the bargaining power of the occupational groups: in the words of a senior manager, 'if you've got your objectives to meet and the workshops cut up rough, you say, "it's OK, we'll manage something on bonuses". The bonus formulae are easy to manipulate'.

Groups such as workshop staff and train drivers who had considerable industrial muscle tended to be able to negotiate favourable agreements for themselves. Management believed that the unions deliberately fostered such pressure in order to create leapfrogging claims and as a way of persuading people of the benefits of joining a union. Industrial relations managers wanted to break away from this characteristic pattern of RENFE bargaining, towards one in which the collective agreement would not be open to subsequent renegotiation by occupational groups.

Third, management wanted to reform the company's pay structure which was characterized by 'complexity, lack of rationality and inequity' (CEFE 1984: 72). Like so many other aspects of industrial relations in RENFE, its irrationality was seen as the direct result of the concessions made to the unions under democratic collective bargaining. Bonuses for particularly onerous or dangerous jobs had been allowed to slip into more general use under pressure from the unions, and had thus lost their original function.[3] (In BR, by contrast, production bonuses, much in vogue in the 1960s and 1970s, had almost all been consolidated into basic pay. Ironically, BR was being recommended by the Monopolies and Mergers Commission to reintroduce incentive payments, although based on group rather than individual performance (MMC 1987: 90).)

In 1986, the issue of production-related bonuses came to the fore in RENFE. The system consisted of over 50 different bonuses, many of which were in practice fixed attendance allowances, paid as a function of the hours spent at work rather than of output (IGAE 1984: 26). Very wide variations existed in the bonus for comparable jobs in different parts of the company, particularly in the workshops. Management claimed that this led to problems with filling vacancies and distorted transfer patterns as employees attempted to move to high bonus areas such as the central repair workshops where the average bonus in 1985 was nearly twice as high as in the zonal workshops. RENFE aimed to rationalize the bonus system, lowering some, raising others, and relating them more closely to changes in output. It also wished to end the practice of paying bonuses to all employees of a particular workplace, whether or not they worked in production-related jobs.

A final area of strategy was the direct reduction of labour costs by a cut in numbers. The 1984 programme contract with the government includéd the objective of a cut of 5,000 in the workforce over three years. In fact, the workforce (excluding military trainees) fell by nearly 6,000 in a single year, from 71,500 in 1983 to 65,600 in 1984, largely as the result of a controversial early retirement scheme (see ch. 8) under which about 10,000 employees left the company. At the same time, RENFE carried out detailed technical studies to determine a new theoretical 'establishment' (i.e. staffing requirements). This was seen as a departure from traditional methods in which staff levels were arrived at by negotiation between the different functions (CEFE 1984: 69). The old establishment which in any case often differed widely from actual staffing levels (IGAE 1984) was reckoned to be too high, and industrial relations management foresaw that further rationalization and a certain amount of new investment would lead to an eventual workforce of 50,000 with a similar size of network and higher traffic.

The changes that RENFE management were seeking were, as in BR, accompanied by organizational reform. Despite numerous reorganizations, the personnel and industrial relations function still bore the marks of its origin under the Francoist labour framework. Its traditional role was largely concerned with the bureaucratic application of labour decrees and regulations, and the administration of social benefits such as housing and the company stores. It also retained a strong legalistic bias, reflecting the important place of legal interpretation and resort to the labour courts in RENFE's industrial relations (see ch. 5).

In the mid-1980s, management set up new structures under an 'organization and rationalization' directorate to examine staffing needs and to reform the entire payment system in RENFE. The growing concern with both flexibility and labour costs raised the question of central headquarters control over the activities of the seven zones. Although the relationship was seen as excessively centralized and bureaucratic, central control was considered to be ineffectual. This was largely because of the inadequacy of management information on matters such as transfers, bonuses, overtime working and so on (see IGAE 1984: 29−42), but it also reflected the lack of clarity of the norms and regulations which led to their being flouted or ignored by the zones, with a loss of credibility for the headquarters personnel function. A new function was established in the industrial relations department to draw up central directives in a clear way, disseminate them throughout the network, and make sure they were adhered to. The computerization of personnel management activities was also pursued. This began to provide headquarters with better control over the zones; for example, by enabling it to compare systematically the amounts paid out under the multifarious earnings heads in different parts of the network. It was hoped to speed up the slow bureaucratic tasks associated with handling the tens of thousands of annual transfers, promotions, detachments, replacements and so on that had brought the largely manual system grinding to a near halt. Better management control would also allow headquarters to decentralize more functions to the zones, and thus increase flexibility in the organization.

Changing Industrial Relations in Practice

In both railways, there was clearly a change in the contents and tenor of industrial relations strategy. But management's success in putting their wider strategy into practice was mixed.

BR

BR hoped that the confrontational approach to flexible rostering would create a momentum for rapid change. This was becoming increasingly urgent for management. New external pressures were being placed on the corporation, the most important being the drastic reductions in the PSO from 1983 which necessitated further efforts to cut labour costs. Management showed its willingness to risk widespread industrial conflict again in order to secure change, for example over the question of driver only operation (see ch. 7). However, progress on most of the other productivity items (with the exception of the relatively uncontentious open station concept) was slow. Five or six years after the 'understanding on productivity', there were still only a handful of driver only schemes in BR. The first passenger scheme had been introduced in 1983 but the introduction of more schemes depended on investment in special trains and equipment, and on overcoming union resistance. Following the confrontation with the NUR over DOO in 1985, progress accelerated and by late 1987 around 1,000 drivers' shifts each day were on driver only trains. The extension of single manning was only agreed in October 1986, following a judgement by the RSNT. The trainman proposals (later renamed the 'train crew' concept) were still far from implementation, and later versions dropped the idea of merging guards and footplate grades into a single line of promotion at lower levels (*Locomotive Journal*, October 1987). Thus management was making slow and rather laboured progress in implementing changes in working practices.

Progress on the reform of the machinery of negotiation and consultation was also limited. Management temporarily abandoned its attempts to abolish the RSNT, although in 1986 it successfully opposed the renewal of the contract of the long-standing chairman of the tribunal. At the beginning of 1988, however, management put forward far-reaching proposals for reforming the machinery. The proposals included the abolition of sectional councils and LDCs, and their replacement by individual staff representatives at local level and by area councils. The existing national tiers of the machinery would be replaced by a single national council to deal with major collective issues. The proposals were aimed at simplifying and speeding up the machinery, and at preventing minor matters from working their way up to higher levels. But beyond this, senior management saw the reforms as a prelude to more decentralized bargaining: the eventual aim was to replace the existing tight national agreements by much looser 'enabling' agreements that would allow local negotiations to suit local circumstances. At the time of writing the fate of management's initiative is still unclear, although BR is aiming to introduce the new machinery by March 1989. In 1987, BR had already taken steps to change the machinery for negotiating pay and conditions of the 800 or so senior managers, telling TSSA and BTOG that it was to end existing bargaining arrangements and would offer managers individual contracts tailored to business needs.

The change to a harder management style led to what the unions saw as a general deterioration in the industrial relations climate which was noted at all levels of the organization. At the RSNT in 1986, the NUR complained that BR was riding 'roughshod over the machinery, and tried to force through change at any cost' (RSNT 1986: 16). There was some evidence to support this contention. In May 1987, for example, BR imposed a new salary structure, including a form of merit pay, on 10,000 middle managers. And in April it imposed a 4.5 per cent pay rise for 138,000 staff even though the unions' claim was going to arbitration at the RSNT. The tribunal, while eventually endorsing BR's offer, warned that cuts in the PSO were having a damaging effect on industrial relations in the railways. It was concerned by the unions' perception that little or nothing of the corporation's improved financial performance was feeding back to their members (*FT* 20 August 1987).

A hardening of attitudes was observed by union sectional council members. Consultation on schemes such as depot closures or service withdrawals became more peremptory, and individual grievances coming up from LDC level were more bitterly disputed. Traditional relationships based on trust and informality started to break up.[4] At local level, the same phenomenon was to be found. It was reinforced by the cost-cutting pressures felt by area management as a result of the demands of business sector managers and tighter budgetary controls. The abolition of the divisional tier of management in the early 1980s led to the devolution of more disciplinary powers to the area manager. Pendleton found a 'dramatic increase in the level of disciplinary action' (1986: 151), which trade unionists saw as evidence of 'the flexing of new-found managerial muscles' at area level (151). The NUR presented evidence to the Monopolies and Mergers Commission about the rising use of disciplinary sanctions in the Southern Region (MMC 1987: 77). The effect of ending the supervisory role of the divisions was reinforced by a changing pattern of career development. A new breed of area managers was emerging, with less knowledge of and commitment to the procedures and traditions of BR's local industrial relations (Pendleton 1986: 175).

RENFE

The transition to a new strategy began two or three years later in RENFE than in BR, and many of the proposed changes were at best incipient. The company's 1984 negotiating 'platform' met with only limited success. The collective agreement significantly watered down management's proposals on matters such as split shifts and polyvalence (Ferner 1987a). The terms of the agreement were so vague and the consultation procedure with the unions so cumbersome that by the time of the 1985 negotiations for the VIth convenio, there were neither split shifts nor new multi-task grades anywhere in RENFE, and progress thereafter was still halting. However, in the VIIth convenio reached in May 1987, polyvalence was extended to all posts with a 'saturation' of less than 50 per cent.

Management's efforts to impose pay restraint in the 1984 settlement, which nominally fell within the government's public sector pay bands, were subverted by the company's loss of control over bonus payments in the following year (see above). In 1987, the pay rise of between 6 and 7 per cent was well in excess of the government's 5 per cent limit for the public sector. And, finally, only slow progress had been made in implementing the other sweeping changes in personnel management, working practices and payment structures that management was planning in the mid-1980s; although a simpler and more flexible procedure for transfers and promotions was agreed in the 1987 convenio.

Despite this, there was, as in BR, a distinct change of style. The drift towards an increasingly tense industrial relations climate was hastened by personnel changes in the industrial relations function. The 1984 negotiating team, which despite its change from 'a passive to a belligerent stance in negotiations' was associated with the post-Francoist period of concessions, was replaced not once but twice by still harder line groups. The new team was criticized by other more consensual senior managers as 'little given to dialogue' with the unions and bent on confrontation. It was argued in return that change by consensus was impossible. This was something of an exaggeration, since negotiated agreement was reached on some changes in the 1987 convenio, albeit with difficulty: the negotiations took three hundred hours, spread over almost three months (*Trenes Hoy*, May 1987: 35 – 42).

Deteriorating industrial relations were illustrated when in 1986 management tried to force the unions to renegotiate the whole bonus system by refusing to apply the agreed pay increase to production bonuses. At about the same time, the police were called to dislodge protesting members of the comité general intercentros. The event created uproar because of the sensitive associations with police repression under the dictatorship. As in BR, there appeared to be a general tightening up of managerial control throughout the network. The change of emphasis emanating from headquarters was reflected in the harsher treatment of disciplinary offences, according to both union officials and some zonal personnel managers. This signalled an end to older paternalistic traditions of discipline that took account of mitigating circumstances such as the family situation of the offender.

Conclusions

In both railways, a change in personnel and industrial relations strategy can be discerned during the 1980s. The turning point occurred during a critical period when attention was focused on quite a small sample of representative, even symbolic issues: the productivity initiatives in British Rail, the attack on 'acquired rights' and the cut in the workforce in RENFE. These were harbingers of wider strategic change, although many aspects of the new policies remained to be addressed, let alone implemented.

The arguments of the chapter raise three central issues that will be discussed in the remaining chapters. The first concerns the timing of change. The new strategy in BR showed more continuity with previous management plans than was the case in RENFE, although the manner of its implementation was a new departure. In RENFE, the break with the past was perhaps more abrupt, both in content and style. The question raised, therefore, is why the changes described occurred when they did. They were of course linked chronologically with the increasing external pressures on both railways, described in chapter 4. Chapter 7 describes the way in which the respective governments changed the framework of rules and expectations, triggering new corporate and industrial relations strategies.

Second, the differing content of the new managerial projects attracts attention. To be more precise, the critical issues in the period of change are significantly different in the two companies. There are of course broad areas of overlap. Both are concerned with productivity, flexibility and working practices. But RENFE focuses its attack more on the notion of acquired rights and privileges, which includes not only working practices but social benefits. The question of the size of the workforce is also central. In BR the critical issues relate overwhelmingly to changes in working practice.

Some of the difference can be explained by different technology and needs of the two networks. For example, the controversial variable day rostering that led to the 1982 strikes in BR has long been accepted practice in RENFE. Conversely, despite the fact that there are 5.2 drivers per locomotive in RENFE compared with 4.6 in BR (CEFE 1983: 31), the questions of single manning and driver only operation are simply not on the agenda in RENFE, because of the technical limitations of the network.[5] Polyvalence for traffic staff has been of central concern in RENFE but of low recent priority in BR. This seems to be because, for lower grades at least, there was generally more flexibility in BR, as a result of the major reform of the occupational structure for station grades that took place in the 1968 Pay and Efficiency agreement (Bagwell 1982: ch. 5).[6]

But beyond these technical differences, it may still be asked why a particular set of industrial relations issues became critical in each company during the 'watershed' period. The way in which these issues were singled out suggests that they fulfilled a symbolic role as well as a practical one in the transition to a new strategy. This question is addressed in chapter 8, where it is argued that the companies' choice of critical issues is influenced by the different kinds of political pressures faced by the railways in the 1980s; that the chosen focus is part of a dialogue between the railway and the political authorities as much as an element of an internal strategy.

Third, in both companies, there was a marked switch from a consensual to a more hard-line, confrontational style of industrial relations. Yet as chapter 9 will show, the contents and style of the new strategy did not emerge at the same time, 'hand-in-hand' so to speak. The policies for change predated the deterioration of industrial relations and the decline of 'active consent', as Pendleton calls it, in both BR and RENFE. It will be argued that it was only after the failure of co-operative strategies for implementing change that the hard-line management style became established. Their failure in both companies has to do with the dynamics of tripartite political exchange between management, unions and the political authorities.

Notes

1 This loose usage is rejected by writers such as Pendleton (1986: 28) who argue that strategy must include 'a coherent set of policy rationales'. This seems unnecessarily restrictive if the object of research is to identify the impact on patterns of management action of changing external circumstances.

2 In BR, 'physical needs breaks' for train crew were regarded as sacrosanct, although management wished to have more flexibility to alter the timing of breaks during the working day (see RSNT 1986).

3 One reason for the prevalence of bonuses in RENFE's pay structure was that consolidation into basic pay would have a severe impact on the employer's national insurance contribution and on the cost of the length of service increment, both of which were directly related to basic pay. This was particularly important with an ageing workforce in the company.

4 This conflicts with Pendleton's finding that 'the near unanimous response of both Regional labour relations managers and Sectional Councillors was that labour relations were being conducted more or less as they always had been, and that values such as trust and respect for the other side were still the most important in bargaining' (1986: 180).

5 This relates to the absence of radio signalling, and of other safety installations, and the high proportion of single track. However, one relatively slight proposal made in 1984 was for the extension of single manning to all 'multiple command' train units.

6 Direct comparison with British practice is not easy since there is a different breakdown of specialisms, reflecting differences in historical development and technology. For example, manually operated points are virtually extinct in the British system, and the responsibility for even the simplest of points maintenance work is strictly that of the signals engineers.

7

Changing the Rules

Introduction

In chapters 3 and 4 it was argued that political control of public enterprises is problematic and that new political objectives have to be *transmitted* to them in a variety of complex ways. It is not enough just to change the statutory framework and formal ministerial directives, although of course these have a considerable impact on enterprise objectives. It is also a question of changing the informal 'rules of the game'. These largely determine how seriously the formal rules changes will be taken. This chapter therefore looks at the British and Spanish governments' attempts to change the rules of the game as far as industrial relations are concerned.

The first section glances back over the formal changes that have already been discussed in previous chapters. Then the role of more diffuse pressures is considered: the changing political climate, the expectations created by committees of inquiry, and direct government intervention in industrial relations questions. It will be suggested that the new rules of the game may be 'communicated' to the enterprise by means of 'demonstrations': dramatic incidents, engineered by government, that illustrate the new priorities. These factors combine to change the relative costs and benefits for management of different courses of action. The chapter also considers the indirect effect of 'rule changes' on industrial relations. The new framework of commercialism has led to business sector management in BR and the beginnings of a similar organization in RENFE. This has its own consequences for industrial relations that may be at odds with the thrust of broad industrial relations strategy. Other tensions arising out of the process of 'changing the rules' are explored, in particular the interaction of external pressures and management's own internal agendas.

Changing the Rules

The Formal Framework — Government Objectives and Industrial Relations

Chapter 4 described the overall changes in the formal framework of government controls for RENFE and BR. Although these changes mainly had an indirect (though profound) effect on industrial relations, both railways were also given new formal industrial relations objectives. RENFE's 'cost reduction objectives' in the programme contract included the reduction in the workforce by 5,130 over the three years of the contract. Costs per employee were to rise by about a third less than the rate of inflation. In exchange for pay increases and the expectation of continuing employment, the workforce would be expected to negotiate an end to 'a series of working conditions and non-economic benefits that represent significant costs for the Network or which hinder or impede the achievement of the proposed productivity objectives, at the same time as representing a comparative advantage with respect to the labour force as a whole' (RENFE 1984a: 54).

These measures, of course, became part of management's platform for the Vth convenio, discussed in chapter 6. Although the final version of the contract appeared in February 1984, when negotiations were well underway, the contents were already known and a draft had appeared the previous autumn. Thus the new formal government objectives became incorporated into management bargaining strategy.

The British government's pressure for change in industrial relations was rarely so direct, but it did lay down formal objectives on at least two occasions. In 1981 the Secretary of State for Transport told the House of Commons that the government's provisional approval of a ten-year electrification programme was conditional on the 'achievement of necessary improvements in productivity' through changes in working practices and manpower reductions (*Hansard*, 22 June 1981: cols 21–6). In 1983, the reform of the machinery of negotiation and consultation became a formal objective of government when the Secretary of State wrote to the new chairman of BR that 'the government wants you to secure improvements to the railways' present industrial relations machinery, which has hampered good communications and slowed down the necessary pace of change'.

Changing the Climate

The government's formal industrial relations objectives for the railways were only the tip of the iceberg. Many of the rules of the game were being changed implicitly by the creation of a new climate of expectations about industrial relations, and the generation of subtle and not so subtle political pressures on the railways.

Government-appointed commissions of inquiry played a part in this in both countries by drawing public attention to aspects of railway industrial relations. In 1980, the report of the Monopolies and Mergers Commission inquiry into services in London and the South East claimed that management had 'not always been vigorous enough in rooting out remaining inefficient working practices'

(MMC 1980: 88), and it was especially critical of working arrangements for train crew (95−7). The report illustrated its case with details of some of the more newsworthy 'restrictive practices'. And a second report, on Network South East, strongly recommended reform of the machinery of negotiation (MMC 1987: ch. 8) (see ch. 5).

In Spain the CEFE commission of inquiry set up by the new Socialist government highlighted features of RENFE's industrial relations in its widely discussed interim and final reports. It was strongly critical of the rigid, rule-bound, bureaucratic administration of personnel and industrial relations. It attacked the inflexibility of labour practices and dismissed the style of industrial relations as 'benevolent paternalism', built around the concession of numerous non-economic 'corporatist' benefits that had once compensated the workforce for low pay but were now unwarranted privileges (CEFE 1983; 27−34; 1984: 69−73).

It is hard to assess how far the pronouncements of such commissions, or of other bodies such as parliamentary select committees,[1] influenced industrial relations within the railways, but they probably helped create a climate of concern about the industrial relations issues that were being aired in the public domain. It then became politically important for management to address itself to those issues. Sometimes management, inadvertently or deliberately, helped bring such pressure on itself. A striking example of the dangers was provided by the proposals for the reform of BR's negotiating machinery. The idea was first floated in public by the then chairman, Sir Peter Parker. By the time management reconsidered the wisdom of immediate reform (see ch. 6), the idea had been taken up by the government and become a formal political objective for the board. Another example concerned the Serpell committee. The BR board had been asking for a broad inquiry into their finances in the hope of ending uncertainty about the railways' role and firmly establishing the government's political and financial commitment to the railways. BR thus saw its relationship with the committee as a delicate political matter of considerable importance to the corporation's future. But there were risks. According to one senior BR manager,

> When changes in the pay structure were being discussed, it became apparent that the costs of doing it would exceed the savings. ... They were in the middle of Serpell. Those closest to the inquiry were aware that the committee were looking for ways of reducing the cost of the railways and that it would be unsympathetic about things that would increase the cost. So people said to Serpell that BR could make further economies on top of the Rail Plan but said nothing about the additional costs of changing the pay structure (fieldnotes).

As a result, the Serpell committee report recommended substantially higher net cost savings than management would have liked.

RENFE managers faced similar pressures at the time of the CEFE inquiry. It will be recalled from chapter 6 that detailed plans for changing industrial relations and reforming working practices were contained in the 'Negotiation White Paper'. Because of their sensitivity as part of management's future negotiating strategy, the circulation of the plans had been carefully restricted even among senior management. But details of the plans were given to CEFE, apparently by senior managers aware of the political ramifications of the investigation: for example, the industrial relations expert on the commission had close links with the leadership of the PSOE, and political 'goodwill' was considered to be at stake.

Changing the Rules and 'Demonstrative Actions': The Case of the Flexible Rostering and Driver Only Operation Disputes

The process of changing the rules, of inducing altered perceptions about the feasibility of different courses of action, could involve diffuse and nebulous elements such as the ideological emphasis of the government. In Britain the aggressive anti-union rhetoric conveyed the need for less consensual styles of industrial relations. In Spain, the central message of the government was of modernization, the restructuring of the economy, the raising of efficiency levels. Sometimes, though, the general messages were reinforced by practical 'demonstrations' by government of how the rules of the industrial relations game had changed. These were important in shaping management perceptions about the balance of costs and benefits of different strategies.

The most important example was a demonstration of the falling costs of confrontation with the unions. Governments' fear of the political unpopularity of public service stoppages had traditionally led to frequent interventions to get management to resolve their differences with the unions. This limited management's freedom of manoeuvre in negotiating change with the unions, weakened hardline bargaining positions and reinforced the tendency towards collaboration rather than conflict.

The post-1979 Conservative government in Britain completely changed the terms of political debate. It successfully exploited anti-union sentiment and created a climate of opinion in which the blame for public sector industrial disputes could be attached to supposedly over-powerful unions. Political virtue was seen to lie in standing up to union claims, rather than in encouraging the peaceful resolution of conflicts.

The political costs of public sector disputes were further reduced by the steps the Conservative government took to limit the disruption caused. A strike on the railways no longer had the same impact once long-distance coach services had been 'deregulated'. The railways' share of freight traffic had been in long-term decline and although basic industries such as coal and steel remained vulnerable to the loss of rail services, the 1984—5 mining dispute showed that quantities of coal could be distributed by road over a long period. Major customers, such as the Post Office, found during the 1982 flexible rostering dispute that they could quite easily move their traffic by road or air. Subsequently the Post Office was able to exploit this to extract a more favourable letters contract with BR. The power of the strike weapon in the public services was also reduced by the government's logistical preparations, of which the stockpiling of coal at the power stations was a notable example.

The practical 'demonstration' that times had changed was the government's attitude during the rail strikes of 1982. In the early summer, disputes were looming over pay and over flexible rostering. The leadership of the Labour opposition played a traditional conciliatory role. The Labour transport spokesman called BR and the unions to a meeting to resolve their differences, and the party leader made last ditch attempts to get the chairman of BR to reconsider ASLEF's counter-proposals. During the strike, Labour party spokesmen condemned the government for its lack of intervention. 'Why', asked one Labour MP with railway connections, 'will the Secretary of State not take an initiative, as his predecessors have done on many post-war occasions, in bringing the parties together round the table to negotiate and resolve this unsatisfactory position?' (*Hansard*, 14 July 1982: col. 1041).

This was the nub of the matter. For the government did not behave in the 'traditional' manner. On the contrary, ministers refrained from meeting union leaders, while they were kept closely informed by the BR board. Even when the board announced that it would close the entire railway system and re-employ striking drivers only if they accepted flexible rostering, the government still declined to intervene (*Hansard* 14 July 1982: cols 1035–45). The Prime Minister argued that 'the handling of (the) strike must be left to the British Railways Board. It cannot be handled in the House or at No. 10 Downing Street' (6 July 1982: col. 145).

The government's readiness to allow — perhaps even encourage — the strike to run its course was evident from the beginning. The Cabinet's contingency committee had begun to meet on the eve of the abortive NUR pay strike at the end of June. When the ASLEF strike was announced, the Secretary of State for Transport told the Commons that

> Faced with that ugly prospect the Government will again take all possible measures to minimise the grievous difficulties for commuters and to protect the public. The police will again make substantial extra car parking spaces available. ... Clearways will be kept free. Roadworks will be postponed wherever possible. It will be vital for hours to be staggered and, above all, for cars and journeys to be shared. There are no legal or insurance obstacles to car-sharing [the Conservative government had removed them], so let every car travel full ... (*Hansard* 2 July 1982: col. 1156).

The government, from the Prime Minister down, made no secret of its support for BR's case against ASLEF. The dispute was blamed squarely on the union for 'its irresponsible and hasty industrial action, which is draining the industry's lifeblood' (5 July 1982: col. 51), and for its failure to consult its members. ASLEF and those who supported it carried 'an immense and direct responsibility for all this damage and all this suffering' (14 July 1982: col. 1035). Ministers emphasized that BR was entitled, indeed obliged, to implement flexible rosters (5 July 1982: cols 44–53; 2 July 1982: col. 1159). 'We must', claimed the junior transport minister, 'support Sir Peter Parker and the British Railways Board in seeking modern working practices which will enable the industry to become the modern, efficient system that the public, the BRB, and most railwaymen want' (5 July 1982: col. 51).

The strength of government support for BR, leading to the crushing defeat of

ASLEF, demonstrated that the rules had changed, that confrontation was politically tolerable, even expected, and that the days of 'beer and sandwiches at No. 10' (14 July 1982: col. 1042) were past. This affected the balance of power between unions and management, and influenced the outcome of subsequent conflicts. In 1985, for example, a dispute between the board and the NUR over the introduction of driver only operation (DOO) came to a head. This was one of the original 'six items' of August 1981 (see ch. 6). Since then BR had introduced a DOO passenger service on the Bedford—St Pancras line, and there had been three freight trials. But the NUR conference had voted in September 1983 not to hold any further productivity talks with BR, especially over DOO which could bring the loss of about 1,750 guards' jobs over five years. In June 1985, BR told the unions that it would resume DOO freight experiments, and extend the passenger services. It was now quite prepared to risk confrontation and force through change without national union agreement.

BR began to implement its policy the following month. NUR and ASLEF refused their co-operation and, with staff being sent home, industrial action by guards broke out in several areas. Striking guards were dismissed in South Wales and Scotland and their jobs were advertised. The union prepared for a national strike. It was reported that, as over flexible rostering, the Cabinet enthusiastically supported BR's uncompromising posture (*Observer*, 11 August 1985).

This time, however, there was a new element to reinforce the change in the rules. Since the flexible rostering dispute, the government's labour legislation had begun to affect the balance of costs and benefits in disputes. The 1984 legislation left unions open to civil action if they failed to hold pre-strike ballots. At its Annual General Meeting in June 1985 the NUR had reluctantly bowed to this and narrowly reversed its previous opposition to ballots. BR showed that it was willing to use the law; in July it obtained a high court order for the NUR to lift its blacking of new railbuses being built for BR by a private company.

When the DOO dispute flared up, therefore, the union's executive balloted its guards for national industrial action. The ballot was narrowly lost, and the union was forced to retreat. Its special delegate conference in September agreed to negotiate with the board on the introduction of DOO services. Like the miners' dispute, it showed the difficulty of getting widespread support for action on issues that would affect only selected groups within the membership.

Conflict and Rule Change in RENFE

The change in the rules had made less progress in the case of RENFE, and there was no 'demonstration' as dramatic as the flexible rostering dispute. In Spain, there was another dimension to major disruptions of public services. Politicians were wary of putting fragile democratic institutions to the test. Thus despite the existence of decrees guaranteeing minimum levels of service during public sector disputes, governments tended to back away from serious conflicts.

This was still the case with the Socialists after 1982. In addition to the concern with political stability, they were constrained by their alliance with the socialist section of the labour movement. The PSOE did show signs of changing the unwritten rules of social consensus. Its plans to restructure and drastically cut back the steel and shipbuilding industries led to lengthy and sometimes fierce conflicts from 1983. But the political cost of these strikes was limited by the fact that they could be contained within restricted geographical areas, often in the peripheral regions of Spain. For example, half of the planned reduction of 17,000 in the shipyard workforce was concentrated in half a dozen sites on the northern coast, and the rationalization of steel mainly affected the town of Sagunto near Valencia. In addition the political benefit of the conflicts for the government was considerable, since they enabled it to achieve a major part of its programme to modernize Spanish industry. Impending EEC membership made it all the more pressing. By contrast, the political necessity or usefulness to the government of forcing a showdown on the railways was more doubtful, especially since RENFE's special social security scheme allowed it to reduce its workforce by voluntary redundancies (see ch. 8) and hence without the massive trauma caused by the restructuring of steel and shipbuilding. The political costs of disruption on the railways were also potentially greater, since conflict would be geographically widespread and more publicly 'visible'. The government was therefore likely to give a much lower priority to change through confrontation on the railways.

In this political context, senior industrial relations managers in RENFE were not convinced that they would be able to rely on unstinting political support from the government in the event of conflict with the unions. This seems to have been an accurate assessment. At no time after 1982 was management able to force a confrontation with the unions on its terms. Strikes continued to be an adjunct to collective bargaining, part of the normal tactics of negotiation, rather than an element in management's strategy for the reform of industrial relations. In 1985, for example, senior managers interviewed expressed their determination to take a hard line in negotiations even if this led to confrontation. But the achievements were limited. According to interviewees, government ministers and senior leaders of the UGT confederation had agreed the basic shape of the pay deal between them and had it accepted by RENFE before negotiations began. The negotiators' hands were tied, since they could no longer trade pay increases for union concessions on working practices. The government's priorities, of avoiding public sector confrontations and maintaining its alliance with the UGT, therefore prevailed over RENFE management's attempts to implement its new industrial relations strategy.

The government sometimes intervened in railway industrial relations for very short-term political motives, rather than to preserve a broader social consensus: because an election was imminent, or a minister feared an impending cabinet reshuffle. In the spring of 1985, for example, a strike called by train drivers over changes in their working arrangements was averted, apparently after direct political pressure.

After 1985, the picture began to change. The alliance between PSOE and the UGT faltered, and by 1987 looked to be on the verge of complete breakdown. The spring saw a phase of unprecedented worker militancy with strikes and demonstrations over pay and restructuring in transport, construction, engineering, cars, shipbuilding and other sectors. In the autumn, senior leaders of the union resigned their parliamentary seats in protest at the limits on civil servants' pay and pensions contained in the government's expenditure plans for 1988. The UGT approached its arch-rival the CCOO to propose a joint campaign of protests against the government. The underlying cause of the breakdown was the UGT's discontent with the government's emphasis on industrial restructuring, austerity and the control of public expenditure. The union argued that, since the working class had borne the brunt of economic adjustment, the government should be more concerned with social justice and the redistribution of wealth. The events of 1987 suggest that the PSOE believed, firstly that the system could cope with a higher degree of conflict than hitherto, and secondly that it could govern effectively without the political support of the UGT. It remains to be seen how far this change in the political context will alter the managerial costs and benefits of confrontation in RENFE.

The Continuing Ambiguity of Government Objectives

It has been argued that conflicting government priorities dissuaded the González government from risking a major confrontation on the railways. But even the Thatcher government, apparently so committed to changing the rules of the game by its attitude to public sector disputes, could still send out conflicting signals. Outside the periods of the major stage-managed disputes, the government had a continuing concern with day-to-day political ramifications of railway industrial relations. Ministers expected to be kept informed about industrial action and its effects on the service. And industrial relations managers, even after the 1982 dispute, continued to ask themselves, 'if we have a strike, is this going to be politically acceptable?'. Management's actions were therefore still influenced by their awareness of ministerial interest. As one senior manager commented during a local dispute in 1983,

> a lot of people at BR are being pestered at the moment because the Brighton guards have gone on strike over a guard sacked for allegedly striking a passenger. Management is being pestered by the Department of Transport who want to know what's going on and why. BR Personnel Department are not ringing up regional managers every five minutes to find out what's happening, they have confidence in the managers on the spot to see that it is sorted out. But on the contrary they do have the Department of Transport chasing them at Rail House several times a day. They ask the Department why it needs this sort of detailed information. The only thing they can get out of the Department is that it is the Secretary of State behind it, because he is responsible for answering questions in the House and needs to have the details (fieldnotes).

The most notable example of ministerial intervention occurred during the 1984 pay negotiations. BR publicly insisted that the pay award would be tied to acceptance by the unions of productivity proposals including driver only operation, single manning of locomotives and the trainman concept. But at the end of May, the unions agreed to a pay offer well above the 3 per cent target for public sector workers, with no productivity strings. Apparently, BR management had become convinced that the unions' campaign of industrial action would be commercially damaging: 'it was not the right time to have either a failure to settle pay, or to force through changes in working practices' (fieldnotes).

There were, however, other influences at work that are revealed in memoranda leaked from the Department of Transport. A note of 2 April to the Secretary of State from the Under-Secretary in charge of the Railways Directorate refers to the government's desire to have the chairman keep 'a low profile and play problems coolly', and to 'Ministers' preference to see BR talks played long, at least while the coal industry remains in dispute' (*Transport Review*, 22 June 1984: 1). Mrs Thatcher's private secretary wrote to an official in the Department of Transport that the Prime Minister

> agrees that BR should increase its pay offer to keep negotiations in play. She accepts that the offer can be increased along the lines suggested so long as the productivity conditions are insisted upon. She would be concerned if the offer were improved beyond this point as it would put the offer made to the miners in a poor light.
>
> (*Transport Review*, 22 June 1984: 1)

The government's direct, if clandestine, involvement in negotiations is evident from these extracts. They also show that its intervention was motivated by its concern with the long-running dispute in the coalmines, and suggest that it did not care to have a war on two fronts. BR was presumably able to convince the government that insistence on the productivity measures would lead to major industrial action on the railways. The episode thus reveals a conflict of priorities. The higher-level strategic aim was to weaken the public sector unions by defeating the miners. In order to safeguard this aim, the change of rules on the railways was put into temporary abeyance.

But there was a deeper ambiguity in the process of changing the rules. For even where government pressure was used to further the rule changes, its very intervention limited management's autonomy. For example, once the government had publicly decided to prepare for a strike by ASLEF over flexible rostering, it became very difficult for the board to back down from its collision course even had it wanted to. The Prime Minister's assertion in the Commons that 'the Government have stood behind the British Railways Board in its negotiations' (*Hansard*, 6 July 1982: col. 145) sounded ominously like a warning that retreat was cut off, a view reinforced by the observations of one well-placed informant who agreed that

> once the government had provided its backing, then the thing had to be seen through and management could not back off. [It is likely that] the Board felt government behind them saying, 'for Christ's sake, railway management, sit this one out' ... The Board cannot afford to have the government minister losing faith or panicking, and the same applies in reverse. The government must say to the Board 'don't come to us in six weeks' time with another fudge' (fieldnotes).

Even though by the time of the dispute BR had lost patience with its failure to pin ASLEF down on flexible rostering, the government's own position must also have been uppermost in the board's mind.

The Transmission of Rule Changes within the Organization: Sector Management and Industrial Relations in BR

Chapter 4 showed how the new framework of commercialism led to major organizational changes in BR and, to an extent still unclear, in RENFE. The new priorities of business sector organization in turn altered the perceptions of those who made industrial relations decisions. In other words, external pressures led to changes in the internal rules of the game.

Sector management was accompanied by the reform of budgetary control in BR. Costs were to be fully allocated to the sectors on a 'prime user' basis (see ch. 4), so that each sector could be responsible for its 'bottom line' results. This, as Pendleton (1986: 137—8) argues, 'has created sharper management accountability and the capacity for more detailed central control ... In budgetary terms, local managers can now be effectively scrutinized *directly* by head-quarters' managers'.

The outcome has been for much greater demands on local management to meet budgetary targets. 'The budget is king', as one area manager put it. 'Before, you used to be able to argue reasons as to why you didn't meet budget. Now excuses are not valid even if they're legitimate' (fieldnotes). A competitive 'league table' approach to achieving objectives prevailed among area managers.

Cost cutting became a priority, even at the expense of quality of service, and in this climate older industrial relations traditions came under pressure. Pendleton (1986: 144) found that the response of production managers to tighter central control and to the 'greater strength and diversity of demands originating from parts of the management hierarchy' took the form of '*ad hoc* variations to traditional patterns of work organization since violations of existing agreements are often the easiest solution'. Sector management's pursuit of commercial opportunities also led to closer central scrutiny of regional labour management practices and to pressures on working arrangements that obstructed sector plans. Pendleton (1986: 140) cites the example of a contract signed by the freight sector with an oil company. The contract violated the traditional 'spheres of influence' of train depots by by-passing an intermediate depot where a change of crew normally took place.

At local level, the situation was a microcosm of the one facing BR as a whole. Area managers generally felt that the rules of the game had changed and that their future careers no longer depended on avoiding conflict. On the contrary,

> You now get 'brownie points' for managing through disputes — as long as you turn out to be right! In disputes managers would now have the full support of higher management. In the framework of corporate objectives there is an allowance for 1.5 per cent of trains to be cancelled: 1 per cent for sickness and holidays, and $\frac{1}{2}$ per cent for managing disputes — not of course 'formally', but generally accepted as a 'strike budget' (fieldnotes, Area Manager).

However, this turned out to be an over-simple view of a complex situation. The signals concerning rules changes were ambiguous. Since sector interest predominated, the order of the day varied with sector priorities. Despite the ethos of managerial assertiveness, sector management appreciated that short-term objectives were sometimes better served by fudging tricky industrial relations questions. Confrontational tactics that led to a dispute could jeopardize bottom line results. This posed a dilemma for some local managers who had enthusiastically embraced the new approach. Sometimes they were like junior officers leading the charge, only to find that their generals were busy concluding a peace agreement with the enemy.

For example, one manager, convinced that he had the backing both of his regional superiors and of sector management, challenged footplate staff over a working practice that contravened the board's traction and train crew instructions. His efforts to enforce the regulations led to simmering industrial action. With new timetables and a major sector initiative approaching, the manager was warned off by regional and business managers, who were able to bring about a compromise arrangement that ended the dispute. 'Macho management', he complained, did not exist: 'I tried it and I now know you don't get any support'.

The manager's disenchantment was understandable. But a more accurate depiction of the situation was that the rules had changed *provisionally*. Timing and tactics were all. Priorities were constantly shifting and senior management wanted to be able to pick their moment to adopt a hard line or to refrain from it. The outcome inevitably confused lower level managers. This echoes the ambivalence concerning changes in the rules of the game that characterized the macro-level of relations between the board and the government, discussed in earlier sections.

Conclusions

Management's perception of the costs and benefits of different approaches to industrial relations has been altered by changes in the formal and informal political rules. In Britain, the new rules raised the costs of consensual industrial relations and lowered the costs of conflict: sometimes directly and explicitly, as when productivity changes were made a condition of government approval for investment, sometimes indirectly as when the government strongly supported BR in its confrontation with ASLEF. In Spain, formal rule changes were not so clearly backed up by 'demonstrative' government action.

As the arguments of chapter 3 would suggest, the problems of conflicting or unclear government objectives persist even in the age of public enterprise commercialism. Governments have different priorities, not all of which can be pursued at the same time, and the logic of electoral politics is ever present. It was only to be expected therefore that even in BR, where the rule changes proceeded further and were more dramatic, their significance was sometimes blurred and it was not always clear how far they had really changed. In RENFE, the continuing preoccupation with social consensus and political alliances blunted the force of formal rule changes, and the government tried to reserve confrontational approaches for issues where it could reap the greatest advantage and minimize the costs.

The chapter also raises questions about the relationship between external rule changes and management agendas. It has been argued that the way in which the new rules of the game were disseminated limited management's freedom to pursue their own internal agendas in the way they thought best. The government had a significant degree of control over the timing and content of the major 'demonstrations' of rules changes, and its priorities and objectives naturally differed from those of management.

Although the content might be the same, it was very different for policies to be embodied in externally set objectives, rather than in management's own internal plans. Once internal policies became part of the political domain, they created formal or informal public expectations and implied commitments by management which could not be quietly shelved if management priorities changed. There was thus a tension between the internal logic of management's programmes, and the conduct of political negotiation with outside bodies.

There was a temptation for management to manipulate information flows so that the resulting political pressures could be used to further internal agendas. But trading information in this way and allowing issues to become public brought a danger of giving 'hostages to fortune'. The dangers became most clear, perhaps, in 1981 when BR management and the unions asked the government to approve higher financial support and more investment in exchange for productivity improvements. Instead, as was seen above, the government seized upon the productivity items and made approval of electrification dependent on their achievement. Thus management could lose control over its agenda, and its energies could sometimes become biased towards the particular aspects of industrial relations strategy that acquired the highest political profile, a theme developed in chapter 8.

Yet the changed external environment was not only a new constraint on management, but a *permissive* factor as well. It enabled management in BR and to an extent in RENFE to 'activate' agendas that had been blocked or were lying dormant. Management was therefore not always opposed to its internal policies entering the public domain, since it could become a way, however risky, of harnessing the external pressures for change.

Note

1 In Britain, the old Select Committee on Nationalised Industries, and the Select Committee on Transport both drew attention to productivity issues at a time when BR was formulating its plans for productivity 'in the broadest sense'. The SCNI recommended reductions in train crews and other changes in working practices (SCNI 1977: xxxiii–xlv), while the SCT endorsed the Secretary of State's contention that productivity improvements should be a condition of approval for electrification (SCT 1982: viii–ix, xxv).

8

The Symbolic Politics of Industrial Relations Change in BR and RENFE

Introduction

A central thread of the argument so far has been that public enterprises have a relative autonomy and bargaining power that makes the exercise of state control problematic. Therefore, the state's new objectives for the railways have to be transmitted through negotiation. This chapter further explores the nature of these political transactions by examining the *kind* of commodities that are exchanged.

On the face of it, there is an antithesis between public enterprise commercialism and political control. Commercialism implies managerial autonomy, and freedom to act in ways analogous to those of private industry. But, as was argued in chapter 3, the drive to public enterprise commercialism emanated from the political sphere, as a political response to underlying problems of state expenditure and economic crisis. Paradoxically, therefore, commercialism is both at odds with and part of the wider framework of political control of public enterprises. The pursuit of commercialism by railway management is a fundamentally political process: 'commercialism' is not only a strategic objective of management but a framework within which the political authorities will evaluate the enterprises' performance.

Railway management is thus faced with a dual task. It must act 'managerially', by putting in place the structures and plans necessary for the more efficient, competitive, 'commercial' organization it is trying to create; and it must act politically to provide the government with evidence that the new strategy of commercialism is being successfully implemented. This 'evidence' constitutes management's bargaining resource in political exchange, in return for which it hopes to secure the continued financial and political support upon which its strategy depends.

The relationship between this evidence and the 'real' plans and practices of management is a problematic one, however. This is because the raw facts of managerial performance must be transmuted into a commodity 'usable' in political exchange, namely one that has value to the political authorities.

The characteristics of such usable commodities flow from the nature of political action. Writers such as Edelman (1971; 1976) have argued the importance of 'symbolic acts' in the political activity of parliamentary democracies. Edelman suggests that symbols are used to evoke responses of arousal or quiescence in the 'mass public'. He borrows Sapir's term 'condensation symbols' to describe phenomena that 'condense into one symbolic event, sign, or act of patriotic pride, anxieties, remembrances of past glories or humiliations, promises of future greatness: some one of these or all of them' (1976: 6). The actual significance of such symbols is 'out of all proportion to the apparent triviality of meaning suggested by its mere form' (Sapir 1937: 493).

It could be argued (whether or not one accepts the psychologistic bias of Edelman's approach) that the symbolic nature of political activity is reinforced by some of the features of the state and representative politics discussed in chapters 2 and 3. The kind of changes being proposed may be essentially long term, as is the case with public sector commercialism, but the electoral logic of parliamentary democracy means that politicians operate according to a shorter-term time scale. Moreover, objectives are complex, varied and changing. Political actors, therefore, are encouraged to mobilize support for policies and objectives by means of symbolic demonstrations of intent that convey a sense of the kind of project that the government stands for. Political acts are in effect signals sent to construct alliances, rally supporters or disarm opponents. They encapsulate and simplify complex and long-term goals. As such, they make use of a kind of short hand, or 'condensation symbolism', which signifies much more than is expressed openly. This suggests that when the railways engage in political exchange, they have to offer the political authorities a *representation* of commercialism that can be used by political actors in the pursuit of their goals. It must be a symbolic 'condensation' of commercialism, capable of concise and public expression, and hence able to enter the conventional discourse of politics.

The following sections examine case studies from BR and RENFE that illustrate the importance of symbolic action in political exchange. The tensions between the symbolic representation of commercialism and the real practice within the enterprise will also be discussed. The cases are taken from the 'watershed' period of changing industrial relations strategies during which, as chapter 6 suggested, attention was focused on a small number of key issues. These fulfilled symbolic political functions over and above the role that they performed within internal managerial plans and strategies.

RENFE: The Symbolic Significance of Workforce Reductions

The symbolic nature of the Vth convenio of 1984 has already been stressed (ch. 6). The agreement was presented by management, and accepted by government, as a break with the concessionary bargaining style of the past; yet its practical impact was very limited. The concessions squeezed from the unions had to be watered down (as a result of the collapse of the UGT's strategy of collaboration in the rationalization of RENFE — see ch. 9) and those that survived proved to be hard to put into practice.

The second aspect of the watershed period in RENFE was the attempt to control labour costs, not only by restricting pay increases, but also by reducing the size of the workforce. It will be remembered that the programme contract laid down the target of a cut of more than 5,000 employees between 1984 and 1986. In March 1984, an early retirement scheme was introduced for workers aged over 55 and with 25 years service.[1] This was made possible by RENFE's special pensions scheme which, for those who had joined the company before 1967, allowed full pension rights to be retained at a lower retiring age than was permitted under the general state scheme. Unlike the latter, RENFE's system also allowed pensioners to retain their pension even if they found work outside RENFE. The 1984 early retirement scheme, together with ordinary retirement, led 10,000 workers to leave the company in little more than a year, and the workforce to fall by a net total of some 7,000.

At one level, the reduction can be seen as part of managerial industrial relations strategy. It cut operating costs rapidly and significantly. Even where leavers were replaced by new recruits, costs were lower because of the higher pay of longer-serving employees: management estimated that the age-related pay increments led to a difference of one-third between pay rates for a beginner and those for an employee with 25 years service. Early retirement was seen as a way of raising productivity, since older workers were considered to be less productive than younger ones. Thus where it was decided that leavers should be replaced, a coefficient of 0.8 was used to calculate replacements for those over the age of sixty. In other words, for every 10 leavers over 60, only eight new employees would be recruited. The early retirement scheme also allowed management to get rid of large numbers of medically unfit or disabled workers; these constituted roughly half of the ten thousand leavers.

Yet the implementation of the early retirement scheme had features that could not be fully understood as part of a coherent internal managerial strategy. There was a disjunction between the rational managerial appearance of the scheme, and the way it was put into practice that suggests that it was also part of an external exercise in symbolic communication with the political authorities.

Studies of early retirement in Britain have noted the advantages of voluntary early retirement such as cost efficiency and the avoidance of industrial conflict. But as Turnbull (1987: 7) argues, 'the pattern of volunteers may well influence the pattern of actual redundancies, and without attempts to control the resultant occupational, skill, age and experience structure of the firm it may well be that the post-redundancy workforce is incompatible with the requirements of the production process'. As a result, as an Institute of Manpower Studies survey found, management control over such schemes has been maintained in practice

> through a tight definition of eligibility, managing the duration of early retirement schemes, and adjusting the terms to ensure take-up by the target group(s) ... management control over eligibility and non-replacement were seen as pre-requisites to using early retirement in any substantial way

... the most common approach was to identify at an early stage those whose skills, qualifications and/or experience meant that they should be ineligible for consideration for voluntary redundancy because they had key skills which the company needed to retain (Gordon 1984: 9, 57).

This approach would be combined with the right to refuse applications for early retirement so that a 'balanced' workforce could be retained.

In RENFE, such a strategy was not adopted. First, the early retirement scheme made no attempt to restrict *a priori* the categories of eligible worker. It was open to all who fulfilled the age and length of service conditions. Second, management did not in practice retain the right to veto applications from among those eligible. In theory, the selection of employees for early retirement from among the thousands who applied was to be done according to 'rigorous norms' to ensure that key staff did not leave. The head of the applicant's workplace had to provide a report approving the request and certifying that the individual was surplus to requirements. In principle this was relatively straightforward for the 5,000 or so applicants with medical disabilities, but rather less so for the remainder. Of the nearly 9,000 applicants for early retirement, almost 6,000 were allowed to leave during 1984, while some 2,700 applications failed to obtain the necessary approval of the head of workplace. Yet by the spring of 1985, all of these had been given permission to leave. The criterion of operational needs had been completely discarded in practice.

The abrupt and more or less random decline in the trained workforce that resulted from the early retirement scheme created inevitable operational problems. Overtime working, which had been declining in early 1984, began to rise again. The zones found themselves with labour shortages, and complained about the lack of planning and consultation on the scheme by the headquarters personnel department:

> The personnel function at the centre has not reached agreement with the zonal directors. As a result of the circular [no. 510, authorising the retirement scheme], there have been too many early retirements and zones may become 'de-populated'. The zones are quite happy to have early retirements as long as there is a plan of recruitment so that they know when and how the people who leave are going to be replaced, so that their level of establishment can be maintained and they can run the services as they need to ... People think that trains are simply run by the Holy Ghost rather than using real people (fieldnotes, zonal manager).

Similar problems were created in the so-called 'structure', comprising managerial and professional grades. In one zone, a third of the 90 or so higher grade posts were vacant, including ones crucial for operations such as traffic control. This was a pattern repeated elsewhere. Between four and five hundred higher grade staff, roughly a third of the total, took early retirement. According to one union leader, 'many of these retired managers have remained at their posts to do the jobs that they were doing before, until RENFE manages to get replacements for them' (although many of the posts were frozen).

A second problem with the early retirement scheme was its cost. Although new entrants were, as we have seen, much cheaper than older employees, the replacement process was itself expensive. This further strengthened the need for selectivity in approving retirement. According to one senior manager, 'since the company had to pay for three years training of its workforce, it could not allow the decapitalization involved in permitting everyone over 55 who wanted to retire to do so'.

An important additional cost of early retirements was created by lump sum payments made, in addition to the normal pension, in order to encourage early leavers. The sums offered to the highest grade manual workers at 55 years of age were just under 2 million pesetas, while managerial and professional employees of the same age were entitled to sums of between 4 million and 15 million pesetas. The total cost of these payments in 1984 was some 9 billion pesetas. It placed a considerable burden on the company's capital account and further reduced the overstretched funds available for investment in much needed physical assets.

Why was the scheme allowed to operate in this manner? Two reasons of a 'managerialist' nature were discernible. First, there was a question of equity. RENFE's own pensions system was due to be phased out, and impending changes in the pensions legislation meant that the pension would be calculated on a less favourable basis. As a result,

> People who were 'good' workers and who were therefore encouraged by RENFE to stay were in danger of seeing themselves penalised for being good, since it was the bad ones who were benefiting from the generous provisions of the earlier legislation. So in the end, RENFE let them all go (fieldnotes, zonal manager).

Second, certain increasingly influential groups in management argued that RENFE's formal establishment of some 67,000 was too high. The early retirements had led to a workforce of some 64,000. Central personnel and industrial relations management saw this as a good opportunity to redefine the railway's staffing needs and cut the theoretical establishment. The zones were therefore instructed to draw up lists of posts that would be abolished.

However, some zonal managers were highly critical of the way in which the new establishments were defined. One manager, for example, complained that staffing levels were arrived at by unscientific procedures. The data used were primarily 'subjective' descriptions of the components of jobs, or tasks, rather than formal work study analysis. It was also claimed that the reduction in establishment took insufficient account of staffing needs due to illness and holiday. Finally, the treatment failed to discriminate properly between zones according to the nature of traffic, equipment and so on; for example, zones with higher than average proportions of suburban commuter traffic would have correspondingly higher staffing requirements.

The burden of the above arguments is that the early retirement exercise and its aftermath did not altogether make good sense from a strictly managerial point of view. The rapid, indiscriminate reduction in numbers was costly, and caused operational problems. But the disadvantages may be considered as a small price to pay for the benefits that become apparent when the episode is viewed from the perspective of the political exchange process.

The sharp fall in numbers had an important symbolic significance. Both RENFE and the government could point to a clear, readily quantifiable success in meeting the targets of the 1984 programme contract. It was a potent political message that RENFE had begun to tackle the problems of inefficiency and over-manning that were believed to plague it. Even more important, perhaps, the early retirements allowed the company to show a reduction in current expen-diture. Because of its obvious bearing on the size of RENFE's deficit, this was a figure of acute political sensitivity. (See, for example, the relentless grilling of RENFE's chairman by opposition members of the budget standing committee of the Chamber of Deputies (Comisión de Presupuestos 1983: 2486−2498).) As a result of the early retirements, current labour costs were immediately cut by perhaps 10 per cent, since the cost of lump sum payments was, as mentioned above, borne by the capital expenditure account.[2] There might well be detrimental effects on the quality of service and investment, but these would take longer to develop, and were vaguer, less quantifiable and less politically visible.

Thus while internal managerial purposes might have been better served by a more gradual and more selective rundown of employment and labour costs, RENFE's political bargaining position was strengthened by the dramatic cut that the early retirement scheme helped to bring about.

In short, RENFE was able, at some cost to a coherent managerial strategy, to offer the government a 'usable commodity' in political exchange. The govern-ment could point to a significant 'restructuring' of a major public enterprise without any of the trauma that accompanied retrenchment in the shipyards, steelworks, mines and ports. This could, potentially, make a major contribution to the mobilization of support for the PSOE's broader programme and the defus-ing of opposition to it. It could be argued that RENFE received its reward with government approval in 1987 for the huge investment plan, the PTF.

BR: The Political Symbolism of Flexible Rostering

The dual nature of management behaviour during the 'watershed' period − the concern with both internal managerial strategy and external political com-munication − may be illustrated in the case of BR by the flexible rostering conflict.[3]

Flexible rostering had a major role in management strategy. It will be recalled that it was seen as a way of minimizing the cost of the introduction of the shorter working week agreed in the 1980 pay settlement. As a result it was the first of the major working practice changes to be reached, and it became a test of the unions' willingness to co-operate in changing working practices. In addition, management considered it to be the key to other changes in footplate work.

The bitter confrontation that arose over flexible rosters, ending in the two-week strike of July 1982, was a remarkable departure from traditional patterns of industrial relations in BR. Although there was a clear managerial rationale for introducing new working arrangements for footplate staff, the costs of con-frontation were extremely high. These costs arguably outweighed the benefits that management could hope to obtain, either directly or from the impetus that would be given to other productivity initiatives.

The immediate costs of the disputes of 1982 were estimated by BR at some £170 million (BRB 1982r: 7; Bagwell 1984: 103). In addition, it seems likely that some traffic was permanently lost, and that BR was forced to make costly concessions to major customers in order to secure their future business. There were other less quantifiable costs. It was admitted that ASLEF and its members were embittered and demoralized by management's hard line approach to the dispute, particularly by threats to sack striking drivers.

Some interviewees believed that the gains from flexible rostering could have been achieved without the July 1982 strike (cf. Bagwell 1984: 100). In a last minute attempt to avoid a dispute, ASLEF proposed a compromise arrangement. It took up an idea originally put forward by BR for a parallel experiment in which, 'by a careful review of the work allocation, and the concentration of more work into programmes, links and rosters, there could be savings to cover the introduction of the 39-hour week at minimal cost and to produce productivity improvements to match the Board's flexible rostering proposals' (*Locomotive Journal*, July 1982: 1). Some considered this offer to be a major concession which in more consensual times would have formed the basis of a settlement. But despite this, BR refused to respond. According to one experienced and well-placed observer, the union's general secretary

> could not get to see BR and they would not allow him to have any leeway on it at all. BR could have got an agreement there and then. But they chose to have the fight ... It was unprecedented for BR not to seek to find a way out of the trouble at the last moment (fieldnotes).

Managers disputed this interpretation. They believed that ASLEF was not to be trusted and that if BR had gone along with the simultaneous trials, 'flexible rostering would not have been in even now'. Even if this view is accepted, however, and the dispute was necessary to obtain the benefits of flexible rostering, the savings were minor. It was estimated that total savings from flexible rostering would reach about £5 million a year after five or six years of operation. From this must be deducted the shift payment to drivers, so that foreseeable net savings were likely to be running at £2−3 million a year at 1982 prices, or about 1−2 per cent of footplate labour costs.[4]

Senior management believed that, by 1987 at least, flexible rostering was working well. But there is evidence that the flexible rosters had significant practical problems, at least in the first few years, partly because of the haste with which they were brought in; some managers interviewed in 1986 doubted whether the estimated savings were in fact being made. Pendleton's detailed examination of the new arrangements (1986: ch. 8) concludes that the aim of reducing unproductive time for driving staff had been largely unrealized. This claim is supported by the Monopolies and Mergers Commission's analysis of the breakdown of driving time on the Southern Region, which shows that the percentage of driving time on rostered shifts rose only slightly, from 45 per cent to 47.5 per cent between 1980 and 1986 (1987: 86). The flexible rostering scheme was constrained from the beginning by the safeguards for drivers laid down by the 1982 RSNT recommendations. For example, 50 per cent of turns had to be of eight hours or less and only 20 per cent could be over eight-and-a-half hours. Already in the summer of 1982, one of the railway's legendary figures, Gerard Fiennes, the former general manager of the Western and Eastern Regions, was warning that the RSNT safeguards would 'be sure if slow death to accept' (*Modern Railways*, August 1982: 369—70). In addition, Pendleton argues that management failed to take into account the way in which flexible rostering would interact with existing local agreements and with the continuing control by local workforce representatives over working arrangements. As a result, rigidities increased rather than diminished. For example, work was traditionally allocated according to seniority. If a nine-hour job arose, the most senior spare driver might be on a seven-hour turn. Since a driver could refuse to accept a turn that involved rostered overtime of more than one hour, the train could be left standing at a station (Pendleton 1986: 245).

There were also serious administrative problems in matching hours over varying day lengths to achieve the stipulated 312 hours over an eight-week cycle, and in reconciling payment arrangements with local practices on mileage equalization and route and traction knowledge (241—4). The managers interviewed by Pendleton were highly critical of the loss of control, reduced flexibility and administrative complexity that flexible rostering had brought (246—8). Union sources claimed that such problems led to big increases in overtime in some areas (see, e.g., *Locomotive Journal*, February 1985: 2).

All these problems were foreseeable. It was not only ASLEF who attacked the notion of flexible rostering in advance. Even before the new system had been fully implemented, some groups within BR management were arguing that it was

> not very suitable for the British railway system. It worked OK on the continent because it was a much more stable system, with longer driving distances and fewer timetable changes. Financial pressures in the British system are leading to pressure to go and find the market and adapt to changing demand. Flexible rostering is hard to accommodate to changing timetables (fieldnotes).

However, some managers argued that the real benefits of confronting ASLEF over flexible rostering went far beyond the relatively meagre savings that it generated directly. One strand of thinking held that a major issue of principle was involved. Senior industrial relations managers considered that ASLEF had failed to honour a clearcut agreement under the 1981 ACAS understandings to accept flexible rostering. This could not go unchallenged, for the breaking of agreements would lead to 'anarchy and indiscipline', and the basis for agreeing future change with the unions would be undermined. The dispute was thus necessary in order to 'get an honourable relationship preserved with the union'. This argument emphasized the unquantifiable dangers of *not* confronting ASLEF.

A second strand suggested that confrontation paved the way for more sweeping changes in working practices: 'There are cynics in the industry saying that the enormous battle that took place was not worth it. But ... the big prize has been to change the attitudes of the unions and the members that were averse to change before' (fieldnotes, senior manager). This argument was partly based on the perception that BR could not hope for further co-operation from the NUR unless it confronted ASLEF: 'flexible rostering was merely the front runner . . . so if this was blocked and ASLEF alowed to escape, how could the NUR membership be expected to swallow other changes affecting them?'.

According to such thinking, it was therefore necessary to include in the benefits of confronting ASLEF the savings that would be made from other productivity items, such as driver only operation and the single manning of locomotives. In 1982, annual savings from the other five of the six productivity items were estimated at about £36 million, a substantial sum, although it still amounted to only about 1 per cent of total operating costs and would not be achieved for several years.

Net savings would be lower, however, because of the need to share benefits with the staff under the terms of the August 1981 understanding on productivity which refers to rewards for staff 'whose responsibilities are directly affected under these agreements.' These payments would foreseeably reduce the value of the savings by several million pounds, up to as much as half. Moreover, they would be paid in full as soon as agreement was reached on an item, while the savings for management could take several years to materialize as displaced staff gradually retired (RSNT 1986: 26).

Payments could turn out to be higher than anticipated, as in the case of single manning. Management tried to reduce the shift payment from £1.50 to £1.25, reflecting the fall in estimated staff reductions from 2,000 to 1,500 and gross savings from £13.9 million (at 1983 prices) to about £11.5 million. However, the RSNT recommended that the payment be restored to £1.50 (RSNT 1986: 35−6). Since the original offer represented a share for drivers of 50 per cent of total savings (*Modern Railways*, February 1986: 71), the workforce therefore would receive more than half of the savings in this instance.

It was therefore possible that annual net savings from all the productivity items might amount to no more than say £20 million (at 1982 values) after several years. However, it is questionable how far the 'investment in change' represented by the costly defeat of ASLEF allowed even these modest gains to be achieved. An optimistic strand of management thinking held that the defeat of ASLEF would create an irresistible momentum for change. In fact, further progress on the productivity items was slow (see ch. 6). The changes were also less ambitious than originally planned. In 1982, single manning and DOO had been forecast to cut more than 5,000 jobs. But by the time the new practices were introduced, the potential reduction in jobs had fallen to some 3,250 (*Modern Railways*, February 1986: 71; *Guardian*, 15 August 1985).

It may also be asked how far changes could actually be ascribed to management's tough stance on flexible rostering. ASLEF's opposition to flexible rostering had been based on a long-standing and deeply felt attachment to the principle of the guaranteed eight-hour day that had been won by the union in 1919 (McKillop 1950: chs 10−11). But the principle of single manning had already been well established by agreements in the 1960s (Bagwell 1982: 51−9). Opposition, while still strong in view of the number of ASLEF members who would be displaced, was not as deep-rooted as to flexible rostering.

Moreover, the eventual implementation of DOO arguably owed more to the Conservative government's 1984 trade union legislation than to the events of 1982. As was seen in chapter 7, a major conflict over the introduction of DOO was avoided only when the NUR leadership narrowly lost the compulsory ballot for industrial action in the autumn of 1985. It might be suggested that the membership refused to back industrial action because it remembered management's determination in the flexible rostering dispute. But it is as likely that the vote reflected sectional interests, with those depots unaffected by DOO plans unprepared to back action in support of other groups.

Flexible rosters in theory benefited another important area of change, depot rationalization, by allowing depots to be further apart. But there was scepticism among some senior managers, who thought that depot strategy was unlikely to be much affected. Rationalization was not dependent on new train working arrangements, and was already underway before the dispute. In any case, the agreement on rosters included the safeguard for ASLEF that 'the introduction of flexible rosters would not involve any alteration in the allocation of work to existing depots', which appeared to limit management's freedom of manoeuvre.

In short, therefore, the confrontation over flexible rostering was an extremely costly investment when viewed from a managerial perspective. Even the relatively small forecast savings were of uncertain achievement; and it was by no means evident that the use of confrontational methods in 1982 was necessary to achieve such savings. Further, as argued in chapter 6, the board had access to major sources of labour costs savings with much lower risks of confrontation. Administrative streamlining, the rundown of marshalling yards, and withdrawal from the collect and deliver parcels service allowed 14,000 staff to be cut between May 1980 and December 1981 at a total annual saving of over £65 million. Such economies were expected to continue in future years, as indeed they did, contributing to a further steady fall in staff numbers (cf. table 5.1).

It is hard to believe that BR's approach to flexible rostering was the result of managerial *miscalculations*, since most of the factors affecting the balance of costs and savings — for example, the need to make offsetting payments to staff in return for productivity changes — were foreseeable in 1982; to the extent that there were uncertainties, these were likely to reduce net savings rather than increase them. One is driven to the conclusion, therefore, that the 1982 strategy was based on calculations other than the internal managerial rationale that has been explored in the preceding paragraphs.

The arguments of earlier chapters suggest, rather, that the flexible rostering dispute was an element in political exchange with the Conservative government in the early 1980s. The government made clear its objectives and priorities by redefining the 'rules of the game' for public enterprise industrial relations. The attack on the power and influence of the unions made tripartite political exchange impossible (see ch. 9). BR became aware that continued political and financial support from government depended on a managerial strategy that publicly broke with the assumptions of the old industrial relations. As one senior manager put it,

it was clear that we needed to demonstrate a significant step forward in the area of making it a more efficient business. The professional advice was that flexible rostering was a good thing to choose as *flag bearer*. Of itself it was not yielding a great deal of money but we were in the game of *showing the flag* (fieldnotes, emphasis added).

It was thus necessary not only to introduce new labour strategies within the corporation, but also to signal the transition clearly to the government. Flexible rostering was suitable for this purpose because it was a clear-cut, single issue whose principle could be easily grasped in public debate. Management's opponent, ASLEF, could be conveniently presented as an obtuse, reactionary union, the living embodiment of 'outdated' craft attitudes, restrictive practices and resistance to change. BR conducted a skilful media campaign which successfully promoted this version of the conflict. Three years later, the NUR's battle to prevent the extension of DOO was to be helped by public sympathy for the union. By comparison, despite ASLEF's vigorous defence of the eight-hour day on safety grounds, there was little public support for the drivers' case. ASLEF's isolation was reinforced by the public recriminations between the NUR and ASLEF over the need to accept change, and ultimately by the TUC's lack of sympathy for its case.

Thus although the dispute was costly from the point of view of a narrow managerial rationale, it had the symbolic properties necessary for political exchange. It was a concrete expression of management's determination to pursue higher productivity, *if necessary against the opposition of the trade unions*. It was the clearest possible demonstration of the demise of the old tenet of industrial relations that the unions had to be taken along with change.

Flexible rostering thus helped to convince the government and the wider 'public' of the credibility of management's new commercial orientation, and hence pave the way for government approval of major investment projects. As the RSNT recognized, 'a failure to agree any proposal for more flexible rostering which makes a positive impact on productivity by improving train working time, will seriously affect the Board's ability to obtain the essential capital it urgently requires for investment and modernisation' (1982: 57).

Because it symbolically 'condensed' a number of assumptions about the new possibilities for management action and the limitation of the role of the unions in public enterprises, the flexible rostering episode was also an eminently 'usable' commodity for the Conservative government in the pursuit of its broader political goals for reshaping industrial relations attitudes and behaviour. It was the visible, public sign that management had taken the government's urgings seriously and had changed the way in which it managed.

Conclusions

It has been argued that the strategies of the railways during the watershed periods have a dual character. They follow both an internal *managerial* rationale concerned with reducing costs and increasing efficiency and flexibility, and an external *political* logic aimed at retaining government and public support. The cases that have been examined can be 'read' in both manners. Flexible rostering in BR and early retirements in RENFE functioned as part of management plans.

But they also had features that only 'made sense' when seen as part of a symbolic exchange with government, representing politically visible achievements around which governments could mobilize support for their broader programmes.

This process, which it could be argued is characteristic of enterprises that have to operate in a highly political environment, reflects one of the major paradoxes of the move to greater commercialism: management's ability to behave commercially and to retain its autonomy depended on its capacity to mobilize political support and to negotiate successfully with the political authorities.

The need for management's actions to be valid both as political symbols and corporate managerial policies extracted a high price. For the symbolic *representations* of commercial strategies used in political discourse could conflict with the *practice* of commercialism within the enterprise. In both BR and RENFE, management felt strong pressure to be seen publicly to adopt a harder, more confrontational approach to industrial relations. The railways' continuing political support depended on it. Thus management was sometimes led into displays of overt 'commercialism' that could wrench policies from their context and upset the careful planning of internal managerial strategies. As Pendleton (1986: 226) says about flexible rosters in BR, 'because of the way [they] were removed from the context of a more comprehensive work re-organization strategy, and because introduction of them came to be of symbolic importance, insufficient attention was paid by BR management to the labour relations processes likely to surround their implementation and the way in which they would interact with existing agreements'.

In conclusion, the case studies have shown how railway managements, in order to win broad political support, have used symbolic acts that demonstrate the break with the past, the *discontinuities* of strategy, rather than the manifest continuities that may be identified (see ch. 6). Thus the salient episodes of the watershed period mark almost a rite of passage from one strategy to another, and constitute what Edelman might call the 'dramaturgy' (1971: 148) of relations between public enterprise and political authorities: a public acting out of management's commitment to the new rules of the game of commercialism.

Notes

1 Normal retirement age in RENFE was 64, but several categories of workers retired at 62, or, in the case of train drivers and some other groups, at 60.
2 Subsequently, new accounting procedures were introduced for the public sector which meant that the costs of early retirement would be borne by the current account.
3 The dispute is discussed in detail in Ferner 1985. The following account draws extensively on that article (see also Pendleton 1986: ch. 7).
4 Management claimed that the real gross savings were higher, since flexible rostering offset the cost of introducing the shorter working week, which BR calculated to be some 2.5 per cent of footplate costs (see MMC 1987: 86). However, this argument seems to beg the question, for it is not clear that management would have accepted the introduction of shorter hours for footplate staff if the cost had not been offset.

9

New Industrial Relations Strategies and Tripartite Political Exchange

Introduction

This chapter continues to explore the way in which new state objectives are introduced into the public enterprise by means of political bargaining. It looks at railway unions as political actors, and examines the extent and limits of their participation in the transmission process.

The idea of the unions' ability to engage in 'political exchange' was discussed in chapter 3. The unions have political power resources that are different from (although often related to) the economic muscle to inflict damage on the employer. They can trade political 'commodities', notably the preservation of 'social consensus' (Pizzorno 1978). In the case of the railways, the unions' political bargaining resources may include their ability to resist or to encourage the change and rationalization that the political authorities and railway managements are seeking. As will be seen, in both Britain and Spain, some of the unions offered their co-operation in implementing managerial strategies in return for political 'goods' that only governments could provide.

The concept of political exchange has been applied by writers such as Pizzorno, and Regini (1984), to what might be termed the 'macro-political' level. They have been concerned with 'corporatist' political relationships between the state and the peak interest groups representing labour and capital. The social contract of the mid-1970s in Britain and the series of tripartite and bipartite pacts in Spain after the death of Franco may be seen as prominent examples of macro-political exchange.

But the concept might also be used to describe lower level 'meso-corporatist' relationships (Lehmbruch 1982; Cawson 1985a) between sectional interest groups and the state; for example, between the state, employer organizations and unions in industrial sectors such as steel (e.g. Rhodes 1985) or, as in this case, the railways. The 'meso-level' may be part of a broader system that includes bargaining between peak organizations, or it may be relatively isolated in a largely 'pluralistic' system in which organized interests play little part in policy formulation (Cawson 1985b: 9). The term 'meso-political exchange' seems appropriate to describe the bargaining that takes place at this level, located somewhere between micro-political processes internal to the corporation and the broader political exchanges between national interest organizations and the state.[1]

The power of governments to affect industrial relations issues such as pay, employment, participation and work organization, and their constant intervention in the objectives and activities of public enterprises, provides a strong motive for public enterprise unions to engage in political exchange. Governments often become *de facto* participants in industrial relations and a potential bargaining partner for the other parties, unions as well as management.

Although the differences between the public and private sector in Britain were eroded by the growth of tripartism and incomes policy in Britain in the 1960s and 1970s, public enterprise unions have traditionally had to adapt themselves to the needs of political action as well as to industrial strategies (Batstone *et al.* 1984: part III). The British railway unions have developed institutional means of political action. The NUR, in common with other large unions in both the public and private sectors, has traditionally sponsored Labour MPs. In 1945 when it had several hundred thousand members, as many as 15 of its sponsored candidates were elected to parliament (Bagwell 1982: 379). ASLEF and the TSSA also have parliamentary spokesmen. The NUR has used its parliamentary leverage to exert pressure on issues such as the Beeching closures, electrification and the Channel Tunnel. According to Bagwell, during a thirty-month period in the mid-1970s, NUR MPs, organized and co-ordinated by the union's political liaison officer, put down over 300 oral and written questions on transport matters (386).

Railway union leaders have cultivated contacts with politicians of both main political parties. But in periods of Labour government, railway union leaders have been able to exploit their links within the labour movement to gain political access and engage in quite successful political exchange. As described in chapter 5, they were able to persuade ministers and even the Prime Minister to intervene in railway negotiations on several occasions. In his autobiography, the former NUR general secretary Syd Weighell recounts the intervention in the 1975 pay negotiations by the Prime Minister Harold Wilson. According to Weighell,

> Wilson warned us of the serious economic problems facing the country. Of course, I was well aware that discussions were going on with the TUC at the time to try to reach an understanding on the next pay round. I wondered whether he would really risk a national rail strike at such a delicate stage of the Government's negotiations with the TUC.
>
> At the end of our meeting, Wilson ... drew me to one side and said we should not do anything drastic and he would see what he could do about getting a settlement (1983: 31).

The outcome was that BR's final offer of 27.5 per cent was improved to 30 per cent. The episode illustrates how the effectiveness of the union's engagement in political exchange depended on its power to cause embarrassment to the government in a particular political conjuncture, rather than on the economic impact of disruption.

In Spain, the context of political exchange was very different. Following the death of Franco, the democratic unions ended 40 years of exclusion from activity in both the labour market and the political sphere. Since then, the priorities of the labour movement have been dominated by the effort to restore democratic institutions, including a framework for industrial relations, and to consolidate the unions themselves (see ch. 5). As a result political exchange has concentrated on national corporatist arrangements designed to preserve social consensus in the difficult conditions of the transition to democracy. Since the 1977 Moncloa Pacts, agreed by the government and opposition parties, a number of national compacts have been reached between one or both of the major union confederations and the employers' peak organization the CEOE, with the blessing if not always the direct participation of the government. The pacts gained the unions' agreement to pay guidelines, and granted important concessions to the labour movement including shorter working hours and employment creation measures (Pérez Díaz 1985; Roca 1983).

The UGT has generally seen greater advantage than CCOO in such political exchange, since it emerged from Francoism in a debilitated state. In return for its contribution to consensus, it has been able to win government support for a model of unionism and industrial relations favourable to its own needs and strategy. Notable examples were the 1980 Workers' Statute which followed a framework agreed between the ruling UCD and the PSOE, and the 1984 law on trade union freedoms. The latter gave legal recognition to trade union branches or 'sections' within companies, and gave them bargaining rights and entitlement to union facilities. This accorded with the UGT's desire to give a predominant role to 'the union as an institution', which led it to emphasize the importance of the branch within the union's structure. By contrast, the CCOO stressed more direct forms of participation (Miguélez 1983: 17) and thus favoured the development of the workplace committees which were more suited to the decentralized, workforce-based organizational strengths of the workers' commissions (see also Zufiaur 1985).

As well as having more to gain from political exchange, the UGT has had greater political access than its rival. It has been able to take advantage of its close links to the PSOE, especially since the Socialist victory in the 1982 general elections. But the CCOO's political strategy has been handicapped by the low level of representation of the Spanish Communist Party in parliament, and in recent years by deepening splits within the party.

Given the close integration of the Spanish railway unions into their national confederations (compared with the much looser association of British unions with the peak organization, the TUC), their political action has to be viewed within this broader framework of macro-political exchange in which the confederations, particularly the UGT, have been engaged since 1976. The Rail unions' main political resource has been their ability to threaten the carefully constructed social consensus. Governments have regarded disruption of the rail network less as an economic problem than as a potential disturbance of still vulnerable democratic institutions. This, as chapter 5 suggested, has led to direct intervention by the government in pay bargaining.

Such leverage may be seen as 'implicit' political exchange, since there may be no direct bargaining between the unions and the other participants. When the PSOE came to power, however, the UGT rail union, acting in the context of the national union's strong (if conditional) support for the PSOE's policies of modernization and restructuring, embarked on a strategy of explicit political exchange. This is the subject of the following section.

The Case of the UGT Railway Union and the Vth Convenio

The UGT Railway Union's Strategy of Meso-political Exchange

We have seen that the new Socialist government introduced measures for containing the crisis of RENFE and other Spanish public enterprises, and that this led to a reassessment of business and industrial relations strategy in the company. The optimistic expansionary plans of the early 1980s were replaced by a strategy that gave priority to retrenchment and rationalization and demanded 'sacrifices' from the workforce. The prominence of RENFE in the Spanish economy and the political weight attached to it made the fate of the new strategy of great importance to the success of the PSOE's economic aims.

The UGT was a close ally of the PSOE. It broadly supported the government's programme of modernization, although it could be critical of particular policies, such as the reform of the social security and pensions provisions; it was only in 1987 that differences with the government over such issues finally brought relations to breaking point. As suggested in chapter 5, the sectoral unions that made up the UGT confederation did not act autonomously but generally responded to the broad political and strategic line of the higher levels in the organization. How, therefore, was the railway union to react to the political pressures facing RENFE and the new strategies being developed by RENFE management?

In contrast to the CCOO, the UGT's impulses to oppose retrenchment in RENFE were balanced by an awareness of the wider political context of the union's support for the government. The union also saw the opportunity to pursue its own objectives by a strategy of meso-political exchange. Thus it gave its broad approval to the government's strategy for the rationalization of the public enterprise sector. The approach was expressed by the general secretary of the UGT transport federation, to which the railway union belonged: 'UGT is prepared to negotiate a reduction in the deficits of [the public] enterprises, to accept sacrifices, not only in wages. But in return we ask to participate in the elaboration and control of the respective plans ' (*El País*, 9 February 1984).

The railway union adopted this strategy in the watershed period of 1983–4, described in chapter 6. In return, it wanted a greater involvement in the management of RENFE and in the conduct of its rationalization strategy. This involved negotiation with both management and the government. Participation in the management of public enterprises was part of the broad agenda of the Socialist government. Its 1982 election programme promised legislation to establish 'co-participation' in the management of large enterprises (PSOE 1982: 20). In early 1983, the minister of transport announced that he would appoint union representatives to the boards of the public sector enterprises controlled by his ministry. Fully-fledged participation, with union representation on the corporate board, was subsequently discussed in government committees, but awaited the publication of repeatedly delayed legislation on public enterprise. In the meantime, the minister decided to institute a limited form of participation in the railways. After consultation with the two unions, he appointed one person from the UGT and one from CCOO to the board of RENFE in February 1983. (Similar appointments were made on the narrow gauge railway, Ferrocarriles de Vía Estrecha (FEVE).) However, the appointees were formally considered to be ordinary board members and were not expected to represent the 'corporate' interests of their unions (Comisión de Industria, Obras Públicas y Servicios 1983: 2497).

The UGT's appointee, Apolinar Rodríguez, was a key figure in the railway union, and was to play a central role in the union's strategy of political exchange. A civil engineer and economist in RENFE, he had been adviser to the PSOE parliamentary group on railway matters since 1977 and worked on the Socialists' transport policy document. His prominence in the union and his professional expertise led to expectations that he would receive an important public sector appointment following the PSOE's election victory. This illustrates the typically politicized workings of public enterprise management in Spain, and suggests the kind of political horse-trading between the PSOE and its ally the UGT that was expected to occur. According to a version of events emanating from the union, the UGT confederation exerted pressure on the minister of transport for Rodríguez to be given a post in RENFE itself where his expertise could best be used. Soon after his appointment to the board, Rodríguez was made an assistant director with responsibility for investment issues. He was later given responsibility for planning as assistant director general (ADG), and played a major role in negotiations for the programme contract. While RENFE management denied that there had been political pressure for the appointment, a senior respondent conceded that, of course, 'you took the whole picture into account in the appointment. Thus the fact that he [Rodríguez] was in the UGT and it was a period in which the firm would like to have got some kind of collaboration with the union was part of the picture' (fieldnotes).

This suggests that management perceived the advantages of establishing links with the politically influential UGT as a way of implementing the changes demanded by the government. Indeed the collaborative strategy began to bear fruits for management. The 1983 emergency retrenchment measures were accepted by the UGT even though they meant a reduction in personnel costs and the failure to honour important provisions of the 1983 collective agreement. The ADG was a pivotal figure in this: the presence of a UGT activist in a strategic management post 'gave the company credibility in the eyes of the workers . . . As a result of his actions, the company's viability plan could be accepted by the UGT because of his great credibility within the union. This has been very useful for the company' (fieldnotes).

The ADG himself claimed that 'nobody has promoted the [retrenchment] policy with more enthusiasm than I have. I have encouraged with all my power the austerity measures, work discipline, labour modernization, joint responsibility of the unions in safety matters, the Emergency Action Plan . . .' (*Cambio 16*, 1 August 1983).

The collaborative strategy reached its apogee in the period of negotiations for the Vth convenio. The negotiations began at the end of 1983 and continued on and off until a final settlement was reached in June of the following year. They were marked by a gradually widening split in the union ranks, between the CCOO on the one hand, and the UGT together with the two small unions, SLF and USO, on the other. The UGT accepted the need to moderate its pay demands to keep within the 6 per cent limit for public enterprises laid down by the government. It was prepared to give up the 'acquired rights' described in chapter 6 and to move away from the paternalist model of 'objective' protection of the workforce through regulations. The more 'subjective' and the less rigid the regulations, it believed, the greater the role for union power and collective bargaining. In return, the UGT demanded that retrenchment should be carried out without forced redundancies, and that participation should be greatly extended. It argued that the unions should have the right to appoint up to 30 per cent of the members of the corporate board. It also wanted a role in headquarters and regional management committees, and in the monitoring of RENFE's restructuring plans. The union believed that through participation it could, in the words of one activist,

> help to provide solutions to the issues facing the railway. It doesn't want the sort of unionism in which the company says, 'I give the orders, and if you are not in agreement with them we can negotiate or you can use your strike weapon and then we will come to some agreement.' The UGT wants direct responsibility in the management of the company (fieldnotes).

The CCOO national confederation was highly critical of the restructuring policies of the government. The railway union followed its lead and refused to accept the logic of 'sacrifices': the participation that UGT saw as the prize of co-operation was viewed by CCOO with suspicion. The union considered its appointee to the corporate board to be a representative of union interests, rather than a board member like any other. The board was seen to be dominated by government appointees representing the different ministries, and to be acting as a rubber stamp for the government's policies and for those of the chairman. CCOO found that debate at the board was limited, the style consensual, and open dissent from decisions or policies usually only expressed by the CCOO appointee. The union thought it could wield only limited influence on decisions through participation in management bodies, and it therefore did not see increased participation as a valuable objective.

Negotiations for a new convenio continued during the first three months of 1984 against a background of strike calls by the unions. After a series of management offers, towards the end of March the divisions between the unions came to a head. The UGT and its allies accepted a management offer of a 6 per cent pay rise in exchange for 'countermeasures'. The draft agreement also offered the unions four places on the management committee and on the important 'central traffic safety committee'. The management committee, the principal executive management body in RENFE, was composed of the chairman, vice-chairman and senior functional directors. The union representatives would be full voting members of the committee. Finally, management agreed to extend participation to other levels of the company, particularly to the zones.

CCOO strongly opposed the draft agreement and it was put to a ballot of the workforce in May. The result was a rejection of the proposals by a 2:1 majority. A period of deadlock was broken by the intervention of an outside mediator, leading to agreement in June. Although some important concessions were made by the unions, they were much weaker in the final agreement than in the rejected draft agreement. For example, the provisions on split shifts and job flexibility ('polyvalence') were so loose that management was unable to implement them. The inclusion of additional benefits such as the completion of a regrading exercise increased the value of the final offer to something over 7 per cent.

But in return, the UGT lost its cherished objective of increased participation. The final agreement allowed only for monthly meetings between the management committee and the unions for the joint examination of 'the general position of the Company, its economic situation, investment policy, the employment situation, planned reorganizations and restructuring, and in general, all those matters having a direct or indirect influence on the situation of the workforce'. Following a change of chairman and other top managers, even this limited provision fell into disuse after a few meetings.

Thus the UGT was placed in the paradoxical position of having to accept unwillingly an agreement that was in most respects more favourable than the one that it had willingly agreed to in March. It grudgingly acknowledged that the ballot result showed that the workforce as a whole put more weight on tangible benefits than on the intangible advantages of participation. The union's strategy of collaboration was therefore in disarray.

The Limits of Political Exchange: Strategy Dilemmas of Union and Management

The strategy of sacrifice coupled with participation had created serious problems for both union and management in RENFE. The tensions became apparent during the negotiations for the Vth convenio when, not long after the debacle of the ballot on the draft agreement, Rodríguez was dismissed from his post of ADG. The dismissal was nominally the result of a disagreement between him and the chairman over the use of external consultants, but its causes ran deeper.

For the UGT, collaborating with management carried great risks, and it subsequently admitted that the strategy had been misguided and 'ingenuous'. It still had to compete as a trade union with the better organized workers' commissions. Since under 50 per cent of the workforce was unionized, and both unions recruited in all grades, the UGT could not afford to lose the support of the railway workforce by neglecting traditional trade union demands. Its policy of sacrifice gave CCOO an opportunity of which the latter took full advantage. This was shown in membership figures. Between March and June 1984 (the period of conflict over the draft collective agreement), CCOO's net rise in membership was over 400, while the UGT's fell by more than 300 and continued to fall into 1985. Participation in management through the ADG merely compromised the union by linking it to managerial decisions unpopular with the membership, without producing tangible benefits.

The debacle of the negotiations led to a period of turbulence in the UGT rail union and a radical shift in its strategy. A phase of internal critique led to the replacement of most of the existing executive. There followed a series of complex struggles in which a faction favourable to continued close collaboration with management and support for government policy briefly came to power. The so-called 'Catalans' were in their turn ousted by the architects of the original political exchange strategy. The latter now argued that the dangers of trying to resolve issues through negotiation with the minister outweighed the attractions, and decided that the 'vote of confidence of the union in the government' was to be replaced by a more critical stance. This was reflected in the deteriorating industrial relations climate of 1985–6, described in chapter 6.

Part of the problem with the UGT's earlier collaborationist strategy had lain in the complexities of tripartite political exchange. The union had to deal with the government as well as management, and it was unable to tie down the government sufficiently to the commitments that were needed to counterbalance the sacrifices. The warning signs were visible well before the negotiations for the Vth convenio began. The programme contract between RENFE and the government was originally supposed to be drawn up with 'participation of the trade unions in the agreement' (RENFE 1984a: 60). But when the document was published in early 1984, the leader of the UGT transport federation expressed the union's 'disillusionment at the complete lack of union participation in the elaboration of the programme contract' (*El País*, 9 February 1984).

Behind this lay an ambivalent attitude in government circles towards political exchange with the UGT. At the macro-political level the government's preferences were revealed in a notorious letter from the economics minister, Enrique Boyer, which argued the advantages of not having a social contract in 1984 because 'no concertation was cheaper than concertation'. Thus a strategy of macro-political exchange was seen as an expendable luxury, if only at that particular conjuncture. Analogous thinking was applied to the meso-political level of rationalization in RENFE. Although some ministers saw the opportunity to 'transmit' government objectives to RENFE by means of political exchange, the price demanded by the UGT was considered, particularly by the economics ministers, to be too high.

First, the union's participation in management was felt to put at risk the government's efforts to promote more professional management and more commercial policies in the public enterprise sector. Second, the government's monetarist-oriented economic policy gave priority to cost cutting, rationalization and retrenchment. But the UGT wanted rationalization and sacrifices to be accompanied by a consolidation of the railway's role. This was expressed in a preference for the 'social model' of railway organization over the 'liberal model' (see UGT 1984; RENFE 1984b[2]). The 'social model', of the kind operating in some of the European railway networks, was based on the co-ordinated planning of transport and the use of social cost—benefit criteria. Given the pattern of social needs, this implied an expanding, high investment railway. The liberal model, more akin to that being pursued by the Conservatives in Britain, entailed the use of narrow economic and financial criteria of performance, cuts in the network, investment and the workforce. It was clearly a coded description of the perceived policy of the PSOE economics and finance ministers.

This struggle was fought out in the preparation of the programme contract. In a speech to a conference on the future of the railways in 1985, Apolinar Rodríguez (by this time no longer ADG), argued that between successive drafts the contract had changed from being 'positive' to 'negative', despite his efforts to persuade the board of its limitations. It had become less a programme contract than 'a programme for RENFE produced by the government'. Under the pressure of economics ministers, the government's financial contribution to RENFE had been reduced, and the idea of line closures introduced. Targets for cutting the workforce by several thousand had been included. The contract, he suggested, concentrated too much on cost reduction and not enough on raising revenue, and its provision for future investment was inadequate. Above all, Rodríguez concluded, it has been a strategic mistake to postulate a policy of sacrifices without also having 'a strategy for the future': the contract had been drawn up in the absence of a broader corporate plan for the future development of RENFE. The position was changed somewhat by the government's approval in 1987 of the ambitious investment plan, the PTF. But it could be considered to tend to the liberal model in that it went hand-in-hand with continued cuts in staffing, and it concentrated resources on the more commercial and potentially profitable parts of the network to the detriment of some of the more 'social' components.

Political exchange was hampered not only by differences of interests between party and union but also by factional divisions that cut across both. The minister of transport at the time of the Vth convenio negotiations, and his leading political advisers, had been associated with a majority section of USO that had joined the UGT in 1977. The minister had also been leader of a political grouping, Convergencia Socialista, which had been brought into the PSOE a few months before the 1982 elections. Hostility between the USO group and the 'ugetistas' in the UGT transport federation was said to date from an episode in which several ex-USO members were disciplined for failure to obey a UGT strike call (Cacicedo 1984).[3] This conflict persisted in tensions and suspicion between the railway UGT and the ministry, which impeded the political bargaining process.

The strategy of collaboration created serious difficulties for management as well as the UGT, and these contributed to its eventual failure. As we have seen, the appointment of a senior UGT militant to a managerial post enabled management to tap sources of political legitimacy, given the links between UGT and PSOE, and gave credibility to the rationalization and cutbacks in RENFE. On the other hand, union participation was perceived as creating a parallel power structure within the organization rivalling the formal managerial hierarchy. Managers complained that lines of authority had become confused and that the 'non-political' professional managers were demoralized by the conflicts arising from the UGT's role. The ADG was seen to play a central role in the union's accumulation of power (cf. Cacicedo 1984). One highly coloured report cited a RENFE manager's view that

> no one knows who is in control in Renfe. When there is a management or personnel question, people talk to 'El Poli' [Apolinar Rodríguez, the ADG], who is the one who calls the tune in Renfe. The executives and directors don't dare move for fear that if they take a step that the UGT ... don't like, they could lose their job (*Cambio 16*, 11 July 1983: 47).

While the lurid and exaggerated tone of the article must be treated with caution, especially in the politicized climate of infighting in RENFE, internal evidence strongly suggested that the power of the ADG was indeed considerable. His position was strengthened by the depth of his knowledge of railway matters, which the chairman as an outsider without previous railway experience did not possess. The ADG's sphere of influence extended from planning and investment to the conduct of RENFE's broad industrial relations strategy. Thus the strange spectacle was presented of the same person acting both as a major force behind management's negotiating position and as the principal architect and co-ordinator of the union's strategy.

The dismissal of the ADG by the chairman in May 1984 was a sign that management recognised that the costs of co-optation outweighed the possible advantages. The extension of union participation in management bodies (as agreed under the draft of the Vth convenio) now seemed an excessive price to pay for the UGT's faltering collaboration. RENFE was prepared to make major concessions to CCOO in order to get agreement to a convenio that did not include participation. As we have seen, the final version provided only for meetings between the unions and the management committee. Subsequently, the involvement of the UGT in management gave way to exclusion (although the two union representatives continued to sit on the board of directors). Indeed the appointment in late 1985 of a new chairman and several senior managers who were active in the PSOE illustrated the practical lesson that the UGT had by now digested: that the union and the party had different objectives. The arrival of the new team further reduced the access of the UGT to the managerial structure and strengthened the industrial relations tensions.

The episode of the UGT's collaborationist strategy illustrates the attractions and limits of tripartite meso-political exchange. Though the initial impetus to political exchange came from the alliance between the UGT nationally and the Socialist government, the railway union, RENFE management and the government all saw advantages in harnessing the co-operation of the union in the company's retrenchment plans. Equally, each had reservations. Perhaps the major one for the UGT itself concerned the risk to its integrity as a union in the face of competitive pressures from CCOO. It is possible to see the demise of the strategy as being over-determined by its combined disadvantages for the parties involved. But equally it could be argued that had the UGT's organizational position been secure in RENFE, the advantages of political exchange would have outweighed the problems.

BR and the Balance Sheet of Change

The Approach to the Government

In contrast to RENFE, the original impulse for tripartite political exchange in BR was primarily internal. It grew out of the tradition of consensual bargaining relationships between management and unions rather than out of the relationship between union and government.

As chapter 6 described, when the pressures for greater commercialism began to mount in the mid-1970s, BR continued to insist on maintaining the co-operation of workforce and unions. Management stressed the theme of progress by consent rather than confrontation (e.g. BRB 1977r: 16), and talked of the 'social partnership of the railway community' (8). Taking the unions along with change meant recognizing their legitimate aspirations, as embodied in the NUR's Railwaymen's Charter. In the 1980 pay negotiations, the unions won a 20 per cent pay award and a cut in the working week from November 1981, in return for agreement to co-operate on changes such as the rationalization of the marshalling yards and the 'collect and deliver' parcels service.

But the strategy of consensual change was endangered by the growing financial crisis on the railways. By mid-1980, recession was badly affecting BR's revenue. The corporation cut back its investment programme and froze recruitment. It forecast that it would overshoot its external financing limit and feared a serious decline in its services unless it could obtain a significant rise in the limit. The situation made it increasingly difficult for BR to satisfy the aspirations of the unions.

At this point, the chairman of BR, Peter Parker, launched an initiative to find a way out of the impasse. The main vehicle was the Rail Council (see chapter 5) set up in 1979 as a high-level forum for senior management and union leaders, separate from the main machinery of negotiation. The choice reflected management's desire for a consensual approach, and to emphasize the gravity of the situation: 'the Rail Council was proposed in order to say they shouldn't have negotiations, but rather a sharing of problems ... It was a question of trying to see issues as responsible people rather than as negotiators' (fieldnotes, senior manager).

The October 1980 meeting of the council recognized that government support was unlikely until outstanding rationalization and productivity issues had been addressed. At a special two-day meeting of the Rail Council in November 1980, the chairman proposed the idea of a 'balance sheet of change' as the basis for a joint approach to the government. The council agreed to ask the minister for a larger EFL and a higher investment level, to endorse a rolling programme of electrification, and to authorize key investment schemes such as the advanced passenger train, and signalling and rolling stock replacement.

But, in return the chairman stressed that there was 'no chance of our going to government rattling the begging bowl, supported only by vague assertions of good intent'. Management and unions had to show that they were undertaking the things that were within their control. The unions were asked to co-operate in the accelerated rundown of services and facilities, administrative cost savings and the continuing small changes that the board called 'good housekeeping'. Their commitment was sought to a speeding up of consultation procedures to enable these changes to be implemented more quickly. Finally, BR wanted the unions to agree to an urgent review of the productivity and working practice changes first discussed at the time of the 1980 pay negotiations (see ch. 6). The balance sheet is summarized in table 9.1.

TABLE 9.1   The Balance Sheet of Change

Proposed Action by the Railways	*Proposals to Put to the Minister*
1 Accelerate rundown of marshalling yards	1 Agree adequate EFL and revised PSO for social railway
2 Withdraw from collect and deliver parcels	2 Recognise need for higher investment levels and provide additional funds from (say) 1983
3 Reduce passenger train mileage and facilities by 5 per cent	3 Endorse electrification rolling programme
4 Accelerate streamlining of administration (e.g. divisional re-organization)	4 Consider freight strategy
5 Continued co-operation in 'good house-keeping'	5 Authorize specific key schemes: APT, 'jumbo' cross-channel car ferries, rolling programmes for electric multiple units, locomotives and freight wagons, West of England signalling scheme
6 Commitment 'to push consultation procedures at all levels to facilitate speedy progress'	
7 RSNC to meet urgently to review commitments in 1980 pay deal concerning changes in national agreements and working practices, especially manning of traction units; recruitment and training of traincrew; open station concept	

Source: BRB.

The balance sheet was pursued in three meetings with successive transport ministers, beginning with Norman Fowler in January 1981. First signs were hopeful and the minister appeared receptive to the idea. The unions stressed that there should be a 'synchronization' of commitments by government and railways. A concession by one party should be matched by an equivalent concession by the other. The minister agreed that many of the problems of the industry were the result of a lack of investment over a long period of time and that there was 'a need for a sensible bipartisan programme' (Weighell 1983: 75). At a second meeting in June the minister told the council of his decision to authorize a ten-year electrification programme. But BR had to justify individual schemes, and the minister also attached productivity conditions to his decision (see ch. 7). The unions were not satisfied. They felt that they had too little to show their executives and their members in return for the progress made by the unions in delivering the railways' side of the balance sheet. There was no concrete indication that the government intended to keep its side of the bargain. In particular, there was concern that the Anglia electrification scheme had not been approved. This had been with the minister awaiting approval for some time, but had been dragged back into the net along with the main electrification programme to be submitted to criteria of profitability.

In September, Fowler was replaced as transport secretary by David Howell, and the carefully developed political understandings between railways and the government had to be rebuilt with a new minister. Howell met the Rail Council in December. Again the need for synchronization was recognized, but it was clear that each party interpreted the concept differently. The minister claimed that the government had moved significantly, pointing to an increase in the PSO and the EFL. BR and the unions felt that the government had not acknowledged the record of change over a period of time. It had moved, but not at the same pace as the railways, or to the extent that the unions required to maintain the co-operative approach.

In late December, the minister announced his approval for the Anglia electrification scheme, the day after the NUR had signed an agreement on flexible rostering for guards. But by then it was too late. BR and ASLEF were already heading towards a confrontation over footplate rostering. Once the dispute had broken out at the beginning of 1982, the fate of the balance sheet approach was sealed. According to Weighell, 'the goodwill that we had painfully built up with the Transport Minister was thrown away, and Howell told Parker that there was no point in having a further meeting of the Rail Council early in the year, as we had planned, to discuss more Government moves to boost investment' (1983: 86–7).

While Weighell blamed the hardening of the government's attitude on 'the flexible rostering nonsense', it could be argued that the root cause of the breakdown was the failure of the government to respond earlier, which had led to growing union frustrations. As a senior manager confessed,

> Though Fowler made all the right noises, when it came down to brass tacks he did not deliver, and the unions felt let down . . . if the East Coast Main Line electrification programme had been authorised, it would have

been a tremendous fillip for the whole business. It would have put the chairman and the top people in a very good light with the unions, even ASLEF ... The government let us down badly. We delivered and they didn't (fieldnotes).

In short, the uncertainty of the government response merely fuelled the unions' suspicions. The more suspicious they became, the greater the concessions that were required from government to satisfy them, and the more difficult it was for management to win their co-operation. This in turn provided anti-rail groups with a weapon for attacking the idea of a deal with the unions.

The Failure of Tripartite Political Exchange in BR

The failure of political exchange owed little to the rivalry that undoubtedly existed between the NUR and ASLEF (see Weighell 1983). BR's unions had well-established spheres of influence, and ideological divisions were muted. Thus the competitive pressures that had forced the UGT away from a collaborationist strategy towards a more traditional trade union position were almost entirely absent.

Part of the reason for the failure may be found in BR management's reassessment of the costs and benefits of the political strategy. In late 1981, management were fearful that the absence of a government response would lead to union accusations that they were being 'sold down the river', and would put at risk the unions' co-operation on productivity issues.

But a radical change in management perceptions was taking place. The high investment strategy articulated in the March 1981 rail policy document was giving way to a strategy of 'realism' that relied much less on investment and more on increasing efficiency and cost savings to run the railway 'within its means'. For example, while the 1980 corporate plan forecast an increasing workload and manpower for the workshops, within two or three years drastic cuts were being contemplated; and the idea of investing in 'jumbo' cross-channel ferries was quietly dropped. With this change in management thinking, one of the props supporting the idea of a joint approach to the government was removed.

The change in management strategy, however, also reflected BR's awareness of a deeper obstacle to successful political exchange: the underlying hostility of the government to the idea. The corporation realized that the 'high investment card was grossly out of tune with government thinking'. However sympathetic successive ministers of transport were to the railways' position, they had to argue their case in cabinet where they were faced by strong opposition. Powerful groups in the government, including the Prime Minister, reportedly, had a rooted objection to increasing government support for the state-run transport sector. These views were forcefully articulated by figures such as the then head of the Conservative's Centre for Policy Studies, Alfred Sherman, who advocated turning railway lines into express coach ways. Another opponent was Alan Walters, the Prime Minister's economic adviser, who was a relentless critic of BR's ten-year electrification programme. Electrification was a key element in the balance sheet of change. A senior manager described it as 'the touchstone' which 'could have been a very good steadying and guiding light for the trade unions if it had been accepted'. But Walters' intervention forced BR to revise the assumptions of the original joint BR/Department of Transport electrification review (Department of Transport/BR 1981), and to prove the viability of each individual route in the programme. Subsequently, BR was to complain of repeated changes in the criteria that had to be met.

The Treasury, as the driving force behind cuts in public expenditure, also provided sustained opposition to some of BR's plans. It was said by one senior respondent to have blocked Fowler's attempts to secure approval for the Anglia electrification scheme in time for the June 1981 meeting with the Rail Council.

The ability of transport ministers to overcome these obstacles to the balance sheet approach depended on their political weight and clout. But the two ministers concerned were in a relatively weak position. The first was an inexperienced minister in his first government post, while his successor's standing with his cabinet colleagues was far from strong: he was soon to lose government office altogether and return to the back benches. When the major East Coast Main Line electrification programme was eventually approved in the summer of 1984 it was under a 'strong' minister, Nicholas Ridley, who was a leading architect of the government's hard line economic strategy and a confidant of the Prime Minister.

More fundamentally, however, one of the main tenets of the Conservative government's political programme was the need to reduce the interference of unions in matters seen to be the prerogative of management. The government was wary, therefore, of the whole idea of union participation in political bargaining. The view was expressed by one well-placed respondent as follows:

> When Thatcher had come in in 1979, a fundamental article of faith was that the trade unions had had much too big a say at a strategic and management level concerning how investment should be carried out in industry. They spent too little time putting their own house in order, and were too taken up with internecine squabbles, especially as one could see in the case of the NUR and ASLEF. Thus it is totally, totally wrong to say that a deal could have been made. Things were moving away from that sort of deal from 1979 and the view was increasingly that managements should manage and not go to government together with the unions to patch up a deal (fieldnotes).

Under these conditions, the delicate negotiations between the transport minister and his cabinet colleagues could be easily upset by signs of the unions' noncooperation. Episodes such as the ASLEF strikes of early 1982 strengthened anti-rail sentiment in the government and forced the end of the experiment with political bargaining.

> The failure to get a move on the abandonment of restrictive practices [over flexible rostering] reconfirmed government's prejudice that they were dealing with the wrong people and that the trade unions would never deliver. It was a question of management managing. Instead of saying 'we'll give investment here, there and everywhere', the government said 'stop coming to us with the trade unions and say to the trade unions that unless they deliver there will never be any investment in the industry'. And that is still the position (fieldnotes).

The Conservatives were thus breaking decisively with the unwritten assumptions of the traditional relationships between public enterprise actors and the state, effectively excluding the unions from political influence. The government's position was a major cause of the change from a consensual style of industrial relations in BR to a more confrontational one (ch. 7). Management now realised that continuing government support depended on its challenging the existing power of the railway unions, rather than on co-operative strategies for change. To put it another way, the *blocking* of traditional tripartite political exchange was used by the government to transmit its political objectives to BR, and indeed constituted part of the very objective the government was trying to pursue.

Conclusions — The Limits of Political Exchange as a Transmission Mechanism

BR and RENFE provide contrasting cases of the use of tripartite political exchange as a 'transmission mechanism' for government objectives. They illustrate some of the classic dangers for the unions of a 'political' strategy. First, as in RENFE, the benefits may be more abstract, nebulous and long-term than those to be derived from traditional trade union strategies. This, as Pizzorno (1978: 284—5) notes, may make it harder for union members to judge whether a good or a bad bargain has been struck on the political market. Pizzorno warns of the danger of an 'interpretation' gap between union members and the leadership; if it becomes too large, a breakdown of representation may occur. In the case of the UGT, for example, the results of the workforce ballot showed that the membership put a different interpretation on the value of participation in exchange for sacrifices. Compared with the BR unions, the UGT faced the additional hazard of falling behind in the competitive struggle with CCOO to occupy the available union 'space'.

The case of BR points to a rather different problem in political exchange, and one highlighted by Regini (1984): how far can the government guarantee the expected outcome? Governments may lack the capacity to deliver their side of the bargain, as in the cases of 'solidarietà nazionale' in Italy and the British social contract in the 1970s. In the Britain of the 1980s, it seems that the eagerness of BR management and unions to pursue a co-operative strategy led them to overestimate the Conservative government's preparedness to engage in serious political exchange. Whatever the view of successive transport ministers, they were too constrained by more powerful forces in the government to be able to deliver what management and unions hoped for.

Alternatively, there may be a reassessment of the costs and benefits of political exchange when it is already in progress, as the Spanish case suggests. The background of the consensual transition to democracy and the political alliance between the UGT and the Socialists provided the initial conditions for meso-political exchange involving the UGT rail union and the ministry of transport. But conjunctural factors led powerful factions in the government to put a greater weight on rationalization and cost reduction, and less on consensual 'concertation' as a way of implementing modernization policies. In other words, the government found it had less motive for engaging in exchange.

This supports Regini's perception (1984: 131−6) that the conditions for the 'stability' of political exchange differ from its 'emergence' conditions. Stability depends on the way in which the actors' complex strategies interact with each other.

In the cases examined, it could be argued that the potential for instability is increased by the participation of three rather than two actors. For each party has to remain satisfied that the benefits of exchange outweigh the costs. Political exchange brings dangers for management as well as for the unions. In RENFE, the creation of parallel authority structures was seen, eventually, as an intolerable cost of the collaborationist strategy. In both BR and RENFE the changing strategies and perceptions of management would probably have diminished their interest in the joint political strategy irrespective of the position of the government. It may be hypothesized therefore that the greater the number of parties to the exchange, the higher is the instability of the arrangement.

Finally, the case studies demonstrate the variability of the unions' *political* power resources. The *economic* strength of the railway unions has been in chronic decline with the gradual eclipse of the railways as a mode of transport. But their ability to disrupt the social consensus − and hence engage in effective political exchange − responds to a more contingent, relatively short-term, political dynamic. As was argued in chapter 7, the British Conservative government was able to construct a framework of rules and political assumptions that minimized the political consequences of industrial disruption on the railways. This greatly reduced the power of the unions to force political concessions from the government. In Spain by contrast, the more vulnerable social consensus gave the UGT more political weight, at least for a time, even though it was organizationally weak and its economic strength was even more limited than that of the British unions.

Notes

1 Cawson's usage of the idea of meso- and microlevel corporatism differs from this notion in that he reserves the microlevel for relationships between individual firms and the state, rather than between sectoral interest organizations (Cawson 1985b: 12−17).
2 Although the 'Balance Social' (RENFE 1984b) was a formal corporate document, it contained a clear expression of the arguments for the social model. This reflected the strong influence of a small group of UGT activists in middle management positions on the drawing up of the Balance. The episode was a further illustration of the tensions created in the power struggle between the UGT and the formal management hierarchy in RENFE during the period of the collaborationist strategy.
3 Among them was a USO activist in RENFE who was subsequently to become the head of the minister's 'cabinet' of political advisers.

10

Conclusions: Commercialism and Industrial Relations in the Public Enterprise

Introduction

As Palmer (1985: 524) has pointed out, studies of the state have failed to reconcile high flown theoretical concerns with detailed empirical observation. On the one hand, recent Marxist debate on the nature of the advanced capitalist state has sometimes seemed far removed from the observable institutions and events of actual states. On the other hand, detailed empirical studies have tended to be the preserve of scholars and policy-makers working within a descriptive or indeed prescriptive tradition of 'public administration'.

This book has attempted to occupy the middle ground between these two extremes by examining concrete state institutions within a broader framework of analysis. First, it has tried to address the impact of the broad sweep of economic crisis and restructuring on the state enterprise sector. Second, it has considered the empirical ramifications of general theoretical ideas about the nature of the state, notably the practical implications of the idea of relative autonomy of, and within, the state.

The basic question that the book has addressed is, what happens to the industrial relations of public enterprises when economic crisis leads to pressures for 'commercialism'? The argument has been constructed around two themes. First, there are *similarities* in the general processes observed in BR and RENFE that derive from the nature of the state, its response to crisis, and the position of public enterprises within it. Second, there are *differences* in the response in each country that result from variations in the political environment, as well as from institutional industrial relations factors. By way of summarizing some of the main arguments of the book, these two themes are considered in turn.

Commercialism, Industrial Relations and the Logic of Public Enterprise

It has been argued that there are certain features of public enterprises that come about because they operate in the state sphere. These features may be summarized as follows.

State enterprises are subject to some kind of political control, but problems of control abound. These derive from the way in which the state operates. First, public enterprises have claims to autonomy, since the activities they engage in cannot be provided satisfactorily without a degree of managerial discretion. This in turn gives rise to internal managerial interests and agendas that may not co-incide with those of the controllers. The boundary between control and autonomy is blurred and shifting. Second, political objectives for public enter-prises are complex and changing, since they reflect the interplay of social in-terests as they are aggregated and mediated through political institutions. There may be considerable continuity in the basic economic task of the enterprise — providing railway services or whatever — but even here, the detailed definition of the task and the priority given to different aspects of it can be highly variable. And the public enterprises are temptingly available instruments for the pursuit of unrelated political ends. This impedes the setting of clear, stable yardsticks for judging the performance of the enterprises. Third, the state is fragmented into separate agencies with different agendas and their own organizational in-terests; co-ordinating their different demands on state enterprises is problematic, hence the enterprises may receive conflicting signals from different parts of the state. Fourth, control of state enterprises is made difficult by problems of access by the controllers to specialized knowledge and their co-option by the enter-prises they are supposed to supervise. Finally, enterprises have countervailing power resources, since their activities and decisions on prices, pay, employ-ment, investment, closures and so on have major economic and political reper-cussions for other state actors and specifically for governments. They are also able to mobilize politically by forming alliances with other interest groups (in-cluding organized labour) within and outside the state.

These characteristics have evolved within a general dynamic of public enter-prise: economic crisis and the related crisis of public expenditure have created cross-national tendencies towards a redefinition of the role of public enterprises, their relationship to the state, and the boundaries between control and autonomy. A principal manifestation of this has been the rise of public sector 'commer-cialism' although its timing and substance has varied from country to country.

Given these typical patterns, the question arises of how the agendas of politi-cians become translated into the strategies and plans of enterprise management; or in the terms that have been used in this book, how are political objectives *transmitted* to the enterprise?

This becomes particularly pertinent at a time of major change in political objectives, and the emergence of explicit government programmes for greater 'commercialism' in British and Spanish public enterprises. The increasing politi-cal pressures on railway management had potentially far-reaching consequences for industrial relations. Commercialism implies the search for greater efficiency and productivity, for a strategy more oriented to the market and competition, for the increased exercise of managerial autonomy and prerogative. All these aspects of the new political climate had serious implications, whether directly or indirectly, for the conduct of industrial relations. How, therefore, were these *potential* effects translated into actual changes in industrial relations?

First, it was argued that change comes about partly through subtle conditioning of the political environment in which the enterprises operate. Although direct political control of public enterprises is limited by the factors considered above, governments can manipulate the wider political environment to change the relative costs and benefits of particular management strategies. This depends not only on the formal regulatory powers of government, but on the government's political will and ability to mobilize power resources to reshape the 'rules of the game': for example, by the marshalling of political and broader electoral support, the skilful manipulation of ideological symbols to create a climate of opinion, and careful logistical preparation.

A second consequence of the fluid relationship between public enterprise and the state is that change is often negotiated. Since both sides have power resources, and the capacity to inflict costs on or withhold benefits from the other, there is room for mutual accommodation, within limits. Thus the cost for railway management of not implementing reforms in working practices or cuts in numbers was the possible risk of a reduction in ministerial goodwill and enthusiasm in fighting for resources or gaining approval for investment. This pervasive negotiation may affect industrial relations directly, as when the government has industrial relations objectives of its own whose implementation it wishes to negotiate with the enterprise. Political negotiation may also have an indirect impact on industrial relations by way of the changes that it brings about in broader managerial strategy.

Third, negotiation between the enterprise and the state takes on a characteristic form. Exchange takes place on the boundary of two different systems, each with its own distinctive logic of action. The enterprise is concerned, formally at least, with the managerial task of co-ordinating material, financial and human resources in order to produce specific services. The outcome is measurable in terms of volume, financial flows and other indices of managerial performance. Governments, by contrast, are primarily concerned with the task of mobilizing political support and building alliances. In this process, political symbols are important rallying points and condensed expressions of government intention. Therefore the currency of exchange in bargaining between the enterprise and the state is frequently action that has symbolic value; form is often more important than substance. Symbolic encapsulations of 'commercialism' provide governments with the leverage with which to pursue their objectives in the political arena. The case studies have shown that this characteristic form of exchange has a considerable influence on management industrial relations strategy.

Fourth, collective bargaining typically extends beyond the boundaries of the enterprise and of the formal machinery of negotiation. On the one hand, the political authorities have a direct interest in the outcome of bargaining and the power to influence it by direct, if sometimes secretive, interventions. On the other hand, the unions have political as well as industrial power, especially a variable degree of power to cause political embarrassment to the government. Thus the basis exists for tripartite exchanges over industrial relations and other questions. This can affect the internal industrial relations dynamic of the enterprise, not only by its immediate impact on bargaining outcomes, but also, as the case studies showed, by creating pragmatic alliances between management and unions and by changing the pattern of co-operation and competition among unions.

A consequence of these general features of the state-enterprise relationship is that the response of industrial relations to the challenges of 'commercialism' is far from automatic. A number of problems and contradictions arise in the course of translating external pressures into managerial strategies.

First, internal management agendas for change repeatedly collide with the demands of operating in a political environment. Even when an enterprise wholeheartedly embraces the ethos of commercialism, the nature of the political environment continues to frustrate management's efforts to implement commercial strategies. However committed governments may be to commercialism, it is only one of a multitude of objectives. Conflicting priorities and changeable short-term aims provide the motive for continuing interventions, for example on pay bargaining. At the least, this undermines the autonomy of management. At worst, it forces it to adopt policies that conflict with its commercial objectives. Even where the government intervenes to reinforce commercial objectives, it may have the contrary effect by undermining managerial autonomy and confirming the expectation of *ad hoc* and changeable political control.

This reflects a more general problem of commercialism that arises even where government priorities are clear, where political signals point public enterprises unambiguously in the direction of commercialism, and where governments abstain from direct interventions in managerial decisions. Management plans and policies have to conform to commercialism not only as an internal managerial objective, but as a *political objective* of governments. This requires the achievement of politically symbolic commercial objectives. As a result, elements of plans are wrenched out of their context within a managerial logic in order to serve the different logic of political exchange. As the case studies have shown, this can distort management's industrial relations strategy by diverting resources to issues that have a high political 'salience'.

In general, the implementation of commercialism depends on management's ability to *negotiate* its autonomy with the state, to gauge how the commercial remit can best be discharged, and to manoeuvre between competing political pressures. Paradoxically, therefore, political skills continue to be as relevant as professional managerial ones.

A second problem of implementing commercialism is that incompatible industrial relations policies may be generated at different levels of management. Thus broad business strategies have created pressure for industrial relations change on the railways. But these changes were often unplanned, *ad hoc* reactions to immediate problems of business management, rather than strategic responses. There was no necessary correspondence between them and overall industrial relations strategies being developed by corporate specialists.

A more fundamental problem of commercialism revealed by the case studies is that it is by no means clear what pattern of industrial relations is appropriate to it. On the one hand, new business strategy may demand reduced costs, labour cutbacks, and greater flexibility in working practices and in the machinery of industrial relations. This may be reinforced by political demands, as notably in Britain, for a firm management line in the face of union resistance to change. Commercialism could therefore imply an industrial relations strategy of change through confrontation. On the other hand, new business strategies of appealing to the customer, seeking new markets, and so on, may require a greater attention to customer needs and hence a high level of employee commitment. This may be undermined by labour strategies that weaken the consent and co-operation of the workforce and unions. In public service industries such as railways, with a 'perishable' commodity, the achievement of commercial business targets requires stable working uninterrupted by disputes. One possible outcome of such dilemmas is an oscillation in management industrial relations strategy between hardline confrontation and renewed co-operation with the unions. This pattern was visible in the case studies; for example in BR's willingness, even during a period of 'robust' industrial relations, to extend the consultative machinery, to run experimental services and to reassure the unions over further line closures.

Thus, it is argued, the comparison of state enterprises in two different 'polities' has enabled certain general conclusions to be drawn. The adaptation of industrial relations to the pressures of commercialism occurs in ways that result, not from the peculiarities of the British or Spanish public sector, but from the nature of public enterprise, its relationship to the state and the dynamics of its development in response to the crisis in state functions and finances. The logic of this line of argument is that similar processes will be observable in other capitalist democracies with different political institutions and different forms of state enterprise: ultimately they derive from the dilemmas of political control versus public enterprise autonomy, the continuing complexity and variability of political objectives even in the face of the crisis of public expenditure, and the characteristic form of political interactions that these give rise to.

Sources of Variability in the Response of Industrial Relations to the Pressures of Commercialism

The book has also tried to illuminate public enterprise industrial relations under 'commercialism' by exploring the *differences* in response in the same industry in two different countries. These variations were linked to differences in the political environment facing the railways in Britain and Spain. In addition, the independent impact of industrial relations institutions themselves was examined, although the emphasis was on the way in which these were influenced by the broader political variables. Some general conclusions may be drawn from the findings about the sources of variation in public enterprise industrial relations. But first the main differences in response between BR and RENFE are summarized.

Responses to 'Commercialism' in BR and RENFE: A Summary

In both Britain and Spain, the underlying economic crisis and the preoccupation with state expenditure brought forth political programmes for reforming and controlling the public sector. The efficiency and performance of public enterprises and their demands on the public purse moved to the forefront of political debate. But the strategies adopted were different.

The 'Thatcherite' Conservatives' prescription for state enterprises not only tightened existing financial controls but questioned the very assumptions on which the state productive sector had grown up. Like Thatcherite ideas more generally, it was a radical reaction to much of the commonly held ground of post-war British politics. The 'Butskellite' consensus had viewed the state's intervention in economic life as both necessary and benign, whereas the post-1979 Conservatives saw it as a harmful distortion of the market, the source of inefficiency and complacency. The ultimate aim, therefore, was not so much to reform the practices of the public enterprise sector as to reduce it to a minimum; hence the massive commitment to privatization. The Thatcherite strategy also questioned another of the tenets of Butskellism: the view of the unions as legitimate actors, whose collaboration was necessary for the preservation of social consensus. Conservative governments, especially during the 1950s and 1960s, had been concerned not to be seen as the party of industrial strife and division, and their labour policies had often been conciliatory. In the railways, management's strategy of avoiding confrontation and taking the unions along with change had meshed well with this prevailing political context. The post-1979 Conservatives aimed to reduce radically the industrial power of trade unions, not least through legislation on strikes, picketing, ballots, the closed shop and so on. They also cut the unions off from political power, downgrading tripartite bodies, refusing to act as in the past to defuse major industrial disputes. The public sector was seen as the main breeding ground for the unions' restrictive practices, since it was not exposed to the bracing effect of private sector competition. The public sector unions also exercised 'power without responsibility'; in the words of one Conservative minister, they were 'all too ready to seek to involve the Government in the interests of their political objectives if not in the interests of the members'. Privatization was seen as the way to 'break the political link' (Moore 1986: 89).

In Spain, post-Franco governments were preoccupied with the politics of the transition to democracy. The accommodations that were made exacerbated the emerging crisis of state expenditure. When the PSOE came to power in 1982, it had to work within and preserve the prevailing consensus, rather than challenge it in the way the Thatcherite Conservatives were doing. Indeed, its alliance with the socialist section of the labour movement was — to begin with at least — one of its main bases of support. Rather than weaken the unions as in Britain, government policy was directed to strengthening their institutional position and rebuilding a framework of democratic industrial relations. The PSOE's strategy was one of modernization, rationalization and control of public expenditure, tempered with a concern for social justice — Thatcherism with a human face, perhaps. The public enterprise sector was not seen as an affront to market values. Its problems of efficiency and the use of resources were viewed pragmatically. Privatization was not considered to be a general prescription but a practical solution in specific cases. (On the other hand, further nationalization was not a cornerstone of government policy.)

Divergent government strategies for the public sector were reflected in different approaches to the railway problem. In Britain, the Conservatives, motivated by a firm belief in the superiority of private transport, severely squeezed financial support for BR and strengthened market pressures by encouraging road competition. The government's uncompromising attitude towards the unions both permitted and encouraged management to seek industrial relations change through confrontation − at first reluctantly, later under a chairman appointed by the Conservatives and more in tune with their approach, with greater conviction.

By contrast, the PSOE was more pragmatic and technocratic. The railways were a fearful and rapidly worsening drain on public resources. The government's strategy aimed in the first place to staunch the flow. New formal mechanisms of control were introduced, notably the programme contract, to put state support on a sounder and more regular footing. The social role of the railways was more narrowly defined, and this led to a reallocation of resources away from little-used rural parts of the network and towards more commercially viable services. But there was little political animus against the railways as a mode of transport. Indeed, after the initial period of financial 'cleansing', the government looked favourably on a large programme of new investments.

In both railways, management responded to the new environment by developing new industrial relations policies that aimed to cut costs, increase flexibility, change working practices. The differences in approach between BR and RENFE largely reflected differences in the respective political contexts (although they also related to the technical characteristics of the two networks). Both companies concentrated on a number of core issues, some of which came to play a symbolic political role in demonstrating to the political authorities that new policies were being pursued. In BR, the controversial questions concerned working practices and the collective agreements that sustained them. The process of reaching agreement through the machinery also came under scrutiny. Cost cutting through continued reductions in the labour force was readily available from other sources, but the political focus was on the unwarranted power of the unions − their 'restrictive practices' and their ability to slow down the pace of change. In RENFE, management emphasized reductions in the labour force, since this was one of the main ways of achieving the government's principal aim, a rapid cut in the deficit. But much attention was also paid to 'acquired rights' and 'privileges', with their echoes of an older paternalistic, authoritarian industrial relations system. There was also a political desire that RENFE workers should be seen to be making some sacrifices, at a time when other sectors were bearing the brunt of the government's strategy of restructuring; compared with steel or shipbuilding, for example, the railways' 'readjustment' was relatively painless. As for much of the transition period, RENFE's prominent position as one of the largest employers in Spain gave it a symbolic role as an example, 'good' or 'bad', for others to follow.

The way in which government objectives were 'transmitted' to the railways varied in two main ways between Britain and Spain. First, the different forms and traditions of state bureaucracy, coupled perhaps with varying relationships between state and civil society, led to different patterns of state enterprise management: the 'professionalization' of management in the British public corporation, compared with 'politicization' in Spain. In turn, this has affected the degree of management autonomy and the development of internal agendas in response to commercialism. In BR, a change in the political climate triggered a managerial reassessment of policies, opening up some avenues of action while closing off others. But political transactions largely took place at the boundary between the board and the government. In RENFE, by contrast, the organization was permeated by political considerations. In a highly politicized public enterprise culture, managers with strong political links were in a better position than 'apolitical' professionals to force through commercial policies within RENFE. Card-carrying PSOE members came to occupy managerial posts below board level, as well as the chairmanship.

Second, the form of the adjustment process on the railways was influenced by the differing role of the unions in political bargaining between the enterprise and the government. The PSOE's rationalization policies were affected by its dependence on the support of the UGT. This enabled the Spanish railway unions to negotiate a relatively mild adjustment process in RENFE. In this they may be compared with their ostensibly far stronger British counterparts, whose organizational strength, membership density, experience of collective bargaining and tradition of political action were all superior. Yet it was the Spanish unions who were able to exploit the political circumstances to bargain with the government across the boundaries of the enterprise. British Rail's unions found their political power greatly reduced by the ability of the Conservative government to alter the rules of the game. In these circumstances, political exchange involving the unions was unlikely to prosper, and an 'exclusionary' strategy became possible, even necessary, for railway management.

The changes in BR appear to have started earlier and gone farther than those in RENFE. The drastic reductions in PSO support provided a particularly strong incentive for management to push through change in working practices and cut employment. This was coupled with the impetus to change (albeit somewhat ambiguous) provided by business sector management. In RENFE, the most notable change was the large cut in the size of the workforce. This was all the more striking when compared with the preceding years of relatively stable employment levels. But job losses were achieved with little conflict, largely because they did not require compulsory redundancies (unlike the massive job losses in BREL, for example). In other areas, change in RENFE was slow. The constraints of the political context made it difficult for management to adopt a confrontational approach to issues such as working practices. This gave the unions greater scope for resisting change, especially since the pressures for change from business sector management had yet to be felt in RENFE. The balance sheet of change in response to the pressures of commercialism was still, therefore, provisional; as indeed it was in BR, where many important issues, such as pay and occupational structure, and the machinery of negotiation were still pending.

Industrial Relations and the Political Environment: The General Causes of Variability

The study has explored different 'layers' of variation in the political environment with different identifiable effects — direct or indirect — on industrial relations. At the most general level lie long-term historical features of the political system that leave a persistent and only slowly evolving legacy of organization, practice and authority structures; what Zysman (1977: 177) calls 'the residue of the political struggles that create the state'. Broad historical differences may work their influence by means of mediating variables, such as the nature of the government bureaucracy. As political scientists (e.g. Richardson 1982; Scase 1980; Zysman 1977) have suggested, there is considerable variation in bureaucratic policy-making patterns in different countries. The British style of generalist civil servants with 'strong leanings towards consultation' and a reluctance 'to develop an *authority* relationship with outside groups and agencies' (Dudley and Richardson, 1987: 171) might be compared with the more authoritative style of, say, France; or with the clientelistic Italian state in 'symbiotic' relationship with political parties. The detailed analysis of the impact of these differences on state-enterprise relations would provide a fruitful area of comparative study.

Another mediating variable is the degree of fragmentation of the political system which, as was argued in chapter 3, affects the extent of managerial autonomy and bargaining power. While fragmentation is a general feature of states for reasons discussed in earlier chapters, its degree varies according to underlying features of the political system. Even in quite similar states with long-standing and continuous democratic traditions, historical variations in formal institutional arrangements, such as the separation of powers between legislative and executive arms of the state, may exert a continuing influence on policy options and outcomes.

Not all such sources of variation are, of course, present in comparisons between Britain and Spain. But other studies suggest their relevance for the sort of analysis presented here. Weaver (1985), for example, has linked the differing patterns of fragmentation in the 'command structure' of nationalized railway companies in Canada and the United States to the differences between the Canadian executive-dominated parliamentary system and the constitutional separation of powers in the United States. Weaver shows how these distinctions affect patterns of negotiation between state and enterprise, and hence the outcomes of policy-making. The United States system makes for complicated bargaining between, on the one hand, the railway companies and, on the other, different parts of the executive and Congress, in order to construct coalitions for particular courses of action. One example with direct industrial relations consequences concerns political exchange over reductions in the workforce in the passenger rail company Amtrak. Organized labour was one of Amtrak's political supporters in the battles between Congress and the administration over plans for cutbacks in the rail network. The company was therefore reluctant to offend labour and only likely to cut the workforce when forced to do so by 'strong countervailing political force' (1985: 253).

A further example of the consequences of fragmentation of political power and authority is provided in the study by Seglow *et al.* (1982: 91−2) of German and British rail unions. They suggest that the rationalization of the German rail network was impeded by the power and autonomy of the *Länder* (regional governments) which benefited from but did not pay for the railway. This provided the main railway union, the GdED, with the opportunity to mobilize and co-ordinate political opposition to cutbacks through its full-time officials who were members of the *Länder* and of the federal Bundestag.

A second 'layer' of explanation looks to more 'conjunctural' shorter- and medium-term variations in political systems. Time periods measured in decades or years rather than centuries show their own political character. The post-war consensus in Britain may be compared with the Francoist period or the 'transition to democracy' in Spain. The initial pattern of industrial relations and its subsequent development in the nationalized industries of both countries was conditioned by such medium-term variables − consensual 'Butskellite' political strategies in Britain, compared with the repressive control and subordination of labour under Francoism in Spain. Underlying these patterns are political alliances and bases of support that show a degree of stability.

These time periods may be in turn subdivided into short-term or conjunctural political variations caused by changes of government, and with them changes of political alliances, ideology and programme. This affects the forms of control, government objectives and patterns of political intervention in public enterprises. The fact that political programmes for dealing with the public sector have been brought to fruition under governments of very different ideology and bases of support in Britain and Spain, has greatly influenced the limits and possibilities of industrial relations change. The case studies have shown, for example, how the power of public enterprise unions is a function of the political skills, will, priorities and ideology of the government; a relational rather than an absolute quality. (It is possible that political exchange will be more sustained and successful in polities with a longer-standing tradition of 'macro-political' exchange between peak organizations and the state, and where therefore the possibilities of exchange do not vary so much with changes in the political conjuncture.)

A corollary of the importance of conjunctural political factors is that some of the changes that have occurred in the past five or six years were, up to a point, contingent rather than inevitable. The political system was faced with different strategic *options* for restructuring the railways. If a Labour government had been in power in Britain, for example, the possibilities of political exchange with the unions might have led to a different pattern of rationalization and investment.

The division between short- and medium-term variations is of course somewhat blurred. The phenomenon that is increasingly known as 'Thatcherism', not least by its adherents, appears to mark not only a contingent short-term variation within the patterns of post-war British politics, but the beginning of a new phase in which the assumptions of future governments of whatever colour are likely to be conditioned by the Thatcherite agenda. The accepted consensus on matters such as the role of public enterprise, and of unions within them, has been fundamentally challenged, and some of the possible alternative political projects that seemed viable at the end of the 1970s have been closed off for the foreseeable future. On this view, it can be argued that Britain, like Spain, has (in some respects) provided its own internal comparison between different medium-term political phases.

As with longer-term political factors, the political developments of the medium or short term also leave a concrete residue in the form of new institutional arrangements, some of which continue to exert an independent influence of their own even after the conjuncture that gave rise to them has passed. An example would be the formal mechanisms of control of public enterprises. The change in the status of, say, the British Post Office from government department to public corporation, or the recent introduction of a new status for Italian state railways granting them a much higher degree of autonomy from central government, resulted from short-term political decisions; but they could be expected to affect the subsequent relationship of the enterprise to its political controllers and hence patterns of negotiation and 'transmission'. For example, one could hypothesize that the more closely an enterprise is integrated into the central state apparatus, the less the possibilities for management to develop an internal agenda for implementing commercialism (cf. Weaver 1985: ch. 6).

The case studies have suggested that, in addition to external political factors, the pattern of industrial relations within the enterprise is a significant explanatory variable. The possibilities for tripartite political exchange are affected by the relationships between the unions in the enterprise. Inter-union competition can make it risky for a union to engage in political exchange, even where external political circumstances are relatively favourable, as they were in Spain in 1984. This suggests a general hypothesis about the conditions for political exchange: other things being equal, political exchange is more likely to occur the less the internal competition between unions within the state enterprise.

Union competition may be seen as a function of institutional industrial relations variables, such as the overall density of union membership and the degree to which one union can monopolize the representation of the workforce, or sections of it, in an enterprise. The work of Streeck, Seglow and Wallace (Streeck *et al.* 1981; Seglow *et al.* 1982), which compared railway unions in Britain and West Germany, relates the 'monopoly of interest representation' to institutional factors such as the extent of union control over job structures and the workings of the co-determination machinery.

Institutional industrial relations factors are also important in explaining patterns of union resistance and accommodation to commercialism and rationalization. For example, in the West German railways (DB), changes in working practices are not a contentious issue, compared with BR and to a lesser extent RENFE. The concept of the 'line of promotion' does not exist, so that the maintenance of existing working practices is not so important for the defence of sectional occupational interests as in BR. The DB's system of movement between grades, based on the widespread availability of retraining, allows for a much more fluid occupational structure. Another example of the mediating effect of institutions is the influence of the formal collective bargaining machinery. In the case of BR and RENFE, management considered the machinery of negotiation to be part of the problem. Yet even where management was in a strong position, changes were not simply imposed, but were still negotiated through existing channels. This affected the scope and pace of change, and encouraged proposals, in BR at least, for reform of the machinery itself.

The book has tried to go beyond an institutional industrial relations explanation of differences by considering the interrelationship of industrial relations and political variables. Thus railway industrial relations systems may be partially analysed as another 'residue', as 'crystallized' forms of political alliances and power balances. For example, the prevalence of extensive negotiation and consultation machinery in British nationalized industries was related to the influence of labour movement aspirations; in Spain, the construction of democratic industrial relations machinery similarly reflected the political forces in operation during the transition to democracy. Moreover, external political forces continue to interact with internal industrial relations institutions. For example, the power struggles between the UGT and CCOO in RENFE were related to wider struggles and political alliances in the post-Franco political system.

We therefore return to the observations of chapter 1. The institutional analysis of public enterprise industrial relations, while it provides useful descriptive accounts, cannot adequately analyse the dynamic of industrial relations development. The nature of changes in public enterprise industrial relations can only be understood in terms of the logic of action of the public enterprise and its changing relationship to the complex political environment in which it operates. It is hoped that the comparative approach to this central theme has allowed both the general processes and the sources of variation to be fruitfully examined.

Bibliography

Aaronovitch, S. and Smith, R. with Gardiner, J. and Moore, R. (eds) 1981: *The Political Economy of British Capitalism. A Marxist Analysis*. London: McGraw-Hill.

Aharoni, Y. 1981a: Performance evaluation and state-owned enterprise: a process perspective. *Management Science*, 27, 1340–7.

Aharoni, Y. 1981b: Managerial discretion. In R. Vernon and Y. Aharoni (eds) 1981, *The State-Owned Enterprise in the Western Economies*. London: St Martins Press, 184–93.

Allen, D. and Williams, G. 1985: The development of management information to meet the needs of a new management structure for British Rail. In K.J. Button and D.E. Pitfield (eds), *International Railway Economics. Studies in management and efficiency*. Aldershot: Gower.

Almendros Morcillo, F., Jiménez-Asenjo, E., Pérez Amorós, F., Rojo Torrecilla, E. 1978: *El Sindicalismo de Clase en España (1939–1977)*. Barcelona: Península.

Amsden, J. 1972: *Collective Bargaining and Class Conflict in Spain*. London: Weidenfeld and Nicolson.

Anastassopoulos, J.-P. 1981: The French experience: conflicts with government. In R. Vernon and Y. Aharoni (eds) 1981, 99–116.

Anderson, I. 1976: British Rail: the machinery of negotiation and the resolution of minor issues in the Eastern Region. Typescript. Coventry: University of Warwick Industrial Relations Research Unit.

Ariño, G. 1985: La empresa pública: mito y realidad. *Economía Industrial*, 241, 49–60.

Armstrong, P., Glyn, A. and Harrison, J. 1984: *Capitalism since World War II. The making and breakup of the great boom*. London: Fontana.

Bacon, R. and Eltis, W. 1976: *Britain's Economic Problem: Too few producers*. London: Macmillan.

Badie, B. and Birnbaum, P. 1983: *The Sociology of the State*. Tr. Arthur Goldhammer. Chicago/London: University of Chicago Press.

Bagwell, P. 1963: *The Railwaymen*. London: Allen & Unwin.

Bagwell, P. 1982: *The Railwaymen*. Vol II. *The Beeching Era and After*. London: Allen & Unwin.

Bagwell, P. 1984: *End of the Line? The fate of British Railways under Thatcher*. London: Verso.

Bain, G.S. and Price, B. 1983: *Profiles of Union Growth. A comparative statistical portrait of eight countries*. Oxford: Blackwell.

Balfour, S. 1984: The origins of Comisiones Obreras. *Spanish Studies*.

Barker, A. (ed.) 1982: *Quangos in Britain: government and the networks of public policy-making*: London: Macmillan.

Barker, T. and Savage, C. 1974: *An Economic History of Transport in Britain*: London: Hutchinson.

Batstone, E., Ferner, A. and Terry, M. 1983: *Unions on the Board. An experiment in industrial democracy*. Oxford: Blackwell.

Batstone, E., Ferner, A. and Terry, M. 1984: *Consent and Efficiency. Labour relations and management strategy in the state enterprise*. Oxford: Blackwell.

Bean, R. 1985: *Comparative Industrial Relations. An introduction to cross-national perspectives*. London/Sydney: Croom Helm.

Beaumont, P. and Leopold, J. 1982: Public sector industrial relations in Britain: an overview. *Public Administration Bulletin*, no. 40, December 2−18.

Beesley, M. and Evans, T. 1981: The British experience: the case of British Rail. In R. Vernon and Y. Aharoni (eds) 1981, 117−32.

Bell, J. 1975: The development of industrial relations in nationalized industries in postwar Britain. *British Journal of Industrial Relations*, 13, 1, 1−13.

Beltrán, M. 1977: *La Élite Burocrática Española*. Madrid: Juan March/Ariel.

BIRF [Banco Internacional de Reconstrucción y Fomento]/RENFE 1971: *Convenio* between BIRF and RENFE, 30 June 1971.

Block, F. 1980: Beyond relative autonomy: state managers as historical subjects. *Socialist Register*, 227−42.

Boada, C. 1985: La empresa pública: reflexiones desde mi experiencia personal. *Economía Industrial*, 241, 89−101.

Bolúfer, R. 1985: Control sobre organismos y sociedades estatales: presente y futuro. *Economía Industrial*, 241, 121−6.

Bouley, J. 1985: The customer must be king. *Railway Gazette International*, May, 336−7.

BRB, various years: *Report and Accounts*.

BRB, 1963: *Reshaping the Railways*. (The Beeching Report). London: BRB.

BRB 1968a: Ministerial control of the nationalised industries. Memorandum submitted to SCNI 1968, 156−90.

BRB 1976: *Transport Policy: An Opportunity for Change. Comments by British Railways Board on the Government Consultation Document*. London: BRB.

BRB 1979: *The Challenge of the 80's*. Mimeo. London.

BRB 1982: *Productivity Performance. An analysis by the British Railways Board of its productivity performance since 1977*. London: BRB.

BRB/Leeds 1980: *A Comparative Study of European Rail Performance*. BRB/Leeds University Institute for Transport Studies.

Brittan, S. 1976: The economic contradictions of democracy. In A. King (ed.), *Why is Britain Becoming Harder to Govern?* London: BBC Publications.

Bryer, R., Brignall, T., Maunders, A. 1982: *Accounting for British Steel*. London: Gower.

BTC (British Transport Commission) 1955: *Modernisation and Re-equipment of British Railways*. London: BTC.

Bulnes, R. 1967: Realidad y perspectivas de la lucha sindical en la RENFE. *Cuadernos de Ruedo Ibérico*, 11, 83−91.

Burawoy, M. 1979: *Manufacturing Consent: Changes in the Labor Process under Monopoly Capitalism*. Chicago: University of Chicago Press.

Burawoy, M. 1985: *The Politics of Production*. London: Verso.

Burgi, N. 1985: Neo-corporatist strategies in the British energy sector. In A. Cawson (ed.) 1985a, *Organized Interests and the State. Studies in meso-corporatism*. London: Sage, 125−44.

Burrage, M. 1973: Nationalization and the professional ideal. *Sociology*, 7, 2, 254−71.
Butler, R. 1982: *The Art of Memory. Friends in perspective*. London: Hodder & Stoughton.
Button, K. and Pitfield, D. (eds) 1985: *International Railway Economics. Studies in management and efficiency*. Aldershot: Gower.
Cacicedo, J. 1984: Intrigas ferroviarias: la lucha por el poder en Renfe. *El Nuevo Lunes*, 4−10 June 1984, 12.
Cameron 1955: *Interim Report of a Court of Inquiry into a Dispute between the British Transport Commission and the National Union of Railwaymen*. Cmd. 9352. London: HMSO.
Cameron, D. 1984: Social democracy, corporatism, labour quiescence, and the representation of economic interest in advanced capitalist society. In J. Goldthorpe (ed.) 1984a, *Order and Conflict in Contemporary Capitalism: Studies in the political economy of western European nations*. Oxford: Clarendon, 143−78.
Carr, R. 1982: *Spain. 1808−1975*. 2nd edn. Oxford: Clarendon.
Carr, R. and Fusi, J.-P. 1981: *Spain. Dictatorship to Democracy*. 2nd edn. London: Allen & Unwin.
Cassese, S. 1981: Public control and corporate efficiency. in R. Vernon and Y. Aharoni (eds) 1981, 145−56.
Castillo, J.-J. 1975: Los sindicatos católicos de ferroviarios y mineros de España, 1913−1920. *Revista de Trabajo*, 25, 191−288.
Cawson, A. (ed.) 1985a: *Organized Interests and the State. Studies in meso-corporatism*. London: Sage.
Cawson, A. 1985b: Varieties of corporatism: the importance of the meso-level of interest intermediation. In A. Cawson (ed.) 1985a, 1−21.
CEFE (Comisión para el Estudio de los Ferrocarriles Españoles) 1983: *Informe sobre el Avance Previo a los dos Meses de su Constitución*. Madrid, mimeo.
CEFE 1984: *Informe de la Comisión para el Estudio de los Ferrocarriles Españoles*. Madrid: Ministerio de Transportes, Turismo y Comunicaciones.
Central Statistical Office: *UK National Accounts*. London: HMSO.
Chambers, D. 1984: Corporate plans as commitments. In V. Ramanadham (ed.) 1984, *Public Enterprises and the Developing World*. London: Croom Helm, 119−38.
Chester, D. 1975: *The Nationalisation of British Industry 1945−51*. London: HMSO.
Clegg, H. 1951: *Industrial Democracy and Nationalization*. Oxford: Blackwell.
Clegg, H. 1976: *Trade Unionism under Collective Bargaining. A theory based on comparisons of six countries*. Oxford: Blackwell.
Clegg, H. 1979: *The Changing System of Industrial Relations in Great Britain*. Oxford: Blackwell.
Comisión de Presupuestos 1983: *Diario de Sesiones del Congreso de los Diputados*, 28 May 1983, no. 35 (appearance of Chairman of RENFE before the committee).
Comisión de Industria, Obras Públicas y Servicios de las Cortes 1983: *Diario de Sesiones del Congreso de los Diputados*, 19 October 1983, no. 72 (appearance of Chairman of RENFE before the committee).
Cordero, G. 1985: La empresa pública en los sectores en crisis. *Economía Industrial*, 241, 65−72.
Croissier, L. 1985: INI: estrategia para recuperar la rentabilidad. *Economía Industrial*, 241, 23−32.
Curwen, P. 1986: *Public Enterprise. A modern approach*. Brighton: Wheatsheaf.
Delion, A. and Durupty, M. 1982: *Les Nationalisations*. Paris: Economica.
Department of Transport 1977: *Transport Policy*. Cmnd. 6836. London: HMSO.

Department of Transport/BRB 1981: *Review of Mainline Electrification. Final Report.* London: HMSO.

Derber, M. 1976: Strategic factors in industrial relations systems: the metal-working industry. *Labour and Society*, 1, 1, 18–28.

Donges, J. 1984: La insuficiencia de productividad en la economía española. Causas y remedios. In J. Linz (ed.) *España: un presente para el futuro.* Madrid: Tablero.

Donolo, C. 1980: Social change and transformation of the state in Italy. In R. Scase (ed.), *The State in Western Europe*, London: Croom Helm, 164–96.

Donovan 1968: Royal Commission on Trade Unions and Employers' Associations 1965–68. *Report.* Cmnd. 3623. London: HMSO.

Dore, R. 1973: *British Factory Japanese Factory: the origins of national diversity in industrial relations.* Berkeley: University of California Press.

Dubois, P. 1975: *Mort de l'Etat Patron.* Paris: Editions Ouvrières.

Dudley, G. and Richardson, J. 1984: The political framework. In J. Grieve Smith (ed.) 1984, *Strategic Planning in Nationalised Industries.* London: Macmillan, 112–34.

Dudley, G. and Richardson, J. 1987: *British Politics and the Policy Process.* London: Allen & Unwin.

Dunleavy, P. 1982: Quasi-governmental sector professionalism: some implications for public policy-making in Britain. In A. Barker (ed.) 1982, *Quangos in Britain: government and the networks of public policy-making.* London: Macmillan, 181–205.

Dunlop, J. 1958: *Industrial Relations Systems.* Carbondale and Edwardsville: Southern Illinois University Press.

Durupty, M. 1986a: *Les Entreprises Publiques. 1 – Rôle économique – Cadre juridique.* Paris: Presses Universitaires de France.

Durupty, M. 1986b: *Les Entreprises Publiques. 2 – Gestion – Contrôle.* Paris: Presses Universitaires de France.

Dyson, K. 1980: *The State Tradition in Western Europe.* Oxford: Martin Robertson.

Eaton, J. and Gill, C. 1981: *The Trade Union Directory.* London: Pluto.

Edelman, M. 1971: *Politics as Symbolic Action. Mass arousal and quiescence.* Chicago: Markham.

Edelman, M. 1976: *The Symbolic Uses of Politics.* Urbana: Illinois University Press.

Edwards, C. and Lloyd, P. 1981: Formal procedure and bargaining power. An examination of workplace industrial relations in the railway industry. Typescript, North East London Polytechnic.

Edwards, P. 1986: *Conflict at Work. A materialist analysis of workplace relations.* Oxford: Blackwell.

Edwards, R. 1967: *Nationalized Industries: A Commentary.* Stamp Memorial Lecture. London: The Electricity Council.

Eisenhammer, J. 1985: The politics of the state steel industry: the art of muddling through. In L. Quartermaine and J. Pollard (eds), *Italy Today. Patterns of Life and Politics*, 35–58. Exeter: University of Exeter.

Elbaum, B. and Wilkinson, F. 1979: Industrial relations and uneven development: A comparative study of the American and British steel industries. *Cambridge Journal of Economics*, 3, 3, 275–304.

Encinas, E. 1986: *Trabajadores y Sindicatos en el Proceso de Ajuste del Sector Público – RENFE 1983–1985.* Memoria de Licenciatura, Universidad Complutense de Madrid, Facultad de Ciencias Políticas y Sociología, mimeo.

Esping-Andersen, G. and Korpi, W. 1984: Social policy as class politics in post-war capitalism: Scandinavia, Austria and Germany. In J. Goldthorpe (ed.) 1984a, 179–208.

Feigenbaum, H. 1982: Public enterprise in comparative perspective. *Comparative Politics*, 15, 1, 101–22.

Feigenbaum, H. 1985: *The Politics of Public Enterprise. Oil and the French State*. Princeton: Princeton University Press.

Fernández Rodríguez, T. 1970: La organización y el control del sector público en España. In E. Verdera y Tuells (ed.), *La Empresa Pública*. Real Colegio de España en Bolonia, 935–68.

Ferner, A. 1983: The industrialists and the Peruvian development model. In D. Booth and B. Sorj (eds), *Military Reformism and Social Classes. The Peruvian experience, 1968–80*. London: Macmillan, 40–71.

Ferner, A. 1985: Political constraints and management strategies: the case of working practices in British Rail. *British Journal of Industrial Relations*, 23, 1, 47–70.

Ferner, A. 1986: Relaciones laborales y dinámica sindical en los ferrocarriles españoles y británicos. *Boletín de Documentación* de la Fundación de los Ferrocarriles Españoles, nos. 3–4, 23–59.

Ferner, A. 1987a: Industrial relations and the meso-politics of the public enterprise: the transmission of state objectives in the Spanish National Railways. *British Journal of Industrial Relations*, 25, 1, 49–75.

Ferner, A. 1987b: Public enterprise and the politics of 'commercialism': changing industrial relations in British and Spanish railways. *Work, Employment & Society*, 1, 2, 179–203.

Ferner, A. 1987c: Industrial relations in a changing political environment: collective bargaining and dispute resolution in British Rail. In T. Hanami and R. Blanpain (eds), *Industrial Conflict Resolution in Market Economies. A Study of Canada, Great Britain and Sweden*, Deventer: Kluwer, 117–41.

Ferner A. and Fina, Ll. 1988: La dinámica salarial durante el Franquismo. El caso de RENFE. *Revista de Historia Económica*, vol. 6, no. 1 (forthcoming).

Ferner, A. and Terry, M. 1985: 'The crunch had come': a case study of changing industrial relations in the Post Office. University of Warwick Industrial Relations Research Unit: Warwick Papers in Industrial Relations, no. 1. Coventry: University of Warwick.

Fina, Ll. and Hawkesworth, R. 1984: Trade unions and collective bargaining in post-Franco Spain. *Labour and Society*, 9, 1, 3–27.

Fine, B. and O'Donnell, C. 1981: The nationalised industries. In D. Currie and R. Smith (eds), *Socialist Economic Review*, London: Merlin, 265–86.

Fishman, R. 1982: The labour movement in Spain: from authoritarianism to democracy. *Comparative Politics*, 14, 3, 281–305.

Fontgalland, B. de 1984: *The World Railway System*. Cambridge: Cambridge University Press.

Foster, C. 1971: *Politics, Finance and the Role of Economics. An essay on the control of public enterprise*. London: Allen & Unwin.

Frankel, B. 1979: On the state of the state. Marxist theories of the state after Leninism. *Theory and Society*, 7, 199–242.

Gallie, D. 1978: *In Search of the New Working Class. Automation and social integration within the capitalist enterprise*. Cambridge: Cambridge University Press.

Gamble, A. 1981: *Britain in Decline. Economic policy, political strategy and the British state*. London and Basingstoke: Macmillan.

Gamble, A. and Walkland, S. 1984: *The British Party System and Economic Policy 1945–1983. Studies in adversary politics*. Oxford: Oxford University Press.

García de Blas, A. 1985: La negociación colectiva en España: situación y perspectivas. *Papeles de Economía Española*, 22, 329–42.

García Fernández, J. 1985: El control de la empresa pública. *Economía Industrial*, 241, 129−47.

Gimeno, J.-A. 1984: Las causas del déficit público. *Hacienda Pública Española*, 88, 85−105.

Giner, S. 1985: Political economy, legitimation and the state in Southern Europe. In R. Hudson and J. Lewis (eds), *Uneven Development in Southern Europe. Studies of accumulation, class, migration and the state*. London and New York: Methuen, 309−50.

Goldthorpe, J. (ed.) 1984a: *Order and Conflict in Contemporary Capitalism: studies in the political economy of Western European nations*. Oxford: Clarendon.

Goldthorpe, J. 1984b: Introduction. In J. Goldthorpe (ed.), 1984a, 1−14.

Gordon, A. 1984: *Redundancy in the 1980's. The take-up of voluntary redundancy schemes*. Aldershot: Gower/IMS.

Gough, I. 1979: *The Political Economy of the Welfare State*. London: Macmillan.

Gourvish, T. 1986: *British Railways 1948−73. A business history*. Cambridge: Cambridge University Press.

Graham, R. 1985: *España: Anatomía de una democracia*. Barcelona: Plaza & Janes.

Grant, W. (with Sargent, J.) 1987: *Business and Politics in Britain*. Basingstoke: Macmillan.

Grassini, F. 1981: The Italian enterprises: the political constraints. In R. Vernon and Y. Aharoni (eds) 1981, 70−84.

Grieve Smith, J. 1981: Strategy − the key to planning in the public corporation. *Long Range Planning*, 14, 6, 24−31.

Grieve Smith, J. (ed.) 1984a: *Strategic Planning in Nationalised Industries*. London: Macmillan.

Grieve Smith, J. 1984b: Strategic planning in nationalised industries. In J. Grieve Smith (ed.) 1984a, 49−64.

Guitart, J.-A. 1981: Renfe acts to turn the tide. *Railway Gazette International*, April, 275−9.

Hannah, L. 1982: *Engineers, Managers and Politicians*. London: Macmillan.

Harris, D. and Davies, B. 1979: Planning procedures in nationalized industry: their evolution in the last thirty years. *British Review of Economic Issues*, 2, 1, 42−60.

Harris, D. and Davies, B. 1981: Corporate planning as a control system in the UK nationalised industries. *Long Range Planning*, 14, 1, 15−22.

Harris, J. and Williams, G. 1980: *Corporate Management and Financial Planning: the British Rail experience*. London: Granada.

Harrison, J. 1978: *An Economic History of Modern Spain*. Manchester: Manchester University Press.

Harrison, J. 1982: Spain: the end of the miracle. In A. Cox (ed.), *Politics, Policy and the European Recession*. Basingstoke: Macmillan, 195−217.

Heald, D. 1983: *Public Expenditure. Its defence and reform*. Oxford: Martin Robertson.

Heald, D. and Steel, D. 1981: Nationalised industries: the search for control. *Public Money*, June, 13−19.

Heath, J. 1984: Public enterprises in the UK: relevant experiences for the developing countries. In V. Ramanadham (ed.) 1984, 109−19.

Holloway, J. and Picciotto, S. (eds) 1978: *State and Capital: A German debate*. London: Edward Arnold.

Holter, 1982: Mineworkers and nationalization in France: insights into concepts of state theory. *Politics & Society*, 11, 1, 29−50.

Hood, C. 1982: Governmental bodies and government growth. In A. Barker (ed.) 1982, 44−68.

Hyman, R. and Elger, A. 1981: Job controls, the employers offensive and alternative strategies. *Capital and Class*, 15, 115—49.

IBRD (International Bank for Reconstruction and Development) 1963: *The Economic Development of Spain*. Baltimore: Johns Hopkins Press.

IETC (Instituto de Estudios de Transportes y Comunicaciones) 1983: *Memoria 1982*. Madrid: Ministerio de Transportes, Turismo y Comunicaciones.

IGAE (Intervención General de la Administración del Estado) 1984: *Red Nacional de Ferrocarriles Españoles. Control Financiero*. Madrid, mimeo.

ILO 1969: *see OIT*.

Jessop, B. 1982: *The Capitalist State. Marxist theories and methods*. Oxford: Martin Robertson.

Johnson, N. 1978: The public corporation: an ambiguous species. In D. Butler and A. Halsey (eds), *Policy and Politics: Essays in honour of Norman Chester*. London: Macmillan.

Jordan, G. and Richardson, J. 1981: The British policy style or the logic of negotiation? In J. Richardson (ed.) 1981, *Policy Styles in Western Europe*. London: Allen & Unwin, 80—109.

Jordan, G. and Richardson, J. 1987: *British Politics and the Policy Process. An arena approach*. London: Allen & Unwin.

Joy, S. 1973: *The Train that Ran Away: a business history of British Railways 1948—1968*. London: Ian Allan.

Kassalow, E. 1968: The comparative labour field. *Bulletin of the International Institute for Labour Studies*, 5, November, 92—107.

Keegan, W. 1984: *Mrs Thatcher's Economic Experiment*. Harmondsworth: Penguin.

Kelf-Cohen, R. 1973: *British Nationalization 1945—1973*. London: Macmillan.

Korpi, W. and Shalev, M. 1979: Strikes, industrial relations and class conflict in capitalist societies. *British Journal of Sociology*, 30, 2, 164—87.

Lawlor, T. and Rigby, M. 1986: Contemporary Spanish trade unions. *Industrial Relations Journal*, 17, 3, 249—65.

Lehmbruch, G. 1982: Introduction: Neo-corporatism in comparative perspective. In G. Lehmbruch and P. Schmitter (eds), *Patterns of Corporatist Policy-Making*. Beverley Hills and London: Sage, 1—28.

Lehner, F. and Widmaier, U. 1981: Market Failure and Growth of Government: a sociological explanation. Discussion Paper IIVG/dp 81—120. Berlin: International Institute for Comparative Social Research, Wissenschaftszentrum.

Leitch, G. 1977: *Report of Advisory Committee on Trunk Road Assessment*. London: HMSO.

Levy, B. 1987: A theory of public enterprise behaviour. *Journal of Economic Behaviour and Organization*, 8, 1, 75—96.

Lewin, D., Feuille, P. and Kochan, T. (eds) 1977: *Public Sector Labor Relations: Analysis and Readings*. Glen Ridge, N.J.: Thomas Horton.

Lieberman, S. 1982: *The Contemporary Spanish Economy*. London: Allen & Unwin.

Likierman, A. 1984: The use of profitability in assessing the performance of public enterprises. In V. Ramanadham (ed.) 1984, 159—71.

Likierman, A. 1986: Nationalized industries. In D. Henley, C. Holtham, A. Likierman and J. Perrin (eds), *Public Sector Accounting and Financial Control*. 2nd edn. Wokingham: Van Nostrand Reinhold (UK), 132—229.

Lindberg, L. et al. (1975): *Stress and Contradiction in Modern Capitalism*. Lexington, Mass.: Lexington Books.

Linz, J. 1981: A century of politics and interests in Spain. In S. Berger (ed.), *Organizing Interests in Western Europe*. Cambridge: Cambridge University Press, 365—415.

Littlechild, S. 1979: Controlling the nationalised industries: *quis custodiet ipsos custodes*. Discussion paper B56. Birmingham: University of Birmingham Faculty of Commerce and Social Science.

Longstreth, F. 1979: The city, industry and the state. In C. Crouch (ed.), *State and Economy in Contemporary Capitalism*. London: Croom Helm, 157—90.

McEachern, D. 1980: *A Class Against Itself*. Cambridge: Cambridge University Press.

McKillop, N. 1950: *The Lighted Flame. A history of the Associated Society of Locomotive Engineers and Firemen*. London: Nelson.

Maier, C. 1984: Preconditions for corporatism. In J. Goldthorpe (ed.) 1984a, 39—59.

Mandel, E. 1978: *Late Capitalism*. London: Verso.

Manwaring, T. 1981: Labour productivity and the crisis at BSC: behind the rhetoric. *Capital and Class*, 14, 61—97.

Maraffi, M. 1980: State/economy relationships: the case of Italian public enterprise. *British Journal of Sociology*, 31, 4, 507—24.

Maravall, J.-M. 1984: *La Política de la Transición*. Madrid: Taurus.

Marsh, R. 1978: *On and Off the Rails. An autobiography*. London: Weidenfeld & Nicolson.

Martinelli, A. 1981: The Italian experience: a historical perspective. In R. Vernon and Y. Aharoni (eds) 1981, 85—98.

Martino de Jugo, J.-L. 1980: *Los Ferroviarios en Comisiones Obreras. Datos para la historia del movimiento obrero 1964—80*. Madrid: CCOO.

Marx, K. 1926: *The Eighteenth Brumaire of Louis Bonaparte*. London: Allen & Unwin.

Mazzolini, R. 1981: Strategic decisions in government controlled enterprises. *Administration & Society*, 13, 1, 7—31.

Medhurst, K. 1973: *Government in Spain. The executive at work*. Oxford: Pergamon.

Miguélez, F. 1983: Los sindicatos en España hoy, 1975—1982. Typescript, Universidad Autónoma de Barcelona.

Miliband, R. 1983: State power and class interests. *New Left Review*, 138, 57—68.

Mintzberg, H. 1978: Patterns in strategy formation. *Management Science*, 24, 9, 934—48.

MMC (Monopolies and Mergers Commission) 1980: *British Railways Board: London and South East Commuter Services*. Cmnd. 8046. London: HMSO.

MMC 1987: *British Railways Board: Network South East. A report on rail passenger services supplied by the Board in the south east of England*. London: HMSO.

Moore, B. 1967: *Social Origins of Dictatorship and Democracy. Lord and peasant in the making of the modern world*. Harmondsworth: Penguin.

Moore, J. 1986: Why Privatise? In J. Kay, C. Mayer, and D. Thompson (eds), *Privatisation and Regulation. The UK experience*. Oxford: Clarendon, 78—93.

Murdoch, J. 1986: Trainman. An analysis of change in the labour market for train drivers in British Rail. MA Dissertation, School of Industrial and Business Studies, University of Warwick.

Murphy, B. 1980: *ASLEF 1880—1980. A hundred years of the locoman's trade union*. London: ASLEF.

Nash, C. 1985a: European railway comparisons — what can we learn? In K. Button and D. Pitfield (eds) 1985, 237—69.

Nash, C. 1985b: Paying subsidy to British Rail: how to get value for money. *Public Money*, June, 35—40.

NEDO (National Economic Development Office) 1976: *A Study of UK Nationalised Industries. Their role in the economy and control in the future*. London: HMSO.

Noreng, O. 1981: State-owned oil companies: Western Europe. In R. Vernon and Y. Aharoni (eds) 1981, 133—44.

Normanton, E. 1981: Accountability and audit. In R. Vernon and Y. Aharoni (eds) 1981, 157−69.

O'Connor, J. 1973: *The Fiscal Crisis of the State*. New York: St. Martin's Press.

O'Donnell, C. 1985: Brought to account: the NCB and the case for coal. *Capital and Class*, 26, 105−24.

OECD 1985: *Economic Studies*, no. 4 (special issue on the role of the public sector).

Offe, C. 1974: Structural problems of the capitalist state; class rule and political system. On the selectiveness of political systems. *German Political Studies*, 31−50.

Offe, C. 1975a: The theory of the capitalist state and the problem of policy formation. In L. Lindberg *et al.* (eds) 1975, 125−44.

Offe, C. 1975b: Introduction to Part III [legitimacy versus efficiency]. In L. Lindberg *et al.* (eds) 1975, 245−56.

OIT (Organización Internacional de Trabajo) 1969: *La Situación Laboral y Sindical en España*. Geneva: OIT.

Palmer, I. 1985: State theory and statutory authorities: points of convergence. *Sociology*, 19, 523−40.

Parker, P. 1978: *A Way to Run a Railway*. Haldane Memorial Lectures, 41. London: Birkbeck College, University of London.

Pathirane, L. and Blades, D. 1982: Defining and measuring the public sector: some international comparisons. *Review of Income and Wealth*, 28, 261−324.

Pendleton, A. 1986: Management strategy and labour relations on British Rail. PhD. thesis, University of Bath.

Pendleton, A. 1987a: Markets or Politics? The determinants of labour relations in a nationalised industry. Typescript. Bath: University of Bath.

Pendleton, A. 1987b: The nature of union power and the breakdown of stable labour relations in British Rail. Typescript. Bath: University of Bath.

Pérez Díaz, V. 1985: Políticas económicas y pautas sociales en la España de la transición: la doble cara del neocorporatismo. In J. Linz (ed.) *España: un presente para el futuro*. Vol. I, 21−55.

Pizzorno, A. 1978: Political exchange and collective identity in industrial conflict. In C. Crouch and A. Pizzorno (eds), *The Resurgence of Class Conflict in Western Europe since 1968*. Vol. II, *Comparative Analyses*. London: Macmillan, 277−98.

Potter, S. and Cousins, S. 1983: State subsidies and the corporate motorist. *Modern Railways*, November, 588−9.

Poulantzas, N. 1969: The problem of the capitalist state. *New Left Review*, 58, 67−78.

Poulantzas, N. 1978: *State, Power, Socialism*. London: New Left Books.

Preston, P. 1986: *The Triumph of Democracy in Spain*. London: Methuen.

Pryke, R. 1971: *Public Enterprise in Practice*. London: McGibbon and Kee.

Pryke, R. 1981: *The Nationalised Industries*. Oxford: Martin Robertson.

Pryke, R. and Dodgson, J. 1975: *The Railway Problem*. London: Martin Robertson.

PSOE (Partido Socialista Obrero Español) 1981: *Política de Transportes del PSOE*. Madrid: PSOE.

PSOE 1982: *Programa*. Madrid: PSOE.

PSOE 1983: *Un Año para la Esperanza. 365 días de gobierno socialista*. Madrid: PSOE Equipo de Documentación Política.

Ramanadham, V. (ed.) 1984: *Public Enterprises and the Developing World*. London: Croom Helm.

Regini, M. 1984: The conditions for political exchange: how concertation emerged and collapsed in Italy and Great Britain. In Goldthorpe (ed.) 1984a, 124−42.

Reid, R. 1984: The link between revenue and resources. *Railway Gazette International*, April, 258−61.

RENFE (Red Nacional de Ferrocarriles Españoles) various years: *Memoria*. Madrid: RENFE.

RENFE 1984a: *Contrato Programa Estado RENFE 1984–1986*. Madrid: RENFE/ Ministerio de Transportes, Turismo y Comunicaciones.

RENFE 1984b: *Balance Social 1982/83*. Madrid: RENFE.

Rhodes, M. 1985: Organized interests and industrial crisis management. Restructuring the steel industry in W. Germany, Italy and France. In A. Cawson (ed.) 1985a, 192–221.

Richardson, J. (ed.) 1982: *Policy Styles in Western Europe*. London: Allen & Unwin.

Rijnen, H. 1985: Representatividad y organización de CC.OO. y UGT: una comparación europea. *Papeles de Economía Española*, 22, 235–43.

Robbins, D. 1986: *Wanted – Railman*. Manchester: Equal Opportunities Commission.

Robens, A. 1972: *Ten Years Stint*. London: Cassell.

Robson, W. 1962: *Nationalized Industry and Public Ownership*. 2nd edn. London: Allen & Unwin.

Roca, J. 1983: Economic analysis and neocorporatism (with special reference to post-Franco Spain). Typescript. Department of Economics, Universidad Autónoma de Barcelona.

Rodríguez Saiz, L. and Parejo Gámir, J.-A. 1984: Déficit público, crisis económica y política monetaria. *Hacienda Pública Española*, 88, 67–83.

Roig, B. 1981: La empresa pública: razón de ser y proceso de dirección. Documento de Investigación 65, Instituto de Estudios Superiores de la Empresa, Universidad de Navarra.

RSNT (Railway Staff National Tribunal) 1982. *Decision no. 77: Proposal by the British Railways Board for the Implementation of Sub-paragraph 2(c) of the 1981 Productivity Understanding*. London: RSNT.

RSNT 1986: *Decision no. 92: Proposals by the British Railways Board for the Easement of Single Manning of Traction Units*. London: RSNT.

Sagardoy, J.-A. and León, D. 1982: *El Poder Sindical en España*. Barcelona: Planeta.

Samuels, R. 1984: Public energy corporations in the industrial democracies: Japan in comparative perspective. *Journal of Commonwealth and Comparative Politics*, 22, 1, 53–101.

Sánchez, V. 1984: Ética e información: la cuenta de resultados en 1983. *Unión Ferroviaria*, June, 13.

Santoro, F. 1985: A new government plan for the reform of the state railways. *Review of Economic Conditions in Italy*, 1, 121–35.

Sanz, F. 1978: Al gobierno solo le preocupa el déficit del ferrocarril. *Informaciones*, 3 October 1978.

Sapir, E. 1937: Symbolism. In *Encyclopaedia of the Social Sciences*, vols. xiii–xiv, 492–5. New York: Macmillan.

Sartorius, N. 1976: RENFE: huelga, cincuenta años después. *Triunfo*, no. 726.

Scase, R. (ed.) 1980: *The State in Western Europe*. London: Croom Helm.

Schregle, J. 1981: Comparative industrial relations: pitfalls and potential. *International Labour Review*, 120, 15–30.

SCNI (House of Commons Select Committee on Nationalised Industries) 1960: *British Railways*. HC 254. London: HMSO.

SCNI 1968: *Ministerial Control of Nationalised Industries*. Vol. II, *Minutes of Evidence*. London: HMSO.

SCNI 1977: *The Role of British Rail in Public Transport*. HC 305 i–iii. London: HMSO.

SCT (House of Commons Select Committee on Transport) 1982: *Main Line Railway Electrification*. HC 317. London: HMSO.

SCT 1983: *Serpell Committee Report on the Review of Railway Finances*. HC 240. London: HMSO.

Seglow, P., Streeck, W. and Wallace, P. 1982: *Rail Unions in Britain and W. Germany*. London: Policy Studies Institute.

Serpell, D. 1983: *Railway Finances*. London: HMSO.

Shalev, M. 1980: Industrial relations theory and comparative study of industrial relations and industrial conflict. *British Journal of Industrial Relations*, 18, 1, 26—43.

Share, D. 1987: Transitions to democracy and transitions through transaction. *Comparative Political Studies*, 19, 4, 525—48.

Shirley, M. 1983: Managing state-owned enterprises. World Bank Working Papers, 577. Washington: World Bank.

Skocpol, T. 1979: *States and Social Revolutions. A comparative analysis of France, Russia and China*. Cambridge: Cambridge University Press.

Smith, 1986: *The British Economic Crisis. Its past and future*. (Reprinted with afterword.) Harmondsworth: Penguin.

Smith Ring, P. and Perry, J. 1985: Strategic management in public and private organisations: implications of distinctive contexts and constraints. *Academy of Management Review*, 10, 2, 276—86.

Streeck, W., Seglow, P. and Wallace, P. 1981: Competition and monopoly in interest representation: a comparative analysis of trade union structure in the railway industries of Great Britain and Western Germany. *Organization Studies*, 2, 4, 307—30.

Tamames, R. 1983: *Estructura Económica de España*. Vol. I *Medio Ambiente, Población, Sector Agrario, Industria*. 15th edn. Madrid: Alianza.

Tamames, R. 1986: *Introducción a la Economía Española*. 16th edn. Madrid: Alianza.

Terry, M. and Ferner, A. 1986: Political change and union democracy: the negotiation of internal order in the Union of Communication Workers. University of Warwick Industrial Relations Research Unit: Warwick Papers in Industrial Relations no. 10. Coventry: University of Warwick.

TEST 1984a: *BR: A European Railway*. Vol. I TEST Report 51. London: Transport 2000.

TEST 1984b: *BR: A European Railway*. Vol. II TEST Report 52. London: Transport 2000.

Therborn, G. 1978: *What Does the Ruling Class Do When It Rules?* London: New Left Books.

Thomson, A. 1983: The contexts of management behaviour in industrial relations in the public and private sectors. In K. Thurley and S. Wood (eds), *Industrial Relations and Management Strategy*. Cambridge: Cambridge University Press.

Thomson, A. and Beaumont, P. 1978: *Public Sector Bargaining: a study of relative gain*. Farnborough: Saxon House.

Tivey, L. 1973: *Nationalization in British Industry*. Rev. edn. London: Jonathan Cape.

Tivey, L. 1982: Nationalized industries as organized interests. *Public Administration*, 60, 1, 42—55.

Tombs, F. 1980: *The Role of Nationalised Industries*. Lecture to Bristol Centre of the Institute of Bankers. Mimeo.

Treasury 1967: *Nationalised Industries: A Review of Economic and Financial Objectives*. Cmnd. 3437. London: HMSO.

Treasury 1976: *Public Expenditure to 1979—80*. Cmnd. 6393. London: HMSO.

Tuñón de Lara, M. 1972: *El Movimiento Obrero en la Historia de España*. Madrid: Taurus.

Turnbull, P. 1987: Redundancy, efficiency and the flexibility of the firm. Typescript. Coventry: University of Warwick.

UGT (Unión General de Trabajadores) 1984: *Presente y Futuro del Ferrocarril*. Mimeo. Madrid: UGT.

Urry, J. 1981: *The Anatomy of Capitalist Societies. The economy, civil society and the state*. London: Macmillan.

Vernon, R. 1984: Linking managers with ministers: dilemmas of the state-owned enterprise. Development Discussion Paper 165. Harvard Institute for International Development: Harvard University.

Vernon, R. and Aharoni, Y. (eds) 1981: *The State-Owned Enterprise in the Western Economies*. London: St Martin's Press.

Vilar, P. 1983: *Historia de España*. Barcelona: Grijalbo.

Wais, F. 1974: *Historia General de los Ferrocarriles Españoles*. 2nd edn. Madrid: Editora Nacional.

Weiner, H. 1960: *British Labour and Public Ownership*. London: Stevens & Ross.

Weaver, J. Kent 1985: *The Politics of Industrial Change*. Washington: Brookings Institution.

Weighell, S. 1983: *On the Rails*. London: Orbis.

Wernham, R. 1985: Obstacles to strategy implementation in a nationalised industry. *Journal of Management Studies*, 22, 6, 632—48.

Westergaard, J. and Resler, H. 1976: *Class in a Capitalist Society*. London: Heinemann.

Williams, K., Williams, J. and Thomas, D. 1983: *Why Are the British Bad at Manufacturing?* London: Routledge & Kegan Paul.

Winchester, D. 1983: Industrial relations in the public sector. In G. Bain (ed.), *Industrial Relations in Britain*. Oxford: Blackwell.

Woodward, S. 1984: Corporate planning, commitment and public enterprises. In V. Ramanadham (ed.) 1984, 138—58.

Wright, A. 1977: *The Spanish Economy 1959—1976*. New York: Holmes & Meier.

Wright, E. 1979: *Class, Crisis and the State*. London: Verso.

Zeitlin, J. 1985: Shop floor Bargaining and the State: a contradictory relationship. In S. Tolliday and J. Zeitlin (eds), *Shop Floor Bargaining and the State: Historical and Comparative Perspective*. Cambridge: Cambridge University Press.

Zif, J. 1981: Managerial strategic behaviour in state-owned enterprises — business and political orientations. *Management Science*, 27, 1326—39.

Zufiaur, J.-M. 1985: El sindicalismo español en la transición y la crisis. *Papeles de Economía Española*, 22, 202—34.

Zysman, J. 1977: *Political Strategies for Industrial Order. State, market, and industry in France*. Berkeley: University of California Press.

Index

Index by Annemarie Flanders